BECOMING CHRISTIAN

BECOMING CHRISTIAN

Race, Reformation, and Early Modern English Romance

Dennis Austin Britton

Fordham University Press

New York 2014

Library of Congress Cataloging-in-Publication Data

Britton, Dennis Austin.
    Becoming Christian : race, reformation, and early modern English romance / Dennis Austin Britton. — First edition.
        pages cm
    Includes bibliographical references and index.
    ISBN 978-0-8232-5714-0 (hardback)
    1. English literature—Early modern, 1500–1700—History and criticism.
2. Religion and literature—England—History—16th century.   3. Religion and literature—England—History—17th century.   4. Conversion in literature.
5. Christians in literature.   6. Jews in literature.   7. Muslims in literature.
8. Race in literature.   9. Conversion—Christianity—History.   I. Title.
    PR428.R46B65 2014
    820.9'382—dc23

                                                                        2013048884

Printed in the United States of America

16 15 14   5 4 3 2 1

First edition

Contents

List of Figures		vii
Acknowledgments		ix
	Introduction: Not Turning the Ethiope White	1
1.	"The Baptiz'd Race"	35
2.	Ovidian Baptism in Book 2 of *The Faerie Queene*	59
3.	Infidel Texts and Errant Sexuality: Translation, Reading, and Conversion in Harington's *Orlando Furioso*	91
4.	Transformative and Restorative Romance: Re-"turning" *Othello* and the Location of Christian Identity	112
5.	Reproducing Christians: Salvation, Race, and Gender on the Early Modern English Stage	142
	Afterword: A Political Afterlife of a Theology of Race and Conversion	173
	Notes	177
	Bibliography	229
	Index	253

Figures

"*Aethiopem lavare,*" from Geffrey Whitney, *A choice of emblemes*
(Lieden, 1586), H1r.   2

Map of Africa, from Ephraim Pagitt, *Christianographie*
(London, 1635)   119

Acknowledgments

I am indebted to a long list of mentors, colleagues, family members, and friends who have supported me and this book. My thinking about race, romance, and religion began at the University of Wisconsin at Madison, where I had the great privilege of studying the early modern period with Heather Dubrow, David Loewenstein, Henry Turner, and Susanne Wofford. I owe special thanks to Susanne for her insightfulness and constant encouragement; she has shaped me as a scholar and this project in innumerable ways. I also wish to thank Steven Belletto and Krista Kauffmann, graduate-school friends who continue to read my work, offer helpful comments, and provide moments of respite.

The University of New Hampshire has been an ideal intellectual home, where I have had the great fortune to work with Elizabeth Hageman, Douglas Lanier, Rachel Trubowitz, and Jay Zysk (I could not ask for a smarter or more generous set of early modernist colleagues), and with Monica Chew, Michael Ferber, Burt Feintuch, Katherine Gillen, Robin Hackett, Nicola Imbracsio, Delia Konzett, Mathias Konzett, Rochelle Lieber, Lisa Miller, Andrew Merton, Sean Moore, Siobhan Senier, Janet Yount, and David Watters. Thank you, Deborah Vernon, for your meticulous eye for detail. I also need to send some special love to Lesley Curtis, Courtney Marshall, Cord J. Whitaker, and especially Reginald A. Wilburn, who "keep it real" and keep me sane through it all.

I owe a special debt of gratitude to Bernadette Andrea, Linda McJannet, and Maureen Quilligan for the support they offered in the development of this project. I am grateful to Heather James (my first teacher of Ovid, Ariosto, and Spenser), who first suggested that I might have something to say about early modern literature and culture. Erika Boeckeler,

Rebecca Lemon, Arthur Little, Mary Helen McMurran, and Ian Smith have graciously offered feedback, words of advice, and/or encouragement in the early stages of my career. Lori Newcomb, Sarah Wall-Randell, and Tiffany Jo Werth are the champions of romance with whom I've had the privilege of sitting on panels and conversing about the pleasure of working with this genre. Versions of chapters were presented at UNH, The Shakespeare Seminar at Harvard's Mahindra Humanities Center, Temple University, the Folger Shakespeare Library, and seminars at Shakespeare Association of America annual meetings. The comments, questions, and suggestions offered by audience members and readers at these venues have greatly contributed to refining of the book's arguments.

Thank you to the no-longer anonymous readers, Margo Hendricks and Joan Pong Linton, for their enthusiastic responses and helpful suggestions. Helen Tartar, Thomas Lay, Eric Newman, and the staff of Fordham University Press have been wonderfully helpful throughout the entire process. I could not have hoped for more from an editorial staff and a publisher.

I have been extremely fortunate to receive financial support at various stages of working on this project. A Junior Faculty Fellowship from UNH's Center for the Humanities provided time away from teaching that was instrumental in the shaping and reshaping of this book. I also wish to thank Senior Vice Provost Julie Williams, UNH's Research and Engagement Academy, Dean Kenneth Fuld and the College of Liberal Arts Gift Fund, the Center for the Humanities (again), and the Department of English for funds offered. I am most fortunate to have been awarded a National Endowment for the Humanities Fellowship from the Folger Shakespeare Library. My time at the Folger was invaluable, and this project was thoroughly enriched by the materials I consulted there. Thank you to the wonderful Folger staff: Carol Brobeck, Erik Castillo, David Schalkwyk, Georgianna Ziegler, and Folger fellows and readers who made my time in Washington both professionally and personally rewarding.

I am most blessed to have friends and family members who remind me that there is indeed life outside the academy. Thank you Adam and Gina Henker and family, who gave me a place to stay and warm meals in the dead of winter (it's not as dire as it sounds), Victor and Dzifa Patterson and family, Lorraine Henry, and my North Star family. Leslie Smith, my friend of many years, has always provided much encouragement, for which I am grateful.

To Maw Maw, thank you for your strength and faith. I owe most to my mother, father, and brothers, whose love, support, encouragement, and prayers sustain me. I dedicate this book to all of you.

An earlier version of chapter 4 appeared as "Re-'turning' *Othello*: Transformative and Restorative Romance," *ELH* 78 (2011): 27-50. Any views, findings, conclusions, or recommendations expressed in this publication do not necessarily reflect those of the National Endowment for the Humanities.

Introduction

Not Turning the Ethiope White

> Let it no longer be a forlorne hope
> To wash an Æthiope:
> He's washt, His gloomy skin a peacefull shade
> For his white soule is made:
> And now, I doubt not, the Eternall Dove,
> A black-fac'd house will love.
> —*Richard Crashaw, "On the Baptized Aethiope"*[1]

Richard Crashaw's poem provides hope for English Christians who might have been discouraged from engaging in evangelistic projects by Jeremiah 13:23 ("Can the black More change his skin? Or the leopard his spottes? *then* maie ye also do good, that are accustomed to do evil") and Geffrey Whitney's *"Aethiopem lavare"* in *A choice of emblemes* (1586).[2] In the book of Jeremiah, God speaks through his prophet to the people of Israel, who have forsaken their ancestral religion and turned to the worship of Baal. Israel's apostasy and its seemingly immutable spiritual condition are compared to the unchangeable physical condition of the Moor's (or, in other translations, the "Ethiope's") skin—Jews are compared to Moors, a comparison that became quite common in early modern racial discourse.[3] Yet Jeremiah is concerned with Israel's spiritual condition and apostasy, not with the Moor's black skin; the black Moor and his skin merely function as figures that are to help the Israelites, as well as later readers, better understand themselves and their spiritual condition. Although God says nothing here about the spiritual condition of Moors, the Moor's black skin becomes a figure par excellence for signifying unalterable spiritual depravity.

As in Jeremiah, the Ethiopian's skin becomes a figure of the unalterable in *"Aethiopem lavare."* Indeed, the unalterable skin of the Ethiopian became

L EAVE of with paine, the blackamore to skowre,
With washinge ofte, and wipinge more then due:
For thou shalt finde, that Nature is of powre,
Doe what thou canste, to keepe his former hue:
Thoughe with a forke, wee Nature thruste awaie,
Shee turnes againe, if wee withdrawe our hande:
And thoughe, wee ofte to conquer her assaie,
Yet all in vaine, shee turnes if still wee stande:
   Then euermore, in what thou doest assaie,
   Let reason rule, and doe the thinges thou maie.

Erasmus ex Luciano.
Abluis Æthiopem fru-
stra: quin desinis artē?
  Haud unquā efficiet
nox sit vt atra, dies.
Horat.1. Epist.10.
Naturam expellas fur-
ca tamen vsque re-
curret.

————————— *equusq;*
Nunquam ex degeneri fiet generosus asello,
Et nunquam ex stolido cordatus fiet ab arte.

Anulus in pict.
poësi.

H   *Non*

"*Aethiopem lavare,*" from Geffrey Whitney, *A choice of emblemes, and other deuises, for the moste parte gathered out of sundrie writers, Englished and moralized. And diuers newly deuised, by Geffrey Whitney . . .* (Leiden, 1586), H1r. By permission of the Folger Shakespeare Library.

proverbial: Its origins are usually traced to Aesop.[4] The lines of verse beneath an illustration that pictures an exercise in futility emphasize the power of nature to maintain the Ethiopian's blackness. Blackness resides within the domain of nature and resists the "all in vaine" efforts of the white figures to turn the Ethiopian into a figure that resembles themselves. There exists within the emblem a tension between a "natural" or literal reading of blackness as immutable—it cannot become what it is not—and the emblem as a literary form, in which blackness is transformed into a symbol for any natural phenomenon that cannot be altered by modes of European ingenuity.

I readily admit that the tension I see residing within Whitney's emblem is likely one he never intended; it is much more likely that he intended the emblem to be read as a more straightforward allegory for the futility of working against the laws of nature. Nevertheless, I see Crashaw's poem as engaging a similar tension, one that emerges as Ethiopians—as well as Moors, Turks, and Jews—are dually recognized in the early modern period as figures of alterity, which are made to stand for modes of experience and being that are foreign to normative white Christianity, and as racial and religious subjects, with souls either to be saved or damned. The speaker in Crashaw's poem proves able to wash the Ethiopian white spiritually, but only by removing the Ethiopian from the confines of figurative readings of blackness that had created nonseverable ties between black skin and sin. Crashaw's poem, especially when read alongside Whitney's emblem, illustrates the vanity of English Christians who seek to create converts that are exact copies of themselves, and it seems to ignore the fact that Ethiopians (and many others in Africa and Asia) had been Christians long before the inhabitants of Britannia were. The speaker insists that although the Ethiopian's skin may not change, the waters of baptism make it possible for a "white soule" to reside within a "black-fac'd house." Baptism and religious conversion sever the usual connection between blackness and non-Christian identity, even as the line "let it no longer be . . ." suggests the newness of this severance. Crashaw's baptized Ethiopian embodies that all-important Christian chasm between flesh (black) and spirit/soul (white).[5]

Even so, the transformation "On the Baptized Aethiope" describes is not as complete as Clorinda's in Torquato Tasso's *Gerusalemme liberata*, which was patterned after Chariclea in Heliodorus's *Aethiopica*, or the sultan's in the anonymous fourteenth-century *The King of Tars*. These characters' black skin and religious identities were radically altered by the miraculous mechanisms of romance; at one time, romance conventions helped close the chasm between the color of the flesh and the color of the spirit. As this book will show, however, in early modern England the powers of romance to transform markers of racial and religious identity were called into question by the Reformation's insistence that all miracles had ceased, and more particularly by the Church of England's theology of baptism. Although Whitney's emblem does not make an overtly theological statement, a reader familiar with the Jeremiah passage may have wondered whether the emblem also suggests that Ethiopians could not be transformed into Christians; the inability to wash the black figure could signify the inability of Protestant baptism either to erase original sin or to produce Christian identity. In contrast, though "On the Baptized Aethiope" does not change the convert's skin color, Crashaw's Roman Catholic faith (he converted to Catholicism at some point before 1645) in the power of baptism and religious conversion made it possible for him to recover a catholic notion of a Christianity that could, at least partially, "love" an African turned Christian.[6] Crashaw's lyric redeploys the infidel-conversion motif—in which Ethiopians, Moors, Turks, and Jews convert to Christianity—after its waning in Reformation England, where the Church of England's theology transformed these figures of sin, as well as Christians, into racialized subjects.

Becoming Christian: Race, Reformation, and Early Modern English Romance argues that the Church of England's baptismal theology transformed Christians and "infidels" into distinctive races, and that this transformation was registered not only in theological writings but also in English engagements with romance's infidel-conversion motif. In romances written by Catholic writers, baptisms and conversions of infidels lead to an important telos of the romance genre: Despite their narrative wanderings and deferrals, romances often contain transformations of identity that lead to the incorporation of the other into Christian community.[7] Whereas Catholic romances feature baptism's magical power—the sacrament's ability to transform infidels into faithful Christians—theologians within the Church of England denied the magical (or, more accurately, the miraculous) power of baptism, even debating whether it was necessary for salvation. Moreover, in various discussions of baptism, English theologians asserted that salvation could be assured not only by faith but also through race and lineage. In *Becoming Christian* I contend that baptismal theology and emerging concepts of race provide an important but not-yet-recognized context for understanding why writers such as Edmund Spenser, John Harington, William Shakespeare, John Fletcher, and Philip Massinger either reform or reject the romance telos and the infidel-conversion motif. English engagements with this quintessential romance motif responded to controversies about the means by which individuals acquire both racial and religious identities, as well as the transformation of infidels from figures of sin and alterity into more fully perceivable religious subjects. *Becoming Christian* charts the intersections of race, Protestant theology, and literary form.

Early Modern Race Studies, the Turn to Religion, and Historical Formalism

The infidel conversion motif's pervasive presence in literary works written by Catholic writers, its reformation and rejection in Protestant England, and the presence of race in Protestant understandings of salvation have not received sustained scholarly consideration.[8] Hence early modern literary studies has not fully understood the role that theology plays in the development of race as a category of identity or the role of emergent theological constructions of race in both initiating and requiring changes in generic convention and literary form. Although this study participates in what is surely a renaissance in scholarly attention to romance, literary form, and religious conversion (about which I will say more later), it primarily adds to the growing body of scholarship on the emergence of race as a category of identity in the early modern period.

A long list of scholars have argued that although race in the early modern period was not yet what it would become following the pseudo-scientific taxonomies of the Enlightenment, the emerging concept nevertheless attempted to give meaning to bodily differences among peoples, cultures, and religions.[9] Of the bodily differences investigated, much groundbreaking work has highlighted the importance of skin color in early modern constructions of race, often drawing from and extending the boundaries of feminist readings of women and their bodies in early modern culture and beyond.[10] Both historically and critically, skin color has been an important marker of difference.[11] More recently, however, studies of race in the early modern period have moved beyond skin color to explore factors such as geographical effects on the humoral body, lineage, language, and the practices of print culture and reading.[12] Commenting on this critical shift, Ian Smith notes, "A new orthodoxy has emerged as a corrective to the predominant but unsustainable—for the period—sole emphasis on skin color. Researchers now typically posit that race in the early modern period is the product of several, often interrelated, categories of identification, a complex amalgam of codes that can be mobilized to ratify group exclusion and marginalization."[13] Smith's "complex amalgam" underscores that a diversity of approaches are necessary for analyzing the concept of race, and that race is a fruitfulness concept for exploring early modern formations of various forms of identity: gender, sexuality, class, nationality, and religion.

Of the interrelated categories Smith observes, I am most interested in the relation between race and religion. My hope is that this examination of baptismal theology and the infidel-conversion motif will flesh out what I see as an underexplained truism in early modern race studies: the inextricable link between race and religion. Labels like "Jew," "Turk," and "Moor" embrace both racial and religious identities, such that when an early modern author writes about a Moor, for example, it is often unclear whether that author is describing a person with a set of ethnic/cultural/racial characteristics, a person holding a set of religious beliefs, or both.[14] Critics usually concentrate on the cultural ambiguities surrounding labels like "Jew, "Turk," and "Moor," but I most closely follow the lead of Janet Adelman in *Blood Relations: Christian and Jew in* The Merchant of Venice (2008), in which she illuminates how early modern theology shaped ideas about Jewish racial difference.[15] But even as I follow her lead, I hope to extend her insights and indeed state more emphatically the need for early modern literary scholars to examine the connections between religious doctrine, confessional identity, and race. Moreover, I depart from Adelman's study in my comparative attention to Jews, Turks, and Moors. I do not assert, however, that these groups were indistinguishable in the early modern English imagination. I compare them only to show that English Protestants defined their elect racial identity in contradistinction to their notion of the infidel. English Reformation theology, and specifically the Church of England's baptismal theology, racialized those deemed *infidelis* so as to racialize those already belonging to the Christian faith.

I therefore accept—with reservation and qualification, however— Kwame Anthony Appiah's influential assertion that religion, not race, was the primary marker of difference in the early modern period. According to Appiah, "it seems that . . . stereotypes were based on an essentially theological conception of the status of both Moors and Jews as non-Christians; the former distinguished by their black skin, whose color was associated in Christian iconography with sin and the devil; the latter by their being, as Matthew's account of the crucifixion suggests, 'Christ-killers.' "[16] Numerous medievalists and early modernists now take Appiah to task for his overly rigid formulation of race, one that posits biology as the concept's only progenitor.[17] Modern science, however, continually illustrates that race is, just as it has always been, a social construction; how else do we explain various genetic similarities among races that are imagined to be very different?[18]

Although the advent of biology transformed racialist paradigms, Appiah's thesis posits biology and theology as completely separate discourses. His argument also seems to reduce theology to the simple articulation of Christian and non-Christian; it ignores the ways in which theology provides much more nuanced understandings of human difference, and how theology draws from and creates concepts of race. Neither in the early modern period nor in our own are race and religion disentangled categories of identity. Although early moderns did not have "biology," they did have the word "race," which enfolded, among other things, blood and lineage.[19] To be sure, Jews, Turks, and Moors were seen as religiously different from Christians, but religious differences were not merely a matter of belief but also of genealogy, so much so that true and false belief, salvation, and damnation were often seen as racial characteristics passed from parents to children. Thus, although Appiah's assertion is borne out in the literary and theological examples I discuss, it is true only to the extent that Protestant theology both drew from and further developed concepts of race.

Recent engagements with Christian theology, moreover, tell a story that differs from Appiah's. The historian Colin Kidd, for example, argues that theology has contributed to racialist attitudes, a fact that has been widely ignored:

> Scholarly discussion of racial constructs has tended on the whole—though there are important exceptions—to drift into the territorial waters of sociology. . . . That race is also a theological construct has hitherto attracted much less attention, though it has occasionally intruded at the margins of the more scrupulous studies of race—albeit as a somewhat anomalous factor . . . 'Race-as-theology' should be an important constituent of the humanistic study of racial construction alongside accounts of 'race-as-biology,' race-as-ethnicity' and 'race-as-class or -caste.'[20]

Kidd is one of the few scholars who have explored early modern theology—or the theology of any period—for instances of race thinking.[21] In addition to Kidd, the theologians J. Kameron Carter and Willie James Jennings have argued that modern concepts of race arose from theologies of bygone but not forgotten waves of Christian thought: Carter traces the modern origins of race to a neo-Gnosticism—in which Christ is disembodied from his Jewish flesh—embedded in Kantian philosophy of rational religion, and Jennings explores the soteriology of Iberian colonial endeavors that rendered peoples with darker skin less able to convert and grasp the mysterious of Christianity than peoples with "white" skin.[22] In a similar vein, *Becoming Christian* explores the origins of the concept of race in Christian theology and how this concept led to a reformation of romance tales in early modern England.

This book begins with the claim that "infidel" and "Christian" became racial categories in early modern England. Moreover, English engagements with romance's infidel-conversion motif encode theological formations of racial difference in the aftermath of religious reformation. With the efficacy and number of sacraments significantly reduced, and with the influence of Calvinist doctrines of predestination, English Protestants were forced to reconceptualize how Christian identity originates in the individual. The answer was simpler in Roman Catholicism: Christian identity originates in baptism, the sacrament of Christian initiation. Baptism should be thought as the premier sacrament of the church: As the first sacrament individuals receive, it is the prerequisite for receiving all others. Moreover, as Karen E. Spierling argues, baptism and beliefs about it have long defined Christian communities:

> As the various forms of Christianity have spread across the world, baptism has continued to be one of the most obvious and public points of dissension among Christian denominations, and sometimes within them . . . . This is precisely because baptism is tied so closely, at one and the same time, to defining the relationship between an individual and God and to defining the shape and limits of any given Christian community.[23]

Baptism has always provided a structure for creating difference and partitioning the Christian from the infidel, but in the context of the theological reformations of sixteenth- and seventeenth-century Europe, it also allowed for new ways of constructing that partition. I argue that the Protestant restructuring of difference between Christian and infidel provides a context for understanding the emergence of a theology of race, in which Christian and infidel identity were engendered less by sacraments than by genealogy and biological kinship. This theology of race did not make the possibility of conversion either to or from Christianity impossible, but it did render converts miraculous and monstrous anomalies in the natural course of things.

The sheer number of texts discussing baptism published in Tudor and Stuart England testifies to the extent of the scrutiny of the sacrament of Christian initiation and the diversity of views about it. In Roman Catholicism, no one could be saved without baptism, a doctrine that Calvinist and Zwinglian strains of Protestantism necessarily rejected in order to assert that sacraments are signs of grace rather than vehicles that automatically bestow it.[24] Protestants usually argued that salvation was granted by faith alone; to believe that sacramental elements like water, bread, and wine conferred grace was to make God's grace beholden to works rather than faith. Nevertheless, Protestants who followed Luther and Calvin rather than Zwingli argued that baptism implanted a seed in an infant that would make future faith possible.[25] Yet even this theological position fostered anxieties about what would happen to children who died before being baptized (the Church of England frowned upon baptisms done by midwives) or, even if baptized, who perished before they were old enough to articulate their faith.[26]

Even as they upheld the doctrine of *sola fide*, numerous theologians within the Church of England attempted to console anxious parents by arguing that Christian identity is a genealogical trait that is passed from parents to children; they pointed to God's promise to Abraham, in Genesis 17, that he would be the God of Abraham and his seed. English Protestants appropriated this promise, emphasizing the ways in which God made a promise with an entire race and lineage of people, in order to assure the salvation of their children. At the same time, English theologians were very quick to define the limits of this promise; they asserted that salvation was only assured to the children of Christians and not to the children of "heathens" and "infidels," the words that most frequently appear in these discussions.

Faith in race, however, not only provided solace for grieving parents; it could also relieve adult anxieties fostered by Calvinist doctrines of predestination. In the letter "To Mistress Wilkinson and Mistress Warcup," for example, the English martyr John Bradford attempts to assure the two women of their salvation: "Wherefore came he into this world, but to redeem you, to marry you unto himself, to destroy the works of Satan, to save and seek that which was lost? Wherefore suffered he so great and bitter passion? . . . Wherefore were you born of Christian parents and in God's Church, but because you were God's children by Christ before you were born?"[27] While Bradford stresses Christ's work in providing assurance of salvation, the ordering of the rhetorical questions points to the power of race to save the soul; in the end, being born of Christian parents proves that these women were Christians even before they were born.

The theological arguments discussed in this book usually derive from Calvin, but I focus on theologians within the Church of England in order to illustrate that questions about race and salvation were well articulated in the English context—though in chapter 1, I often point to the Calvinist origins of English arguments. I also focus on the theology of the Church of England in order to set more practical limits. Revisionist historians have taught us that it is no longer appropriate to discuss "The Reformation" and to believe in its teleological narrative.[28] To do so is to ignore not only projects of counter-Reformation but also doctrinal differences within both Protestant and Catholic communities. Consequently, even as I discuss "the Church of England's baptismal theology," I need to acknowledge that opinions within the English Church were not univocal.

Nevertheless, I hope to demonstrate that despite tensions between more conservative and puritan voices within the Church of England, there emerges a desire to construct religious identity in racial terms. I also do not claim that this study fully excavates a deep repository of race thinking in Protestant theologies or even in the Church of England; I acknowledge that explorations of other theological controversies within other confessional communities may reveal very different understandings of racial formation.

Even so, as the theology of the national church that all but radical dissenters would have encountered through participating in communal worship, the Church of England's understanding of baptism seems like a natural starting point. Regardless of how any author might be identified with a particular confessional community, I am careful not to read literary texts as merely reproducing doctrine; I read literary works as multifarious expressions of the habits of belief that English readers and audiences would have encountered through communal worship. The literary works I examine reproduce, revise, and extend the Church of England's theological arguments concerning race and religious identity. I hope to show that the study of theology and not just what we usually consider religion tells a story that links the development of race in the Protestant world to fundamental Christian understandings of salvation and damnation.

Becoming Christian thus participates in what Ken Jackson and Arthur F. Marotti identified almost a decade ago as a "turn to religion" in early modern studies, evidenced in part by a more general interest in confessional identities.[29] This work has questioned the New Historicist tendency to conflate religious identities with political and social identities and sometimes with "culture."[30] Within this turn, both Marotti and Molly Murray have emphasized religious conversion, with Murray illuminating the connection between conversion and poetic practice.[31] But unlike much of the recent work on conversion that focuses on movements among Christian sects, or previous studies that read conversion primarily as a trope of empire, I focus on non-Christian to Christian conversion as a theological concern in its own right. Although conversion from one Christian sect to another was surely believed to be a matter of salvation and damnation, different issues arise when we consider nonwhite, non-European converts—namely, how race, lineage, and cultural background affect conversion.[32] On the one hand, as Ania Loomba argues, "Religious conversion, by signaling the possibility of crossovers, necessarily engenders several kinds of anxiety about authenticity. If the faithful constitute a permeable and changeable body, then the purity of both the original body and those who are allowed to join it is always suspect."[33] On the other hand, such anxieties made theologies of race, which sought to make bodies less permeable and changeable, all the more desirable. Scholars who have most fully turned to religion usually ignore race, and scholars of race have not turned fully enough to religious systems of belief (theology) rather than religion as a form of social identity.

Since, Thomas Kirkpatrick argues, "the word 'religion' is now used to refer to so many different things that it has become virtually synonymous with 'culture' and 'society' in the broadest sense," the term requires delimiting.[34] In early modern literary studies, Julia Reinhard Lupton has provided one of the most precise articulations of what is and is not religion: "*Religion is not identical with culture. . . . Religion is a testing ground for struggles between the universal and the particular. . . . Religion is a form of thinking.*"[35] To maintain that religion is not culture, she continues, "is not to say that religion does not participate in culture or ideology, but rather that what makes religion religion (distinguishing it from identity such as nationality or ethnicity) is its absurd insistence and unlikely persistence beyond the logics of custom and habit, practice and power."[36] I fully accept Lupton's position that religion is not culture (to take it as such would be to ignore the places where religion conflicts with and challenges cultural practices), as well as her insistence that religion is distinct from nationality and ethnicity. In Lupton's argument, religion provides the "form of thinking" (by which she means "formal theology, philosophy, and hermeneutics, but also with ordinary acts of rumination") to which culture variously responds.[37] My examination of the Church of England's baptismal theology suggests that theology ("the form of thinking") transformed Christians and infidels into races, but I maintain that this transformation was the consequence of a form of thinking and not the form of thinking itself. This is a "which came first" argument, but I follow Geraldine Heng's assertion that "race thinking, in premodern contexts, does not require races as such to exist a priori but will produce races at need, in answer to specific historical imperatives and occasions."[38] In the theological writings I examine, salvation is the primary concern, and race emerges to provide assurance of salvation. Although there are surely many instances when constructions of race draw from religious discourse, this study examines how a theology created race in order to resolve doctrinal controversies.

Although *Becoming Christian* participates in the turn to religion, it is equally invested in the return to genre and literary form. Some are calling this trend "Historical Formalism," the practitioners of which are pursuing a course parallel to those who are turning to religion.[39] Whereas the latter are concerned with disentangling religion from culture, the former question premises of New Historicism and partly attempt to disentangle literature from history and culture.[40] According to Stephen Cohen, "Unlike the historicity of texts, the historicity of form emphasizes the particularities of literary discourse, insisting not only that literary texts have historical roots and function, but that they do so by virtue of their discourse-specific forms and conventions as their extratextual or interdiscursive ideological content."[41] Genres, forms, and literary conventions generate historically bound meanings; at the same time, historical formalism acknowledges that genres, forms, and literary conventions carry transhistorical baggage that is integral to understanding their ideological work within a given historical moment. The infidel-conversion motif in early modern England retains its power to transform. Consequently, English authors can explicitly reject the motif (as Spenser does in Book 2 of *The Faerie Queene*), reappropriate it by deracializing the infidel in the narrative (as Harington does in his *Orlando Furioso*), or affirm its validity with qualification (as is done in *The Merchant of Venice, Othello, The Island Princess,* and *The Renegado*). But the rejections, reappropriations, and affirmations all attempt to hold in balance—though in very different ways—the ideological obligations of the motif and an English Protestant confessionalism that transformed Christians and infidels into different races. Romance and its motifs in early modern England negotiate with what they have already done in previous texts. If the New Historicism usually positions itself against the ahistoricity of New Criticism's formalism, Historical Formalism (like the turn to religion) places itself in the nexus of the ahistorical/universal and the historical/particular.

My engagement with religion, race, genre, and form reflects the influences of the critical methodologies discussed above. The analysis of the Apostle Paul's writing by the Talmudic scholar Daniel Boyarin, who reads Paul's epistles as a spiritual autobiography of a Jewish social critic, provides a useful conceptual bridge between the two. I am especially interested in

Boyarin's discussion of Pauline universalism, which, he argues, is born of an opposition between the flesh and the spirit and bespeaks the allegorizing of Jewish history and circumcision. According to Boyarin, in Paul's writings

> literal circumcision, which is for Jews alone, and for male Jews at that, is re-read as signifying baptism in the spirit, which is for all. Jewish history, the history of Israel according to the flesh, is taken as a sign for the meaning of Christ and his Church, Israel according to the spirit, in the world. . . . The very impulse toward universalism, toward the One, is that which both enabled and motivated Paul's move toward a spiritualizing and allegorizing of Israel's Scripture and Law as well.[42]

The universalism and accompanying flesh/spirit opposition that the allegory creates is inherited by early Church fathers like Augustine and Origen; both argued that Jews were unable to accept the truth of Christian scripture because they were excessively carnal.[43] Boyarin observes, "This way of thinking about language had been initially stimulated in the Fathers by Paul's usage of *in the flesh* and *in the spirit* to mean, respectively, literal and figurative. . . . hermeneutics becomes anthropology."[44] Allegory, then, seeks to transform and convert Jewish particularity into Christian universalism. At the same time, Jewish fleshiness is read as resisting transformation—indeed, it must be so read for the allegory to work. There is a mimetic relationship between how Jewish figures are read within the allegory and how actual Jews are constructed and racialized for the sake of that allegory. In other words, because Jews must represent flesh in the allegory, actual Jews are said to be carnal by nature and thus unable to accept spiritual truth. As Jews become associated with the literal, their literal bodies are said to be resistant to Christianity. In this context, the Christian telos posits an eternally present and unchanging Jewishness to which it counterposes itself.[45] Boyarin's provocative statement—"hermeneutics becomes anthropology"—also allows us to recognize the causality between human classification and the interpretive practices required by allegory as a mode of figuration, a causality suggesting that figures derive their meaning from seeming bodily realities; figures can produce bodies, and bodies can produce figures.[46]

Jewish bodies, of course, were not the only ones that became important to Christians' understandings of themselves. For instance, the black woman in the *Geneva Bible*'s version of Song of Solomon, which, according to the

Argument, are *"moste swete and comfortable allegories,"* is read as figuring the Protestant Church: The gloss to 1:4, "I am blacke, ô daughters of Ierusalém, but comelie," reads, "The Church confesseth her spots & sinne, but has confidence in the fauour of Christ." The allegory requires the ability to imagine a real black and beautiful woman—an impossibility given the standards of early modern beauty. While blackness is still associated with sin, the black and comely woman embodies the paradox of Christian identity: the simultaneously beautiful bride of Christ who bears a mark of sin that should make her undesirable.[47]

Allegorizing the black bride's body in this way requires that the bodies of real, contemporary black Christians be erased and ignored. Medieval and early modern Europeans were both aware of and had contact with black African Christians, primarily those located in the dominion of the legendary Prester John. In the 1555 English translation of Joannes Boemus's *Omnium gentium mores, leges & ritus* (or *The fardle of facions conteining the aunciente maners, customes, and lawes, of the peoples enhabiting the two partes of the earth, called Affrike and Asie*), English readers would have learned that "The people of Inde, & Ethiope, under the gouernaunce of *Presbiter* Iohn, perseavere in Christiane godlinesse, howbeit after a sort, muche different from ours."[48] Not only were Ethiopians known to be Christians, but they were also viewed as a potential ally that might join Europe's fight against Muslim Turks and Moors.[49] Consequently, the Ethiopians' skin color could not always be viewed as an outward sign of infidel identity.

Nevertheless, it does not appear that the English had firsthand knowledge of Ethiopians or Prester John, and in comparison with Jews, Turks, and Moors, Ethiopians appear infrequently in early modern English writings. What the English knew about either real or literary Ethiopians came from English translations of Boemus, classical and continental romances (for instance, Chariclea in *Aethiopica,* the Ethiopian sodomite in *Orlando Furioso,* and Clorinda in *Gerusalemme liberata*), and occasional acknowledgements of their ancient Christian origins in more general histories of Christianity. Given the presence of Ethiopians in continental romances, it is striking just how little contact (actual, textual, or artistic) the English had with Ethiopians. Apart from English translation of *Aethiopica, Orlando Furioso* and *Gerusalemme liberata,* and occasional references to "Ethiops" in English literary works, I have only been able to locate one English work in which Ethiopians play a significant role: Richard Johnson's prose romance, *Tom a Lincoln* (1599 and 1607). Yet not only is there no mention of Ethiopian religion in *Tom a Lincoln,* but Prester John and his daughter also have white skin in the narrative.[50] Thus, although Ethiopians can provide an obvious counterexample to the theological formations of race that at times drew from a dichotomy of white-cleansed spirit and black-sinful flesh, their paucity in the early modern English imagination may be understood as a cultural act of suppression, one that lends credence to figurative readings of black, Jewish, or Muslim bodies in theological discourse and English romance.

In this book I explore links between racialized bodies both figurative and real, an endeavor that arises from attention to the period's heated doctrinal controversies about hermeneutical practices and increased traffic between European Christians and non-European Muslims and Jews. Moreover, I argue that romance's infidel-conversion motif—with its figurative trafficking in foreignness and miraculous transformations—and baptismal theology are ideal places to explore the historical convergence of hermeneutics and racialized bodies. Exploring this convergence will also help us see how figurative readings of Turks, Moors, Jews, and other non-Christians help create racial stereotypes.

Early Modern Romance and the Problem of Kind

A revival in studies of romance has uncovered its varied uses in early modern England, revealing its immense popularity (in spite of those who argued that it is a particularly wanton and Catholic genre) and the ways in which its conventions spurred a reimagining of cross-cultural interactions.[51] These studies have also addressed the difficult question, "What is romance?" Whether as a genre or a mode, romance is notoriously difficult to define, in part because it takes on so many different forms, but also because of debates—both early modern and contemporary—about what constitutes a genre as opposed to a mode.[52] Although the term *romance* was first used to describe twelfth-century French vernacular literature, it has come to embrace vastly different kinds of texts, from medieval ballads and tales of chivalry (which are commonly said to embody aristocratic values) to sixteenth-century prose fiction (which increasingly appealed to popular tastes).[53] Even so, romance is often associated with the motifs (concealed identity, shipwreck, and religious conversion, for example) that, as Helen

Cooper puts it, "grew up with the genre of which they formed a part and which they helped to define."[54] In other words, among a variety of literary forms and narrative types, romance emerges and makes itself known through the repetition of the motifs that have come to be associated with the genre.[55] Moreover, the identification of romance by its use of specific motifs can help us understand how this generic categorization can enfold vastly different types of literature, from Ariosto's epic romance to Shakespeare's late plays that we now call "the romances." This understanding of romance also opens up the possibility that works thought of as belonging to other genres—epic, tragedy, or comedy, for example—can employ romance by incorporating its motifs.[56]

Defining romance is further complicated by its vexed relationship to epic. In sixteenth-century Italy a controversy arose (most famously in the debate between Giraldi Cinthio and Torquato Tasso concerning the *Furioso*) about the nature of romance: whether it is a distinct kind of literature or simply a degenerate form of epic. Cinthio insists that there is something unique about romance, whereas Tasso argues that romance is epic that has rejected Aristotelian unity.[57] In England, however, this debate seems to have been bypassed through the use of the phrase "heroic poetry," which Harington uses to describe both the *Furioso* and the *Aeneid* in the "Preface" to his translation of Ariosto's poem.[58]

In the controversy surrounding the *Furioso*, I believe that we see a prefiguring of contemporary debates about the nature of generic classification; the debates concerning the *Furioso* and romance recognized degrees of similarity and difference between romance and epic, and questioned whether or not romance is different enough from epic to warrant a distinctive category. But in terms of generic classification, Alastair Fowler urges us to focus on similarity. As he extends Ludwig Wittgenstein's analogy between generic classification and familial resemblance, he asserts, "In literature, the basis of resemblance lies in literary tradition. What produces generic resemblances, reflection soon shows, is tradition: a sequence of influence and imitation and inherited codes connecting works in the genre. As kinship makes a family, so literary relations of this sort form a genre."[59] Fowler's theory is Aristotelian. Literary works imitate earlier works; Aristotle has this kind of imitation in mind in the *Poetics* when he lays out a taxonomy of the epic.[60]

Extending Fowler's observations to her study of recurrent motifs in romance, Cooper argues that we should recognize recurrences of specific motifs or "memes" as evidence that texts belong to a generic genealogy, even as she asserts that we should not expect such recurrences to be exact replications:

> The romance genre—any genre, indeed—is best thought of as a lineage or family of texts rather than as a series of incarnations or clones of a single Platonic Idea. A family changes over time as its individuals change, but equally, those individuals can be recognized through their 'family resemblance': a resemblance such as might lie in a certain shape of the nose or mouth, or colour of hair, or laughing in a particular way at a particular kind of joke. . . . [61]

Fowler's and Cooper's discussions of genre and family resemblance are provocative because they allow us to consider not only how families and genres are constructed around similar principles—the ability to recognize similarity among difference—but also how historically situated individuals and works of literature belong to larger transhistorical categories. Early modern English texts that use the infidel-conversion motif belong to the family of medieval and continental Catholic texts that they resemble, but only as rebellious teenagers that self-consciously assert difference and independence from the Catholic doctrinal status quo.[62]

Cooper rightly recognizes that genres, like families (and religious communities, I would add), often need to deal with and even incorporate others. But there are other understandings of genre. "The law of genre," John Frow writes, "is a law of purity, a law against miscegenation. . . . Yet lodged within this law is another . . . which registers the impossibility of *not* mixing genres."[63] Frow is extending Derrida's famous utterance at the beginning of "The Law of Genre": "Genres are not to be mixed."[64] Such a law circulated in early modern England. Shakespeare, for example, while never refusing to do what Philip Sidney scornfully calls "mingling kings with clowns," still showed an awareness that mixing literary kinds can be taken too far.[65] What begins in *Hamlet* as Polonius's praise of the actors' skills morphs into a comical consideration of the seemingly endless possibilities of mixing genres: "tragedy, comedy, history, pastoral, pastoral-comical, historical-pastoral, tragical-historical, tragical-comical-historical-pastoral."[66]

We thus might ask Cooper what resemblances count or can be used as evidence of belonging to a family or genre. Cooper's examples suggest that familial affiliations—perhaps in a time before DNA paternity tests—

are most clearly established through visible or audible traits. But are individuals with the same laugh or nose but with different skin colors likely to be recognized as belonging to the same family? Can individuals with similar religious beliefs but very different physical traits be part of the same religious family? What factors (historical, theological, racial), when introduced into a "family," override resemblances, even perceptible ones? Genre mixing, like racial miscegenation, complicates efforts to establish resemblances or distinctions. Yet in its ability to enfold so many different types of narratives and many different types of people, romance seemingly defies laws against mixing mandated by both the law of genre and early modern racial and religious politics.

Despite their impurity, and even as they move toward the transformation and incorporation of difference, romances also illustrate that not all types of difference can be embraced or ignored; various works of romance, then, evince various degrees of acceptability for such differences. In *On Romances* (1554), Cinthio notes that romance, of which *Orlando Furioso* is the prime example, is best fit to make the distinction between opposing categories clear: "The function then of our poet, as regards the inducing of mores, is to praise virtuous action and censure the vicious; and by means of the terrible and the miserable to make the vicious actions odious to him who reads."[67] Cinthio has much to say about romance, but here he speaks of romance's didactic function as part of his apology, and this didacticism clearly depends on a clear distinction between good and evil.[68] Fredric Jameson, however, has noted the paradoxical use of dichotomies and opposites in romance—the tendency to make distinctions between things that, in fact, may be similar—and identifies this as a chief characteristic of the genre:

> Romance in its original strong form may then be understood as an imaginary "solution" to this real contradiction, a symbolic answer to the perplexing question of how the enemy can be thought of as *evil* (that is, an other than myself marked by some absolute difference), when what is responsible for his being so characterized is quite simply the *identity* of his own conduct with mine.[69]

For Jameson this "solution" comes at the moment of recognition, when the unknown knight reveals himself and is then "reinserted into the unity of social class."[70] This conception of romance is helpful because it illuminates both the mode's movement toward the incorporation of *seeming-but-not-actual difference* and its reliance on a paradox that inheres in the tension between similar and different as sharply distinct categories—and romance seems to reproduce on the level of plot questions about similarity and difference that pertain to its own distinctiveness as a genre. Jameson's "historicized" construction of romance as "solution" rightly points to ideological contradictions as problems that seem to work themselves into romances, and it has come to inform much of our contemporary understanding of this genre.[71] His reading of romance as fostering class consciousness in the feudal nobility points toward what he sees as *not-yet-recognized sameness*, difference as merely illusory.

As valuable as it may be, Jameson's theorizing of romance obscures the fact that its goals may not be so singular, especially in an early modern world of ever-shifting political, religious, and theological alignments, and in its engagement with emergent views about human difference.[72] In her groundbreaking readings of race and early modern romance, Elizabeth Spiller, too, questions Jameson's reading:

> What happens . . . when difference does not collapse into the sameness of identity? This question becomes urgent in the printed romances that circulated in sixteenth- and seventeenth-century Europe. Renaissance romances will be transformed not so much by the appearance of ethnically diverse characters—which are central to the genre from the outset—but by the introduction of new models of identity that challenged the genre's assumptions that identity was both fixed (established by birth) and manifest (affirmed by social practice).[73]

My study builds upon Spiller's insightful response to Jameson, and like her I see early modern romance as engaging concepts of race that often work at odds with narratives of religious conversion.[74] Nevertheless, our studies differ methodologically and in our understanding of the relationship between race and religion. Spiller's comparative study—which mainly addresses texts written in Catholic contexts—explores how a "phenomenology of reading" illuminates much of the early modern antiromance discourse, which responds to anxieties about how acts of reading transform readers. I primarily explore the intersections of Protestant theology and thinking about race.[75]

As I highlight the predominance of romance as a genre that can be used to create and define religious communities, I also draw from Northrop Frye's well-known reading of romance as "secular scripture." Frye observes that "Christian mythology," such as hagiography and apocrypha like the harrowing of hell, "expanded to include a large body of romance," and that cultures also "kidnap romance, that is, [use] romance formulas . . . to reflect certain religious or social ideas."[76] Although I am more interested in the theological than I am with the broad category of the "social," Frye's observations provide a conceptual frame for exploring how romance and the infidel-conversion motif simultaneously and dialogically bolster "Christian mythology" and even theology, and how romance can be "kidnapped" to articulate religious questions. That romance should do this kind of work in Protestant England seems at odds with the numerous religious voices that condemned romances for being wanton and Catholic. Tiffany Werth, however, has shown that despite widespread opposition to romances, English authors attempted to reform it and continued to use its motifs and conventions.[77] Romance remained a powerful religious tool in Protestant England, and uses of the infidel-conversion motif both register and inform tensions between the inclusive claims of Christianity and emergent concepts of racial difference.

The Infidel-Conversion Motif: A Brief History

The infidel-conversion motif may be read as upholding Paul's assertion in Galatians 3:28: "There is nether Jewe nor Grecian: there is nether bonde nor fre; there is nether male nor female; for ye are all one in Christ Jesus." This does not mean, however, that race, ethnicity, and gender became inconsequential to matters of religion. Although the Church of England's theology would necessarily maintain that whoever believes and is baptized will be saved, salvation appears to be an even greater miracle when bestowed on an Ethiopian, Moor, Turk, or Jew who converts to Christianity. Thus, rather than understanding the infidel-conversion motif and the passage from Galatians as disavowing differences among people, they can be read as attempting to erase differences within the Christian community; Galatians may be the best example of that "original strong form" of romance Jameson describes. The infidel-conversion motif and Galatians may suggest that race, ethnicity, and gender obscure not-yet-recognized sameness among Christians, even while recognizing race, ethnicity, and gender as real categories that denote differences between infidels and Christians.

In what follows I provide a brief overview of the infidel–conversion motif in Catholic romances. The examples I discuss show that although uses of the motif maintain that baptism and conversion have the power to erase the religious significance of racial signifiers, the motif also reifies racial difference by asserting that baptism and conversion radically transform the subject, creating in that subject a radically different embodied religious identity.

The infidel who converts to Christianity, usually because of an erotic attachment he or she has with a Christian, is ubiquitous in romances written by Catholic writers. It is especially prevalent in, but not limited to, Charlemagne romances and *chansons de gestes* depicting the religious wars between the Franks and the Saracens.[78] In perhaps the most famous of these *gestes, La Chanson de Roland,* Charlemagne overthrows Saragossa and kills the city's Jewish and Muslim inhabitants who refuse to be baptized; baptism is both a spiritual and martial weapon. But Charlemagne has a special plan for Saragossa's queen, Bramimond. In deference to her noble lineage, he desires her to convert on her own free will: "*Ço voelt li reis par amur cunvertissett*" ["The King wishes her to become a convert out of devotion"].[79] The poem concludes with Bramimond's baptism and incorporation into Christendom, the ultimate victory.[80]

Bramimond's conversion also illustrates one of the primary desires of romance: to transform and then incorporate that which is different but desirable. A distinction emerges between the all-but-forced conversions of the Jews and Muslims in Saragossa and that of Bramimond, a difference in which race is a factor. In this context race refers explicitly to her noble lineage (and race will continue to connote lineage, though also much more, well into the early modern period). Because of her race, her conversion to Christianity is enfolded within Charlemagne's desire, his recognition that the willing conversion of a Muslim noblewoman to Christianity will be seen as a greater Christian victory than the forced conversions of ordinary citizens. Although the Jewish and Moorish converts are unambiguously labeled "*Veir chrestïen*" ["True Christians"], with the verity of their Christianity upheld by a medieval Church that recognized the spiritual efficacy of forced baptisms and conversions, the poem and the Church nevertheless portray conversion by choice as producing a more sustainable Christian identity.[81] Because of Charlemagne's will, Bramimond is Christian by true understanding *("Chrestïen est par veire conoisance").*[82] The poem suggests a distinction between those made *"Veir chrestïen"* by coercion and Bramimond, who is converted *"par veire conoisance."* Even so, *Chanson de Roland* not only provides an example of the infidel-conversion motif in a work that so profoundly influenced later continental romances, but it also demonstrates how "respect of persons"—which Paul says God has none of in Romans 2:11—became an important factor in romance negotiations of racial and religious difference.

Indeed, within (and outside) romances, conversions to Christianity are often predicated upon modes of European desire. In *Bevis of Hampton,* for example, the fourteenth-century English metrical romance that was repeatedly printed in sixteenth- and seventeenth-century England, Sir Bevis tells the priest who will baptize the Saracen princess Josiane, "she will, for my sake, / Christendom at the take."[83] There are other examples that would have been well known in early modern England, such as Ruggiero's conversion in *Orlando Furioso* and Clorinda's and Armida's in *Gerusalemme liberata.*[84] Beloved by the female Christian knight Bradamante, the Saracen knight Ruggiero eventually converts to Christianity in Ariosto's account of the wars between the Franks and Saracens. Ruggiero actually says to Bradamante that he will be baptized "if it be [her] desire."[85] In *Gerusalemme liberata,* which is sometimes considered Tasso's epic response to *Orlando Furioso,* the Muslim female knight Clorinda is baptized on her deathbed by her love interest, Tancredi—though in this poem, the relationship is left unconsummated. In works like *Bevis of Hampton, Orlando Furioso,* and *Gerusalemme liberata,* English readers encountered a convention that emerges in the infidel-conversion motif: romantic feelings that lead to religious conversion.[86]

Linking romantic love and religious identity was conventional in romance, but it was usually inverted and demonized in early modern England. Recent work on European engagements with Islamic peoples and nations has revealed that erotic desire often led to "turning Turk," or Christian-to-Muslim conversion, in English plays set in the Mediterranean. Scholarship on turning Turk has shown that anxieties about Christian-to-Muslim conversions were often sexualized, betraying the pervasive fear that political and economic intercourse between European Christians and North African and Turkish Muslims could lead to the loss of European,

Christian identities.[87] I believe that the intensively studied turning-Turk motif is an inversion of the infidel-conversion motif of romance. The turning away from the turning-Turk and toward the infidel-conversion motif reveals that Protestant doctrines made becoming Christian no less a cause for anxiety than turning Turk.

To focus on Protestant doctrine, however, is not to ignore the economic and political circumstances that gave rise to the turning-Turk motif. Numerous studies have brought attention to the complex systems of trade, piracy, and state-sanctioned privateering that circulated in the early modern Mediterranean; ignoring this scholarship would mean missing the opportunity to explore the alternating currents of collaboration and competition among Christian doctrine and political and economic agendas.[88] In the highly charged context of Spain's distrust of Moriscos, the fear of Christian-to-Muslim conversion is placed side by side with the infidel-conversion motif in "The Captive's Tale" in Miguel de Cervantes's *Don Quixote* (1605)—coincidentally, published at about the same time as the performance of *Othello* in England and similarly concerned with Venice's fight to control Cyprus.[89] "The Captive's Tale" is a fictional captivity narrative, a genre that insists on the maintenance of Christian identity, even in the face of Islamic powers that encourage or try to force Europeans to forsake their Christian faith.[90] Cervantes, who participated in the 1571 battle of Lepanto, was captured by pirates on his way back to Spain in 1575; he remained the captive of a Greek renegade in Algiers until he was ransomed in 1580.[91] It is thus suggestive to read "The Captive's Tale" not only in the tradition of romance that so often engages with Islamic/Christian relations but also in relation to captivity narratives that so profoundly reject "turning Turk."

Of particular interest here is the captive's narration of how he came to marry Zoraida, a beautiful Moor who provides both the means and impetus for escape. The captive's first interaction with Zoraida occurs when she lowers from her window a handkerchief filled with gold coins and then a small cross. The captive assumes that Zoraida is a renegade Christian because of "the whiteness of her hand" and because "often the Moors are glad to marry slaves of this sort, whom they value more highly than women of their own people" (357).[92] As it turns out, Zoraida is not a renegade Christian but a Moor who hopes to become a Christian. The initial assumption about Zoraida's identity, however, is made not only because of

her cross but also because her whiteness should—but in this case does not—
signify Christian identity. María Antonia Garcés notes Zoraida's enig-
matic status: "uncertainty regarding Zoraida's identity is marked by the
symbols which mark her appearance. . . . Incarnating the maximum value
of Christianity and a distinct representation of Moorish economic suprem-
acy, these symbols arise as images of two conflicting systems, which col-
lide against each other with the full weight of their metaphorical charge."[93]
I am interested in Garcés's attention to the religious significance of material symbols, the cross and white skin, that both inconclusively and indeed
incorrectly signify racial and religious identity.

Zoraida's paradoxical status, Garcés also notes, is pronounced not only
here but also when she first enters an inn in Spain. She is veiled and mysterious, and upon seeing her Dorothea asks, "Is this lady a Christian or a
Moor? For her dress and her silence make us think that she is what we
hope she is not," to which the captive responds, "Moorish she is in body
and dress; but in her soul she is a very good Christian, for she has the
greatest desire to be one" (338). The captive does everything but answer
Dorothea's question. He suggests that she is both Christian and Moor:
Moorishness seems to reside in the body and in clothing, whereas Christianity seems to reside in the soul and in desire. Despite her white skin,
prior to conversion her body is still Moorish. Yet like the Ethiopian in
Crashaw's poem, her untransformed body contains a Christian soul. Zoraida, also like Crashaw's Ethiopian, is a study in figurative disunity; her
outward signs do not point toward the seemingly already-present inter-
nalized Christian identity. Unlike the baptized Ethiopian, however, baptism (along with a change of clothes) will create such a unity—fortunately
for her, she already has white skin.

In an Arabic letter Zoraida sends to the captive, she explains how she
acquired this hybrid Christian/Muslim identity, and she makes a connection between religious identity and location, one which explains
why she cannot become a Christian in Barbary: "When I was a girl my
father had a woman slave, who taught me Christian prayers in my own
tongue, and spoke to me often of Lela Marien. This Christian died, and
I know that she did not go to the fire but to Allah. For I saw her twice
afterwards, and she told me to go to Christian lands and see Lela Marien,
who loved me very much" (358). A renegade who is imprisoned with
the narrator translates this letter into Spanish. The renegade stands as a

cultural and linguistic mediator between the narrator and Zoraida, and his religious transformation from Christian to Muslim is an inversion of the one for which Zoraida hopes. Moreover, the presence of the renegade is a reminder of the allure of Barbary, where religious identity is mutable, and of anxieties about verifying true religious identities in the Mediterranean.[94]

Zoraida's need to leave Barbary and travel to "Christian lands" or *"tierra de cristianos,"* a phrase that appears throughout the tale, suggests that she cannot truly be a Christian as long as she remains in Barbary.[95] As long as she is there, she has only partial access to Christianity; there her devotion is to *Lela Marien* and Allah, not to the Virgin Mary and God. Here religious difference is marked through language. Although the renegade tells the captive that "where it says Lela Marien, it means Our Lady the Virgin Mary" (358), curiously, he chooses not to translate them and leaves the words in their Arabic form, suggesting that, at least in his opinion, there is no direct correlation between her present faith and "true" Christianity.

This linguistic gauge of true Christianity has a historical precedent. Deborah Root discusses the case of Maria de Molina before the Spanish Inquisition; she notes that language played an important role in the Inquisition's attempts to distinguish true from false converts.[96] Molina is asked to describe the nature of God. To the inquisitor's chagrin, Molina uses the Arabic words for Father, Son, and Holy Ghost. Molina is then convicted as a heretic because, Root argues, "her failure to speak proper Castilian was evidence of heterodoxy. . . . The word *Allah* was determined to mean 'the god of the Muslims' rather than the Arabic rendering of the Castilian *Dios.*"[97] In the mind of the Spanish inquisitor, Allah and God are not the same. Just as the Church maintained that God and Allah are not equivalent, Zoraida's use of Arabic words for Mary and God suggests that she embodies a hybrid Muslim and Christian identity that connotes doctrinal heterodoxy.[98]

Zoraida's religious hybridity is also the consequence an early modern geo-religious mapping of the world (it is one that Shakespeare's *Othello* engages, which I discuss in greater detail in chapter 4) in which geographical locations are given distinct religious identities. Finally arriving in Spain, Zoraida is transformed by the power of the land, especially as the narrator notes the astonishment of the townspeople: "They were astonished by Zoraida's beauty, which was at its height at that moment, by reason of the exertion of the journey and of her joy at finding herself on Christian soil" (379). Zoraida's beautiful elation upon reaching Spain reflects her hoped-for transformation: She will be baptized and become the wife of the captive. Christian soil allows her to partake of the two Christian sacraments so prominent and at times yoked in romance: baptism and marriage, both of which signify new identity, incorporation, and salvation. After baptism and marriage, she becomes the Christian that she had long seemed to be. Moreover, as William Childres argues, "'The Captive's Tale' presents a serious challenge: the integration of converts from Islam through mixed marriages, pointing toward a future society in which the ethno-religious conflict would be overcome"—of course, Cervantes could not have known that Moriscos were to be expelled from Spain just a few years later.[99] Despite anxieties about religious apostasy, or the Inquisition's questioning whether racially and culturally different Moriscos and *conversos* were really Christians, in "The Captive's Tale" the power of the infidel-conversion motif and romance remain firm and stand in opposition to the racial, religious, and economic politics (having been a captive, Cervantes would have been all too aware of them) that conflicted with the power of Catholic sacraments and the inclusive claim of Christianity to embrace all who believe.[100]

"The Captive's Tale" demonstrates that cultural history is not always the primary source of the literary artifact; in this case, the ahistorical and universal elements of romance and Christianity resist the cultural politics of Cervantes' day. Still, if Cervantes' affirmation of the infidel-conversion motif and its willingness to yoke romantic love and religious identity draws from Catholic sacramental theology, the inversion of the motif that so often linked apostasy with lust also responds to the Church of England's distinctively historical version of Christianity—its rethinking of the sacraments and their ability to foster Christian identity. Given the connections between race, lineage, and salvation in Protestant baptismal theology, neither in English churches nor in English romances could baptism be taken unequivocally to transform infidels.[101] English responses to the infidel-conversion motif will often reject the romance telos (the transformation and incorporation of the other) and thereby reinforce a theological view that religious identity is largely fixed and racial.

A byproduct of this theological view is that racial purity helps to assure salvation. Consequently, English responses to the infidel-conversion motif often criticize the erotic impulses that usually lead infidels to convert to Christianity. Romance, after all, is often associated with errant eroticism. Frye suggests that "The central element of romance is a love story, and the exciting adventures are normally foreplay leading up to a sexual union. Hence romance appears to be designed mainly to encourage irregular or excessive sexual activity."[102] (Consider, for instance, Aeneas's tryst with Dido, Ruggiero's with Alcina, or Redcrosse's with Duessa.) Erotic desire often prompts romance digressions, but desire can also be sublimated through Christian evangelism. Romances like *Orlando Furioso* and *Don Quixote* redeem the erotic by establishing baptism and marriage as complementary sacraments. Even so, early modern English authors often reject this sublimation and what we now might label "interracial marriages" in part because Protestant theology linked race and lineage with salvation.

Continental romances are replete with moments that uphold a belief that baptism and religious conversion fundamentally alter identity. Early modern English authors did not only have to confront romances that were foreign to its national literary history, however; its own literary past contained instances of a motif that a Protestant theology could not support. Although it is true that medieval English romances were influenced by their continental predecessors and peers, they become English—much in the way Harington's *Orlando Furioso* does—as they speak to English proto-imperial and proto-national fantasies.[103] An investigation of the infidel-conversion motif in medieval English romance might consider the various English Charlemagne romances, including *The Sowdone of Babylone, Otuel and Roland*, and *Rauf Coilyear*; tales in the Auchinleck manuscript; and medieval romances that remained in print in early modern England like *Bevis of Hampton* and "The Man of Law's Tale" in Chaucer's *Canterbury Tales*.[104] But I would like to consider briefly *The King of Tars*, not only because it has become an important text in medieval race studies but also because it radically imagines the miraculous power of baptism and religious conversion to erase racial characteristics and indeed create human identity.

The sultan of Damascus, whose "hid, þat blac & loþely was" [hide, that was black and loathly], hears of the rare beauty of a Christian princess who is "As white as the feaþer of a swan" [As white as a Swan's feather]. He threatens to begin a war with the Christian kingdom of Tars unless the princess marries him (ln. 928 and ln. 12).[105] She agrees to marry him in order to stop the war, but the sultan then refuses to marry her unless she converts to his belief in Jove, Pluto, Termagant, and Mahoun (ln. 469–80). The princess tells the sultan that she will convert, but the narrator suggests otherwise:

> & þei sche al þe lawes couþe,
> & seyd hem openliche wiþ hir mouþe,
> Ihesu forȝat sche nouȝt.
> Wher þat sche was, bi norþe or souþe,
> No minstral wiþ harp no crouþe
> No miȝt chaunge hir þouȝt.
> Þe soudan wende niȝt & day
> Þat sche hadde leued opon his lay,
> Bot al he was bicouȝt.
> For when sche was bi hirselue on
> To Ihesu sche made hir mon,
> Þat alle þis world haþ wrouȝt. (ln. 505–16)

[and although she knew all the laws (of Mohammed) and professed them openly with her mouth, she did not forget Jesus, wherever she was, by north or south. No minstrel with harp or crwth might change her mind. The sultan thought night and day that she believed his law, but he was deceived. For when she was by herself, she made her prayer to Jesus, who has made all of this world.]

The princess maintains a private, interior Christian identity that seemingly cannot be undone by superficial devotion to the sultan's gods. In a poem in which skin color coincides with already established reader expectations about religious affiliation (white skin signifies Christian identity, and black skin does not), it is possible that the princess is viewed as a Christian because of her whiteness.

So insistent is the poem's investment in skin-color-coded religion that when the sultan's skin miraculously changes from black to white after the priest gives him the Christian name Cleophas, almost out of necessity the sultan becomes a Christian:

> Þe Cristen prest hiȝt Cleophas;
> He cleped þe soudan of Damas

After his owhen name.
His hide, þat blac & loþely was,
Al white bicom, þurth Godes gras,
& clere wiþouten blame.
& when þe soudan seye þat siȝt
Þan leued he wele on God almiȝt. (ln. 925–32)

[The Christian priest was called Cleophas; He named the sultan of
Damascus after his own name. His hide, that was black and loathly, became
entirely white, through God's grace, and clear without blame. And when
the sultan saw that sight, then he believed well on almighty God.]

To be white and not a Christian is a figurative impossibility in *The King of
Tars.* The sultan's transformation also raises questions about Appiah's coun-
terposition of religion and biology; Heng argues, "The Sultan's conversion
demonstrates that, in medieval romance, the odd notion that religion
might trump ontology all erupts *within* a more clearly defined moment of
racial marking, in which visual evidence specifically pivoting on skin color
and a hierarchical aesthetics of color, is the operative determination."[106] In
The King of Tars, white skin indeed has the power to induce Christian belief in the sultan, and the poem unifies skin color and belief. The narrator,
moreover, conjoins white skin with Christian identity by describing the
sultan's new skin as being "wiþouten blame," implying that black skin was
a marker of his sin.[107] *The King of Tars* affirms that white is, as Bruce Holsinger's argues, "the color of salvation."[108]

The sultan's is not the only miraculous transformation in the poem. In
fact, an earlier miracle is what leads him to convert to Christianity. Before
his conversion, the princess gives birth to a child without form:

For lim no had it non.
Bot as a round of flesche yschore
In chaumber it lay hem bifor.
Withouten blod & bon. (ln. 579–82)

[For it had no limbs. But round as a cut lump of flesh, it laid before him
(the sultan). Without blood and bone.]

The sultan blames the child's formlessness on his wife's insincere conversion, but the narrative implies that the sexual and reproductive incompat-

ibility of Christian (white) and Mohammedan (black) is the result of ontological difference.[109] Nonetheless, after the sultan's prayers to change the formless flesh into a child go unanswered, the princess has the flesh baptized. Afterward, it becomes a beautiful boy. Although the miracles of white skin and human form may seem different, Jane Gilbert argues that they materialize from the same racializing religious ideology: "Before the christening, father and son are deemed sub-human to the degree that each represents only the crude form of a human being, lacking that spiritual dimension which properly distinguishes humans from other animals. Baptism refines the animal-heathen substance and creates a superior being."[110] Accordingly, black skin equals formlessness, the mark of a nonspiritual, not fully human ontology.[111]

Catholic baptism and the magic of romance engender (white Christian) humanity, but with a suggestion of the flexibility of racial formation in medieval thought. Lisa Lampert argues in her discussion of *The King of Tars* and *Parzival*, "Unlike modern notions of racial essence, these texts point to the possibility of change, although this change requires conversion and is based on a fixed belief in Christianity as the only true religion."[112] That blackness is not indelible does not negate blackness as a marker of racial difference; rather, it suggests that Catholic structures of belief governed the prevailing constructions of race. As different and reactionary as they are, English Protestant theology and romance, too, sought to govern the construction of race.

The texts I discuss illustrate that English responses to the infidel-conversion motif and Protestant concerns about race and salvation were far-reaching. Although the infidel-conversion motif originates in romance and thus carries within it the genetic material for romance's reproduction, English authors incorporated this motif into works that have other genre designations, such as epic, tragedy, and (tragi-)comedy. The motif's assertion that Christianity can embrace all who believe, regardless of race, must then negotiate with the prevailing ideologies of the primary genre; English authors find it difficult to reconcile romance telos with epic's project of nation building, tragedy's purgation of moral and political evils, and comedy's social/sexual reproduction imperative.

Chapter 1, "The baptz'd race," takes its title from a phrase in King James VI & I's *Lepanto* (1591), a poem about military conflict between Christians and Muslims. I suggest that this phrase accurately summarizes a Protestant understanding of Christian identity as a racial identity. This chapter surveys writings by important English Protestant theologians—including William Tyndale, Thomas Becon, John Hooper, and John Whitgift—and shows that English theologians consistently linked salvation to race and lineage; it further demonstrates just how often the figure of the infidel appears in theological discussions of baptism. This chapter also shows that the rhetorical force of theological arguments about baptism often presupposes a belief among English readers that infidels were racially different from themselves.

Chapter 2 argues that Edmund Spenser's *Faerie Queene*, which is highly imitative of Italian romance epics, is unable to imagine that the Saracen knight Pyrochles can "renounce [his] miscreaunce" because of emerging concepts of unalterable racial difference, difference that Reformation baptism could not erase. Like previous critics, I read the Nymph's well episode at the beginning of Book 2 as registering sixteenth-century baptismal controversies. I also explore the reasons behind Spenser's use of Ovid to examine theological debates. I argue that Spenser uses Ovid's *Metamorphoses,* in which characters retain a portion of their premetamorphosis identities, to explore the incomplete natures of baptismal, romance, and allegorical transformation. The incomplete natures of these transformations, and the concept of transformation itself, contend with the epic's intent to establish a racially pure and religiously stable Protestant national identity.

Where baptism fell short, reading came to the rescue. Chapter 3 situates Sir John Harington's influential translation of Ludovico Ariosto's *Orlando Furioso* in the context of Protestant Bible translation and in beliefs that reading facilitated religious conversion and sanctification. In this chapter I extend work done by Katherine Craike, Elizabeth Spiller, and Tiffany Jo Werth on reading as a practice that was believed to transform readers. This belief created anxieties about reading Catholic texts and romances, which were believed to alter passions, inspire lust, and spread Catholic belief. Reading the English Bible, conversely, especially heavily annotated ones that assured "correct" reading, was believed to help individuals restrain the concupiscent desire that lingers after baptism. Harington's *Orlando Furioso* emerges in the middle of these two beliefs; he produces a distinctly Protestant *Furioso* that seeks to teach readers how to restrain sexual desire. To do so, however, Harington finds it necessary to disavow the kinds of affective bonds that romances portray between Christians and infidels, and even those bonds that romance narratives create between Christian readers and non-Christian characters. We see this disavowal primarily in the infidel-conversion motif. Harington allegorically transforms the Saracen knight Rogero into a Christian long before the actual conversion. By stripping Rogero of his preconversion infidel identity and transforming him into a figure for the Christian reader, Harington repurposes the infidel-conversion motif to tell the story of a Christian's quests for sanctification. Harington thus links the process of translating *Orlando Furioso* to religious conversion; he transforms an infidel Catholic romance into an English Protestant heroic poem.

After chapter 3 I turn from English heroic poetry to consider romance on the early modern English stage. Chapter 4 argues that Shakespeare's *Othello* both reveals the work of genre and geography in the formation of religious identities and enacts a debate about the uses of romance's two competing goals: to transform and to restore identity. Because the play makes it very clear that Othello has been baptized, the Moorish hero closely resembles Ariosto's Ruggiero—in fact, there are allusions to *Orlando Furioso* in Shakespeare's play. Just as in *Orlando Furioso,* the transformative power of baptism and marriage to a Christian woman ought to assure Othello's Christian identity. Yet Iago seeks to undo romance telos and manipulate the infidel-conversion motif in order to restore what is presumably Othello's prior Muslim identity. To undo Othello's conversion, Iago disrupts the romantic ties between Othello and his wife, thus underscoring the ways in which romances cement religious identity through romantic relationships. If romantic love can cement a religious identity, Iago shows that dissolving the relationship between Othello and Desdemona can undo Othello's Christian identity, transforming him into a "turban'd Turk" at the end of the play.

The final chapter explores the dynamic interplay among race, gender, and salvation in tragicomedy, a genre in which the conversion of the infidel to Christianity reflects the formal shift from tragedy to comedy. My discussion of Shakespeare's *The Merchant of Venice,* John Fletcher's *The Island Princess,* and Philip Massinger's *The Renegado* begins, however, with two observations about the early modern English stage: One, more infidel women convert to Christianity than infidel men; and two, early modern English dramas appear to be more comfortable staging relationships between Christian men and infidel women than vice versa—though plays usually end, for the sake of comedy, with the woman converting to Christianity. The frequency with which Jewish, Turkish, and Moorish women convert to Christianity and then marry European men in English drama signals the convergence of the theological and medical discourses that highlighted the role of the male seed in creating a child's identity and that viewed female sexuality as a shortcoming that could be redeemed through childbirth. These discourses suggest that infidel women could be more easily incorporated into the Christian family than infidel men. Moreover, Fletcher's and Massinger's plays employ the discourse of martyrdom in order to verify the women's acquisition of true Christian faith. Nevertheless, the relegation of relationships between Christian men and infidel women to tragicomedy raises questions about the ability of infidel women to reproduce Christian offspring, reflecting the reigning theology's linkage of spiritual and sexual reproduction.

Becoming Christian is the study of a single romance motif. Yet it illustrates that uses of this motif are in dialogue with theological controversies, new forms of confessional identity, and emerging concepts of race. Uses of the motif also show that emergent concepts of race and Protestant theology altered the imaginative possibilities of romance.

I. "The Baptiz'd Race"

... by baptisme we enter into the kyngdome of God.
—*Archbishop Thomas Cranmer,* Catechismus *(1548)*

Betwixt the baptiz'd race / And the circumcised Turban'd
Turkes ...
—*James VI and I,* Lepanto *(1603)*

The above epigraphs sit uncomfortably with each other.[1] Archbishop
Cranmer's statement draws from a traditional, indeed universally accepted,
understanding of baptism. No Roman Catholic would have disagreed
with this statement; baptism has long been understood as the sacrament of
Christian initiation.[2] Disagreement emerges only when we ask how "by
baptisme we enter into the kyngdome of God." Answers to this question
varied greatly among Protestant reformers: Martin Luther asserted the
importance of the sacrament for salvation; Ulrich Zwingli argued the opposite; John Calvin's position was in the middle.[3] English Protestant beliefs about baptism were influenced by continental reformers and hence
equally conflicted.[4] Whereas Cranmer's seemingly ecumenical statement
offers a glimpse of the wide-ranging contestations that underlay baptismal
theology in the mid-sixteenth century, James's statement intimates the
incipient role of race in this heated theological controversy, implying a
racial criterion for legitimate baptism. Yet the king's sense of what the
term "race" means in this context is anything but transparent. Is he referring to a religious group demarcated by the sacrament of baptism, thereby
differentiating baptized Christians from circumcised and turbaned Mus
lims? Or does "baptiz'd race" imply not only sacramental ties but also

genealogical kinship? If so, how does that kinship group "enter into the kyngdome of God," especially if "baptiz'd" is not merely a religious category but also a racial one that presupposes invidious distinctions among kinds of people?

These questions surface not only from a juxtaposition of the passages from Cranmer and James; they also arose within reformed English baptismal theology. In this chapter I argue that the concept of race that emerged from the Church of England's baptismal theology became a powerful tool for clarifying theological arguments about salvation and the origins of Christian identity. When I use the word "race" in this chapter, I intend the early modern meaning, which denotes genealogy and lineage.[5] In this vein, race functions in two ways in the Church of England's baptismal theology: one, in arguments against English Anabaptists, because the Church of England asserted that the children of Christians should be baptized just as the children of Jews were circumcised; and two, in arguments asserting that the children of Christians who died before being baptized were nevertheless saved because God is also the Father of Christian "seed." John Calvin was the most influential source of these arguments, but I focus on English writings to show how widespread was the connection between race and salvation in the Church of England's theology.[6]

English theologians, drawing as they did from the work of Calvin, deemphasized the importance of baptism by asserting that the children of Christians were themselves Christians, even before they were born. This doctrine is contrary to Catholic theology, in which all humans are born as infidels and consequently need to be converted through the sacrament of baptism. It is also contrary to Tertullian's famous maxim, "Christians are made, not born." [7] English theologians repeatedly asserted that Christians are in fact born, a theological position that is also incompatible with Paul's assertion in Romans 9:7 and 8, "Nether *are thei* all children because thei are the seed of Abraham. . . . they which are the children of the flesh, are not the children of God," which was used to construct Jews as children of the flesh rather than of the spirit. Protestants condemned Judaism for what they saw as its genealogical understanding of election while turning a blind eye to their own racialization of salvation. The Church of England's baptismal theology reified concepts of racial difference by suggesting that conversion to Christianity was only for those not born into the baptized race; the need to convert thus marked the convert as racially different from Christians.[8] By questioning the role baptism played in the work of salvation, the English Church's baptismal theology fundamentally altered how individuals were believed to acquire religious identities. Moreover, just as this theology implied a racial difference between infidels and Christians, it both drew from a tradition in which infidels—especially Jews and Turks—were used to figure religious alterity and also transformed those figures into real spiritual subjects who might become Christians.

Understanding Baptism: Sacraments and the Stories They Tell

Reformed baptism arose from reformed sacramental theology. William Tyndale was among the first in sixteenth-century England to articulate a reformed sacramental theology in his *A briefe declaration of the sacraments* (1548).[9] Tyndale writes that he desires to help his readers "understand the pith of the sacraments, how they came up, and the very meaning of them" (347). He argues "that our sacraments are bodies of stories only; and that there is none other virtue in them, than to testify, and exhibit to the senses and understanding, the covenants and promises made in Christ's blood. And here ye see that where the sacraments, or ceremonies, are not rightly understood, there they be clean unprofitable" (358).[10] The "virtue in the sacraments" was a point of contention among Protestant theologians, but for Tyndale the efficacy of sacraments comes from the right understanding of the stories, covenants, and promises made through Christ's crucifixion— and "understanding" is so important for Tyndale that here he uses some form of this word twice.[11] As "bodies of stories," then, Tyndale's sacraments arise from traditional Christian typology (in which Jewish ceremonial rites prefigure Christian sacraments) and gain power from the participants' understanding of them. Tyndale's sacraments, then, are metonyms that point toward multiple narratives; they give the laity a variety of ways of grasping how sacraments work and what they do.

The Church of England's baptismal service, too, emphasized the met-onymic quality of sacraments—although Tyndale found fault with the English Church's statement about the sanctification of the water. The various stories that baptism tells were repeatedly announced to congregations in the opening prayer (indeed, the prayer would have been heard every time a child was born and baptized) to the baptismal service of the "Black Rubric" in the 1552 Prayer Book:

> Let us praye. Almightie and euerlasting God, which of thy great merce diddest saue Noe and his familie in the Arke from perishing by water: and also dyddest safely leade the chyldren of Israel, thy people throughe the redde Sea: figuring thereby thy holy Baptisme and by the Baptisme of thy welbeloued sonne Jesus Christe, dyddest sanctifye the floud Jordane, and al other waters, to the mistical washing away of sinne: We beseche thee for thy infinite mercies, that thou wylt mercyfully loke upon these chyldren, sanctifie them and washe them with thy holy ghoste, that they, beyng deliuered from thy wrath, may be receued into the Arke of Christes Church, and beyng stedfast in fayth, joyeful through hope, and rooted in charitie, may so passe the waues of this troublesome world, that finally they maye come to the lande of euerlasting lyfe, there to reygne wyth thee, worlde without ende, through Jesus Christ our Lord. Amen.[12]

The Church of England's service is remarkably different from the Latin Sarum Rite, the most commonly used order of service in pre-Reformation England.[13] The first prayer of the baptismal service, now said in English, is structured to mirror the interrelationship between understanding and sacramental efficacy. The actual beseeching, marked with the "We beseche thee," occurs only after the congregation has been reminded of instances in which God saves his chosen ones through and from water. God is beseeched to sanctify and wash the child only after the congregation has been reminded of God's saving power. Here the efficacy of the sacrament is implicitly linked to the theological concept of *fides aliena,* in which the understanding and faith of the believers make the sacrament effective for the infant.[14] Additionally, the work of baptism is explicitly linked to the narratives mentioned in the first part of the prayer, when the minister asks God to receive the child "into the Arke of Christes Church" so that the children "may so passe the waves of this troublesome world, that finally they maye come to the lande of everlasting lyfe." In the service the story of Noah provides the dominant metaphors through which the congregation understands what baptism does and how it works upon the child.[15]

One of the other stories baptism tells is that of the covenant God sealed with Abraham through the rite of circumcision. According to Tyndale, "instead of circumcision came our baptism; whereby we be received into the religion of Christ" (350). English reformers often followed medieval scholastic interpretations of the promises God made to Abraham and his decedents in the Hebrew Bible; English theologians, however, differed from medieval scholastics in their understandings of the effectiveness of the sacrament in relation to and apart from faith.[16] Nevertheless, in order to understand baptism, theologians like Tyndale explained the sacrament in relation to the covenant of circumcision. Tyndale first explains the origins of circumcision and the nature of God's covenant with Abraham as accounted in Genesis 17: "I wil establish my covenant betwene me and thee, and thy sede after thee in their generacions, for an everlasting covenant, to be God unto thee and to thy sede after thee . . . . This is my covenant, which ye shal kepe betwene me and you, and thy sede after thee. Let everie man childe among you be circumcised" (7 and 11). Tyndale's explanation of circumcision closely follows the covenant made in Genesis: Circumcision is the "covenant God caused to be written in the flesh of Abraham, and in the males of his posterity . . . circumcision was the seal and obligation of the said covenant" (349). Circumcision becomes for Tyndale a primary example of how God works: God engages in covenants with humans and seals them with rituals.[17] But to understand baptism in particular, Tyndale asserts that believers must first understand circumcision.

Neither Protestant reformers nor their medieval predecessors invented the circumcision/baptism analogy, which has its origins in the writings of St. Paul. Paul's analogy lends itself to a view of Jews as Christians' spiritual ancestors; within the logic of Christian typology, Jews become types of Christians. Drawing from postwar reconsiderations of Paul that seek to recover the connection between his theology and his Jewish identity, Julia Reinhard Lupton argues that, chiefly because of Paul, Christianity is significantly loaded with "Jewish tropes, ideas, and commitments, even when they function under the sign of disavowal."[18] Because understanding circumcision became crucial to understanding the sacrament of Christian initiation, baptism carried with it resonances of genealogical election—albeit with anxiety because Christianity finds it impossible to forget its Jewish heritage even as it distinguishes itself from it.

Justifying Pedobaptism: Circumcision and English Election

Although they departed from Catholic teachings concerning the sacramental efficacy of baptism, Tyndale and the Church of England after him maintained that the infants of Christians should be baptized. They do so, first, by drawing from traditional Christian typology that suggests baptism is analogous to the Jewish rite of circumcision, and second by arguing that just as the infants of Jews were circumcised so too should the infants of Christians be baptized. But comparing the baptism of Christians to the circumcision of Jews did more than just help English Protestants justify baptizing their infants; it also significantly shaped the Church of England's conceptualization of Christian identity. In the English Church's baptismal theology, then, English Protestants often identified themselves with Jews. As Achsah Guibbory has shown, Jews were not always figures of alterity in Reformation England:

> English people spoke about England and her reformed Church in language that figured her as the true Israel and recalled the history of biblical Israel. We see, indeed, a slippage between the idea that England was 'an' elect nation, part of the universal church of God, and 'the' elect nation. Both the New Testament and the Protestant emphasis on election revised but did not dismiss the idea of chosenness and 'chosen people,' as described in the Hebrew Bible.[19]

The circumcision/baptism analogy provides but one example of how English Protestants used Jewish history and religion to imagine their own election. Just as baptism was understood as a retelling of the story of the circumcision covenant God made with Jews as both a race and a nation, so in Reformation England baptism tells a story that allowed English Protestants to see themselves as an elect race and nation, and maybe even elect because of their race.

Advocates of pedobaptism often used the circumcision/baptism analogy to confront arguments made by sixteenth-century Anabaptists.[20] To be sure, the Church of England was careful to define its baptismal and sacramental theology in opposition to that of the Catholic Church. Yet theologians in the Church of England also went to great lengths to refute Anabaptist baptismal theology.[21] This doctrinal stance is quite clear in the work of Thomas Becon, a prolific writer and prominent theologian of the Church of England. In Becon's *A New Catechisme* (1564), which takes the form of a dialogue between a son and his father, the son turns from his vehement attack on Catholic theology toward his belief that the Anabaptists misinterpret Mark 16:16 ("He that shal beleve & be baptized, shal be saved") to mean that belief must precede baptism.[22] According to Anabaptists, infants should not be baptized because they are not yet able to believe. The son uses the circumcision/baptism analogy to confront Anabaptist belief:

> For as the infants of the Hebrews were not secluded and put away from the circumcision, which was also a sacrament or sign of God's grace, mercy, and favour to the Jews, even as baptism is now to the Christians, although [infants] cannot profess their faith commanded by God notwithstanding to be circumcised . . . even so in like manner ought the infants of the Christians to be admitted into the sacrament and sign of grace, (I mean baptism) . . . forasmuch as God is now no less the God of the Christians and of their children, than he was in times past the God of the Jews and their children. (208)

Becon was not the only Englishman to use the circumcision/baptism analogy to defend infant baptism. Thomas Cranmer argued, "Infants in the old law were circumcised; *ergo*, in the new law they ought to be baptized. Again: infants pertain to God, as it is said to Abraham, 'I will be thy God and the God of thy seed after thee.' "[23] Alexander Nowell, Dean of St. Paul's from 1560 until his death in 1602, also defended infant baptism by comparing baptism to circumcision in *A Catechisme* (1570): "Seeing God, which never swerveth from the truth, nor in anything strayeth from what is right, did not exclude infants that were in the Jewish church from circumcision, neither ought our infants to be put back from baptism."[24]

Temporality is important in these arguments. Although circumcision and baptism are analogous, illustrating the unchanging nature of God and how he works through covenants and ritual acts, baptism and Christianity are figured as the fulfillments and perfections of circumcision and Jewish identity.[25] The very verbs used in the argument of Becon's son illustrate this point: Circumcision "was," baptism "is now," and "God *is now* no less the God of the Christians and of their children, than he *was in times past* the God of the Jews and their children" (my emphasis). The manner in which God bestows favor, through covenants made between Himself and a chosen people, is characterized as immutable; the object of that favor, however, has changed from Jews to Christians. Although this belief that baptism supersedes circumcision was not new within Christianity, what is new is the use of God's covenant with Abraham to confront Anabaptist arguments and to think about Christian posterity. Christian supersessionism takes on a new racial logic. Before the Reformation, and even in Tyndale, the Church used the circumcision/baptism analogy mainly to understand more fully how sacraments tie God to man. In Becon and Nowell we see, by contrast, an interest in making sure that the children of Christians are included in God's covenant, which the Anabaptist insistence on the believer's baptism could never assure.

Just as English theologians like Becon and Nowell introduced the circumcision/baptism analogy into their justifications of infant baptism, so they introduced in England the view that Christians constitute an elect nation and race. As Becon argues that the children of Christians should be baptized, he goes beyond the traditional circumcision/baptism analogy—seen, for example, in Tyndale's discussion of the sacraments—in order to articulate the notion that Christians are a race. Like Tyndale, the son in Becon's catechism turns again and again to what becomes the key scriptural text, Genesis 17:7, to support his argument. The biblical examples Tyndale used to argue that God's covenants extend to the children of the faithful are later employed by Becon to assert that the children of Christians should be baptized because the children of Jews were circumcised.

Protestant uses of the Genesis 17 covenant to justify baptizing their infants suggest that Protestants of the time viewed the Jewish "chosen-race" theme as a model for their own self-understanding of "chosenness." Early moderns did indeed understand "Jew" as a racial category of identity, a point that scholars like Janet Adelman and James Shapiro have argued at length.[26] Moreover, the racialization of Jews, Sharon Achinstein suggests in her study of John Foxe's *Acts and Monuments*, was not separate from theological concerns: "Reforming Protestantism supplied the explicit ideological framework through which such social antipathy towards the cultural or racial other could be expressed," and Foxe's "textual incarnations of Jews reflect the emergence and intersection of both theological and racialist discourses on Jews."[27] In his sermon on the conversion of a Jew, Foxe refers to Jews as the "circumcised Race."[28] Although we need not read the word "race" in Foxe in "scientific" Enlightenment terms, his usage nevertheless betrays a belief that Jewish lineage marked Jews as different from European Christians. Moreover, as Adelman suggests, "Insofar as Jews constituted both a lineage and a people, perhaps they were ideally situated to mediate between the older and the newer senses of 'race' and hence to be early victims of racism."[29]

If Jews were viewed as a race, then, the Church of England's theology—which explained baptism by comparing it to the covenant God made with not only Abraham but also an entire race of people—provided a theological foundation for the construction of a Christian racial identity: As an elect race, Christians have the right to baptize their infants.[30] Protestants of that era thus laid claim to a racially elect identity analogous to that of the ancient Jews even as they denigrated Jews as a race.

The circumcision/baptism analogy and the emphasis on the covenantal right to baptize the children of Christians eventually led the son in Becon's *A New Catechism* to entangle race and lineage with notions of faith. Becon's attack on Anabaptist arguments requires a step beyond simply appropriating the Genesis 17 covenant; he further contends that infants have faith: "Infants and speechless children have faith," the son says, "therefore they also ought to be baptized" (211). This view aims squarely at Anabaptist arguments and their interpretation of Mark 16:16. The son speaks of "this sentence of our Saviour Christ, which the ungodly Anabaptists wrest and wring for the condemnation of the baptism of infants, making nothing of them, but rather stablisheth the baptism of your children against them and against their most devilish doctrine" (211). Indeed, both Anglicans and Anabaptists see faith as crucial for salvation; this is not where they disagree. The son thus challenges the Anabaptist assumption that the children of Christians do not have faith in Christ. The son's statement is a radical one, conflicting not only with Anabaptism but also with defenders of infant baptism like Calvin and Heinrich Bullinger.[31] As influential as the continental theologies of Calvin and Bullinger might have been in England, Becon argues that even faith itself, not just Christian identity, was a function of race.[32]

The key question is how infants get faith. The father rightly asks, "How do they obtain faith?" The son replies, "By the Holy Ghost" (212). The answer is convenient, but the son then seeks to demonstrate that individuals can be filled with the Holy Ghost in their mother's wombs. He quotes and comments upon Jeremiah 1:5: " 'Before I fashioned thee in thy mother's womb, I did know thee.' (That is to say, I favored and loved thee.) 'And or [sic] ever thou wast born, I sanctified thee' " (212). The son then provides the example of John the Baptist, about whom the angel said, "He shall be filled with the Holy Ghost, even from his mother's womb" (212). The son's argument implies that Jeremiah and John the Baptist are examples of God's treatment of all Christian children.

Becon asserts that God does not fill all infants with faith, and the emergence of race in discussions of baptism and salvation becomes clearer when Becon notes the limits of God's conferment of faith on infants. After the father asks, "What sayest thou though of the heathen and unbelieving," the son responds,

> Foreasmuch as they belong not to the household of faith, neither are contained in this covenant, "I will be thy God, and the God of thy seed;" again, "I will pour out my Spirit upon thy seed, and my blessings upon thy buds;" therefore leave them to the judgment of God, to whom they either stand or fall. With the children of the faithful God hath made a sure and everlasting covenant. (214)

Here, Genesis 17 is coupled with a passage from Isaiah 44:3. The use of this passage from Isaiah is itself significant, for the two verses preceding this one reaffirm the election of the nation of Israel: "Yet now heare, ô Iaakób, my servant, and Israél, whome I have chosen. Thus saith the Lord, that made thee, and formed thee from the wõbe: he wil helpe thee. Fear not, ô Iaacób, my servant, and thou righteous, whome I have chosen" (Isaiah 44:1–2). Becon uses God's promise to pour his spirit on the children of Israel—even from the womb—to support the idea that, inasmuch as God's promises now pertain to Christians, the spirit of God is now poured on the children of Christians, even before their birth. The elect status of the children of Christians is further emphasized by the exclusion of the children of unbelievers from this promise. Although the son does not explicitly say that faith is coupled to lineage, this conclusion follows inescapably from the position that the children of heathens do not have faith and the children of Christians do. The son does not go so far as to say that the children of heathens are damned; nevertheless, they are excluded from the assurance of salvation that is granted to the chosen "seed."[33]

This belief that the children of Christians are born into the Christian faith was pervasive and enduring in the Church of England, and both Anabaptists and Catholics, despite their radical differences, understood this belief as linking Christian identity to race and linage. Although both

groups focused on the Church of England's views concerning the salvation of infants, Anabaptists criticized its justifications for pedobaptism,
and Catholics criticized its deeming infants as Christians without baptism.
In *The character of the beast: or The false constitution of the church . . . concerning*
true Christian baptisme of new creatures, or new borne babes in Christ: and false
baptisme of infants borne after the flesh (1609), for example, the English Anabaptist John Smyth seeks to demonstrate that the Church of England's
theology linked salvation to race. Smyth advances various arguments
against the practice of baptizing infants, including the fact that Christ,
bridegroom of the Church, "wil not contract in marriage with a bride or
spowse that is vnder age."[34] But what is particularly relevant here is his
critique of the Church of England's uses of the circumcision/baptism
analogy to justify pedobaptism:

> You are to know . . . that all the old Testament was carnal taken from
> the Elementes of the World, thereby to type out & teach them heavenly
> things: & therefore their Church was carnal to type to us in the New
> Testament a Spiritual Church: The matter of their Church was a carnall
> Israelite: the matter of the Church of the New Testament is a true Israelite
> in whom there is no guile: The forme of their Church was a carnall
> circumcision a carnall seale. . . . The forme of the Church of the New
> Testament is the circumcision of the hart. . . . Their carnall Church in the
> matter & forme came by carnall Genealogie . . . our Spirituall Church in
> matter & forme is in the Genealogie of the Fayth of Abraham the Father
> of vs all vnder the Spirituall New Testament. . . . Thus if you would
> compare the Type and the Truth together, you should easily discerne
> the sandy foundation of your false Church ruinated & you false baptisme
> quite abandoned: *who continue a Church by succession of a carnall line.*[35]

Smyth's refutation of the Church of England's baptism employs long-
standing figurative readings of Jews as carnal and Christians as spiritual,
but here these readings come into conflict with each other. Both Anabaptists
and the Church of England understood Judaism as prefiguring Christianity,
but Smyth's Anabaptist reading entails a greater rupture between the old
and new covenants in its assertion that God ceased to work in and through
human genealogy. His accusation that the Church of England "continue[s]
a Church by succession of a carnall line" demonstrates that its baptismal
theology made Christianity a matter of race.

Although Anabaptists rejected the English Church's racial baptismal theology because it slighted faith, Catholics condemned its assertion that baptism was not the only way to become a Christian, seemingly rendering race more important than baptism.[36] This belief clashed so sharply with Catholic teaching that Thomas Harding, an English Catholic exile in Louvain, felt the need to respond to the notion that children were born into the Christian faith precisely because it undermined the importance of baptism. In *A confutation of a booke intituled An apologie of the Church of England* (1565), itself a response to the Bishop of Salisbury John Jewel's *Apologia Ecclesiae Anglicanae* (1562), Harding condemns Jewel's theology of baptism. In one instance, Harding attacks Jewel's use of Calvin, whom Harding criticizes for denying the necessity of baptism and saying that the children of Christians are born holy: "He seemeth to derogate much of the necessity of baptism of Christian men's children; where he saith that by reason of God's promise 'the issue which cometh of faithful parents is born holy, and is a holy progeny, and that the children of such, being yet inclosed in the womb, before they draw breath of life, be nevertheless chosen into the convent of life everlasting.' "[37] Jewel does not deny Harding's accusation. Rather, he responds by clarifying his position concerning the "holy progeny" and defending Calvin's theology:

> Whereas you charge M. Calvin for saying "the children of the faithful are born holy," ye should rather herewith have charged St. Paul. For thus he saith. *Nunc liberi vestri sancti sunt:* "Now are your children holy." Ye should have remembered, M. Harding, that these be St. Paul's words, and not M. Calvin's. His meaning is, that the children of the faithful, notwithstanding by nature they be the children of anger, yet by God's free election they be pure and holy.[38]

Harding's response to Jewel demonstrates that the Church of England's theological position was indeed viewed as a radical and potentially dangerous departure from Catholic teaching. Harding's main concern is that the doctrine of "holy progeny" and what Becon labeled "Christian infants" seem to render baptism unnecessary; he believes that if this is the case, Christians will no longer esteem the sacraments, and thus they may "easily be induced either to receive Mahomet's religion, or some other."[39] According to Harding, the belief in the sacredness of sacraments is what separates Christianity from Islam and other religions; it is hardly surprising, then, that sacraments became such a point of theological contention, and that baptism became such a concern in controversies over Christian-Muslim contact. Consistent with Protestant teaching, Jewel defends himself against Harding's attack by contending that although outward signs should not be conflated with spiritual grace (a position that reformers attributed to Catholics), sacraments are necessary. Harding's critique, nonetheless, illustrates the implications of what became a significant aspect of English baptismal theology. Harding contends that Jewel and Calvin believe that baptism is not necessary because holiness is passed down from parents to children. While Jewel rejects Harding's claim he views baptism as unnecessary, Jewel does not deny the point that the children of Christians are holy; instead, he uses the authority of St. Paul to defend his position.

Harding was correct that the notion of a "holy progeny" has its origins in Calvin's baptismal theology. Denying the necessity of emergency baptism by the laity (and especially by women), Calvin asserts in *Institutes of Christian Religion* (1536) that the children of Christians who die without being baptized are still included in God's covenant.[40] Calvin also argues in the *Institutes* that the children of Christians are baptized not in order to be saved but rather to reaffirm their chosenness: "The children of believers are not baptized, in order that though formerly aliens from the Church, they may then, for the first time, become children of God, but rather are received into the Church by a formal sign, because, in virtue of the promise, they previously belong to the body of Christ."[41] It must be acknowledged, as John Wheelan Riggs argues, that this justification of infant baptism needs to be read in isolation from Calvin's later theologies of predestination; Calvin does not develop his doctrine of predestination until after 1539.[42] But in *Institutes,* baptism does not inaugurate spiritual, Christian identity; rather, it marks the child's induction into the church as an earthly community of the elect, an induction that is itself predicated upon the belief that the child is already among the elect. Becon's and Jewel's assertions that lineage could assure election certainly echo Calvin; for them genealogical differences have spiritual significance, and English theologians used Calvin's arguments to support their belief that race, not baptism, was the key to salvation.

Nevertheless, the basic tenets of Christianity mandate that Becon, Jewel, and Calvin acknowledge that all humanity is fallen. The English racialization of salvation drew from the theology of Calvin, who attempted to reconcile this understanding of election through lineage with the Christian belief that all humanity is damned without Christ's death and resurrection: "For those who imagine that some sort of seed of election was sown in them from birth itself, and that by birth itself, and that by its power they have always been inclined to piety and the fear of God, are not supported by Scriptural authority and are refuted by experience itself."[43] Calvin's statement seems to coexist uneasily with his earlier assertion; he argues here that Christians should take assurance in Christ's sacrifice rather than in a "seed of election"—though we may see in this a gesturing toward a theory of invisible "second election" that Calvin developed later in his doctrine of predestination.[44] The all-too-human behavior of the elect, here understood to be inherently depraved, is used as evidence that even those who are elect are only saved through Christ.

Race became a more explicit part of this argument in Calvin's sermon on the second chapter of Galatians:

> Now then he sayeth that the Iewes are indeede separated after a sort from the Gentiles, not that the Iewes are of more worthinesse, or that they haue any righteousnesse in themsleues: but because God of his own goodnesse voutsafed to choose them: like as at this day the children that are borne of beeuing parents, are not better than the children that are born of Paynims & Turks, if a man consider them both in their owne nature. For we all be a corrupted and cursed lump. . . . But yet neuerthelesse, S. Paul sheweth that they be sanctified, and that they be not vncleane, as those are which are borne of vnbeleeuers or Heathen folke.[45]

Although Calvin makes it clear the elect are not racially superior, he does not challenge the belief that Christians and heathens are different races, and that racial difference has spiritual consequences; he maintains that the children of the elect are born holy and that the children of Paynims and Turks are not. Calvin's point is not so much to deny that election comes through lineage as it is to remind the elect that they are so only because of God's promise to them.

Saved by Race: Salvation Without Baptism

The Church of England's vigorous defense of pedobaptism did not entail a belief that baptism was necessary for salvation. A sacramental theology that insisted that sacraments are metonyms, narratives, and signs of grace rather than vehicles that bestow grace would not allow English Protestants to view them as prerequisites of salvation. The Catholic Church had argued just the opposite, that no one could be saved who does not receive baptism. Thomas Aquinas articulates this position quite clearly in *Summa Theologica*: "Three sacraments are necessary for salvation. Two of them are necessary to the individual; Baptism, simply and absolutely, and Penance, in the case of mortal sin after baptism" (91).[46] Aquinas's phrase "simply and absolutely" underscores baptism as a necessary condition of salvation. This theology justified infant baptism in Catholicism, for only baptism could erase the original sin that all humanity inherited from Adam. In Roman Catholicism, consequently, infants who died without the sacrament were believed to die outside of God's grace and thus denied entrance into heaven. Such a belief led to lay baptisms—often performed by midwives—in cases where an infant was likely to die before a priest could arrive.[47] And the unofficial Catholic belief in Limbo provided partial solace to parents who grieved the deaths of their nonbaptized children.

With the dismissal of what they would have considered the superstitious belief in Limbo, Protestant parents surely must have wondered what happened to their children if they died before being baptized. While English Protestants like Tyndale, Nowell, and Becon maintained that infants should be baptized, their assumptions about and arguments for pedobaptism did not imply that nonbaptized children of Christians were damned—although surely the vehemence with which these theologians defended infant baptism may have resulted from latent and unacknowledged fears about the fates of nonbaptized infants.[48] English Protestants thus yoked their interpretations of Genesis 17 to their understanding of sacraments as signs of grace rather than as instruments that bestow it, thus arguing that the children of Christians who die without baptism are still saved. As it attempted to save nonbaptized children from hell's flames, English Protestant theology denied that baptism was necessary and asserted instead that race and lineage could save the nonbaptized children of Christians.

Despite the scriptural mandate to circumcise male children, Tyndale's sacramental theology does not allow him to esteem circumcision—or baptism for that matter—as efficacious in and of itself. Following St. Paul's argument in Romans 2, he asserts, "males, having the flesh circumcised, yet not believing nor loving God, whereunto the outward circumcision bound them, were uncircumcised unto God, and God not bound to them. . . . so that neither circumcision, or to be uncircumcised, is aught worth (as St Paul saith, Rom. ii.) save for the keeping of the law" (349). We should not be surprised that Tyndale stresses the importance of belief. Accordingly, circumcision has no efficacy without accompanying belief— and we can see here how this reading of circumcision via Paul informs a Protestant view of the sacraments of the Lord's Supper and baptism. Performing and receiving circumcision, as well as Christian sacraments, are necessary because God requires them. Obedience is important, not the act itself. Because obedience and belief rather than the act provide surety of the covenant (and one has no need to be obedient if, as Tyndale puts it, one is "not believing or loving God"), Tyndale can assert that male Jewish children are born into the covenant of Genesis 17, and that the covenant pertains to them even before they are circumcised: "The covenant, made between God and Abraham saved the man-child as soon as it was born, yea, as soon as it had life in the mother's womb" (350). This assertion is the logical extension of the promise of Genesis 17: that God is the God of the seed even while it is in the mother's womb.

Tyndale's assertion that uncircumcised male children of Jews were covered by the covenant may reflect his wish to confront the unhappy consequences of the Protestant rejection of Limbo. To do so, Tyndale simply applies to baptism arguments made about circumcision. Because "instead of circumcision came our baptism," he asserts,

> then it followed, that the infants that die unbaptized, of us Christians, that
> would baptize them at due time and teach them to believe in Christ, are
> in as good case as these that die baptized: for as the covenant made to the
> faith of Abraham went over his seed as soon as it had life, and before
> the sign was put on them: even so must need the covenant, made to all
> that believe in Christ's blood, go over that seed as soon as it hath life in the
> mother's womb, before the sign be put on it. For it is the covenant only,
> not the sign, that saveth us. (350)

More important than baptism is the intent of Christian parents to baptize their children and teach them to believe in Christ; intent seems to be enough to fulfill the human part of the covenant. Moreover, Tyndale's need to specify that the covenant only applies to the nonbaptized children "of us Christians" not only points to the ways in which the promises of God were believed to be inheritable through lineage but also defines genealogical and racial limitations on which children can be saved without baptism and which cannot.

Tyndale's emphasis on the importance of parental intent also responds to the occasional practice of baptizing Jewish or Muslim children against the will of their parents. Thomas Aquinas's criticism of this practice in *Summa Theologica* indicates that such baptisms were performed in the Medieval Church.[49] Notwithstanding his criticism, Aquinas does not deny the efficacy of such baptisms; rather, he suggests only that children who are baptized against the will of their parents may lose the benefits of that baptism: "for they may be liable to lapse into unbelief, by reason of the natural affection for their parents" (161). Before this statement, moreover, Aquinas asserts strongly that the unbelief of a child's parents does not negate the efficacy of the baptism: "Nor is it a hindrance to their salvation if the parents be unbelievers. . . . And the unbelief of their own parents, even if after Baptism these strive to infect them with the worship of demons, hurts not the child. . . . But the faith of one, indeed the whole church, profits the child through the operation of the Holy Ghost" (158–9).[50] This was not solely a Catholic belief. Martin Luther argued a similar point. Anticipating future arguments made by Anabaptists, he writes in *The Babylonian Captivity of the Church* (1520),

> some might cite the baptism of infants who do not comprehend the promise of God and cannot have the faith of baptism; so that therefore either faith is not necessary or else infant baptism is without effect. Here I say what all say: Infants are aided by the faith of others, namely, those who bring them for baptism. . . . Nor should I doubt that even a godless adult can be changed, in any of the sacraments, if the same church prayed for and presented him.[51]

For both Aquinas and Luther, baptism acquires power from the prayers of the Church and its belief in the efficacy of the sacrament—and for Luther, sacraments accompanied by the prayers of the Church even have power to change an unbeliever. Unlike Aquinas and Luther, for whom baptism and the faith of the Church itself have power to change the ungodly into the godly, Tyndale's emphasis on parental intent establishes an intimate connection between spiritual transformation and familial relations.

Tyndale's argument about parental intent, then, as well as arguments advanced by later English theologians who defend infant baptism, departs from both Roman Catholic and Lutheran understandings of baptism's power. This theological departure was reiterated by later English theologians as they rejected the emergency baptisms performed by midwives and attempted to assure grieving parents that their infants who died without baptism were still saved. Like Tyndale, the son in Becon's *A New Catechism* asserts, "Hereof then may we truly conclude, that, forasmuch as the outward baptism, which is done by water, neither giveth the Holy Ghost, nor the grace of God, but only is a sign and token thereof; if any of the Christian infants, prevented by death, depart without baptism (necessity so compelling), they are not damned, but be saved by grace" (217).

The ordering of the arguments in *A New Catechism* is revealing. Becon asserts that "Christian infants" who die without baptism are saved only after his argument establishes that such infants have faith. Faith, that all-important element in Protestant notions of salvation, becomes the primary means through which infants are saved. The category "Christian infants" is itself noteworthy. Not only is it a phrase that appears throughout discussions of infant baptism in *A New Catechism,* but it also suggests that a child is born with an established religious identity that is independent of the sacrament. If one is born a Christian, baptism and conversion seem unnecessary.

So important was the belief that the children of Christians are holy at their birth and thus saved without baptism that William Hubbock devoted a whole sermon to the topic, *An apologie of infants in a sermon, prouing, by the reuealed will of God, that children preuented by death of their baptisme, by Gods election, may be saued* (1594). The sermon poses the question, "and is [God's] compassion shut up from the seed of Christians" and answers it emphatically by demonizing the Catholic position: "O pitifull & cruell sentence, whose ears will not tingle at it? Infants who cannot speak, think, or do ill, the child whose flesh is scarce curded in the wombe: whose bondes scarce grislted out of the wombe: from the darkenes of the wombe passe to the vtter darkness for euer. Thus speaketh the dragon all gorged with blood."[52]

As commonplace as this theological position became in early modern England, there were dissenting voices. During his tenure as bishop of London, Richard Bancroft was less certain about nonbaptized infants: "the state of the infant, dying unbaptized, being unknown, and to God only known.'"[53] David Cressy argues that Bancroft's view reveals that "the Church of England had no consistent or satisfactory answer to the problem of the 'infant which die unbaptized.' "[54] This, however, is a bit of an overstatement, for despite uncertain voices like Bancroft's, numerous English theologians used race to assure a salvation outside of baptism.

The Nonbaptized Infidel: Figure of Difference and Religious Subject

English theologians both transformed Christians into a race and argued that salvation could be assured by race, yet these thinkers never asserted that infidels could not become Christians. Race, however, remained an issue as Protestants considered the process by which Jews, Turks, or Moors could convert to Christianity. In fact, English Protestants often used the presumed racial otherness of infidels to clarify their arguments about baptism. Nowhere do the issues of infant baptism and the racialization of infidels conjoin more closely—indeed in the same sentence—than in this passage from *A Brief and Clear Confession of the Christian Faith,* by the Bishop of Gloucester, John Hooper (1581):

> I believe that this baptism with water is not so necessary to salvation, that one may not be saved without it in case of necessity . . . even as in time past under the law the little children dying without circumcision were saved by the faith of their parents. But this only I do understand of the children of the faithful, unto who the promises of God do appertain, and not of the infidels and reprobate.[55]

In Hooper we see the rearticulation of many of the arguments that were made earlier by Tyndale, Becon, and others: Baptism is not necessary for salvation; baptism is analogous to circumcision; the promises of God pertain to the children of the faithful; and the children of infidels are excluded from the promise of salvation. Hooper makes a sharp distinction between the children of Christians and the children of infidels; only the children of Christians can be saved without baptism. This theology raised the following question: Could an infidel be saved without baptism? In what follows I consider how the infidel—as both a figure of alterity and a religious subject to be saved or damned—was used to clarify reformed views of baptism in England.

Tyndale and Becon argue that an infidel, too, can be saved without baptism. Tyndale writes, "And as the circumcised in the heart, and not in the flesh, had part in God's promises; even so a Turk unbaptized (because he either knoweth not, that he ought to have it, or cannot because of tyranny,) if he believe in Christ, and love as Christ did and taught, then hath he his part in Christ's blood" (351). Tyndale's emphasis on the efficacy of belief over that of the sacraments is hardly surprising. What is surprising is the entrance of the infidel into this theological discussion; the Turk, both as a figure of alterity and as a real person who might be saved, helps to illustrate the view of baptism as no more than a sign. His assertion that salvation is available "even so a Turk" who dies without baptism yet believes in Christ is a logical conclusion to his arguments about baptism. The son in Becon's catechism concurs: "and it is not to be doubted that, even among the Turks and the other heathen, there are many spiritually baptized, and so are saved, although their bodies want the water of baptism" (221). Although these statements affirm that belief rather than baptism has the power to transform the Turk from an infidel into a Christian, the contexts of their statements illustrate that Tyndale and Becon are not so much concerned with the salvation of actual Turks as with the following three points: one, vehemently attacking Catholic doctrines on baptism; two, asserting that Christians are now God's chosen; and, three, saving the children of Christians from hell's flames. For both men the Turk is above all a rhetorical figure of alterity, one that serves to strengthen the assertion that baptism is not necessary for salvation. The logic of their arguments requires, however, that this figure of alterity also be appreciated as a real Turk who can be saved; Tyndale and Becon thus transform the Turk from figure to real religious subject.

In Tyndale and Becon we also see a rhetorical shift from Jew to Turk: from using Jewish lineage as an analogy to the emerging concept of Christian lineage to introducing the Turk as a figure of alterity. Concepts of Jewish lineage proved most helpful for understanding how Christians might be understood as a baptized race, but Jews are absent from discussions of baptism where a figure of racial alterity is needed to prove a theological point. Jews were demonized in many theological treatises, but not in discussions of baptism where the sacrament was compared to circumcision or in discussions of baptism that proposed analogies between Christians and Jews. For this reason, I suggest, the Turk entered discussion of baptism; the Turk became the figure of alterity that could prove that baptism is not necessarily for salvation.

We gain a better understanding of the rhetorical power of Tyndale's and Becon's respective "even so a Turk" and "even among the Turks" when we consider how the Turk functioned figuratively in religious polemics. The Turk, as Matthew Dimmock has shown, held a special place in theological debates and in the religious practices of the Church of England.[56] Turks were the proverbial enemy of the Christian "West," most especially because of their conquests of lands once considered to be part of Christendom (the conquests of Constantinople in 1453 and of Cypress in 1571, for instance). But the Turk was seen not only as a proverbial enemy but also a real one, so much so that the Church of England devised both prayers of petition and thanksgiving concerning their imperial actions. Following the defeat of the Turks at Malta, for example, the Church of England issued *A short forme of thankesgeuing for the delyuerie of the isle of Malta from the inuasion and long siege thereof by the great armie of the Turkes both by sea and lande, and for sundry other victories lately obteined by the Christians against the said Turkes, to be vsed in the common prayer within the prouince of Canturburie on Sondayes, Wednesdaies, and Fridaies, for the space of syx weekes* (1565), a prayer that makes it difficult to distinguish religious and spiritual concerns from imperial ones. Additionally, the Turk was a frequent presence in Christian worship through *The homilie against disobedience and wylfull rebellion* (1570). Lamenting the fall of Christian lands into the hands of Turks, the homily states,

> So manie goodly Cities, Countreys, Dominions, and Kingdomes, some time possessed by Christians in *Asia, Africa, Europa*: the miserable fall of the Empyre and Church of Greece, sometime the most flourishing parte of Christendome, into the handes of the Turkes: the lamentable diminishing, decaye, and ruine of christian religion: the dreadfull increase of Paganitie, and power of the Infidels and miscreantes.[57]

The Turks' presence in the homily suggests that an English man or woman could hardly think of them without considering their supposed antipathy to the Christian faith.

As different as the Turk was in the minds of early modern English readers, not all Protestant writers represent the Turk as the absolute evil. In Tyndale's early writings, the "Turk" is as a figure of racial and religious difference, a kind of placeholder against which the reader can fathom the more radical alterity of Catholics. For example, the figure of the Turk is ubiquitous in *Answer to Sir Thomas More's Dialogue* (1531), Tyndale's response to Sir Thomas More's *Dialogue Concerning Heresies* (1529). There is hardly a discussion in Tyndale's *Answer* that does not use the figure of the Turk to help readers understand the evils of Catholics; in contrast to Catholics, Turks emerge in a favorable light. Tyndale asserts that in contrast to Catholics, "The Turks . . . believe many things of God." (*Doctrinal Treatises*, 53); he further contends that the "pope's life and doctrine are more wicked than the Turks and all the heathen that ever lived" (*Doctrinal Treatises*, 145). It is important to remember, however, that Tyndale is less concerned with actual Turks than he is with Catholics; in his anti-Catholic polemic, the Turk cannot represent the greatest of all evils.

Nevertheless, Tyndale's argument exploits his readers' likely assumption that Turks are an absolute spiritual evil, especially within an early Reformation print culture in which Protestant and Catholic authors wrote books responding to the books of their religious opponents. In *Responsio ad Lutherum* (1523), for example, Thomas More devotes the entire thirteenth chapter ("*Lepide refellit insulem Lutheri Lemma impugnantis diuturntiatem fidei catholicae, illata partier diuturnitate superstitionis iudaicae Turcharum et gentilium*" ["He wittily refutes Luther's silly premise attacking the long duration of the catholic faith by referring to the equally long duration of superstitions of the Jews, Turks, and heathens"]) to criticizing Luther's comparison of Catholics to Jews, Turks and other "heathens."[58] Luther, as More summarizes his argument, suggests that the "public faith of the Turks lasting through several ages and of the heathens lasting through several thousand years is erroneous . . . ; therefore, the public faith of the catholic church, maintained through however many ages, can be erroneous."[59] Putting Luther's logic aside (or the lack thereof according to More), what is significant here and throughout the chapter is the triangulation of Protestant, Catholic and Turk. Reformation debates seem to need this third, outside figure (like the Turk or the Jew [in other theological contexts]) to prove the deficiency and error of the primary opponent—of course, More will turn the table and align Luther with the Turk.[60] In Reformation debates, then, the Turk is often less evil than the Catholic in the eyes of some Protestants—or less evil than a Protestant in the eyes of some Catholics. Moreover, arguments suggesting that Catholics are less godly than Turks gained their power from readers' likely previous assumptions that there is nothing more evil than a Turk.

Consequently, Protestant-Catholic polemics do not allow Tyndale or Becon to view Turks as unredeemable, and thus the Turk's status as figure of evil gives way to the Turk as a spiritual subject who might receive Christian salvation. In Tyndale's theology, to view Turks as beyond salvation is to have a reprobate mind. At the beginning of *Answer,* speaking very generally of an individual who does not have the Holy Ghost to teach him, Tyndale writes, "He believeth that he loveth God, because he is ready to kill a Turk for his sake, that believeth more in God than he; whom God also commandeth us to love, and to leave nothing unsought to win him unto the knowledge of the truth" (7–8). As illustrated in his mentioning of the Turk in *A brief declaration*, here, too, Turks can be redeemed, and indeed should be loved so that they might convert to Christianity.

The main function of the Turk in Tyndale's and Becon's writings is to serve as a foil to Catholic sacramental theology and to clarify their Protestant views. The construction of the Turk within Protestant discourse, however, begs the question: If a Turk, as different as he may be, can become a Christian without the sacrament of baptism, what real good does baptism do the Christian progeny? Tyndale answers this question by asserting that they ought to be baptized because it reminds the congregation of their covenant with God: "Neither our salvation so greatly standeth in [baptism] or any other sacrament, that we may not be saved without them, by preaching the word only. Nevertheless God hath written his will, to have his benefits kept in memory" (359). Salvation comes from two other means: faith, which comes from preaching and through which Turks and indeed everyone can be saved; and through God's covenant that he established first with Jews and later with the baptized race, Christians and their posterity. Although both infidels and the children of Christians can be saved without being baptized, it is important that they are saved through different means. While nonbaptized infidels can be saved through faith and belief, the children of Christians are saved through the covenant. Infidels can be saved in spite of their race, while the children of Christians are saved because of their race.

Despite its use of race to ensure salvation and to prove the inefficacy of baptism, the Church of England never went so far as to say that Turks, Moors, Jews, or any other infidels could not become Christians. The English Church nevertheless created a Christianity defined mainly by race and lineage, in which the customary route to salvation was birth into the

Christian faith. Tyndale's and Becon's belief that even Turks could be saved without baptism thus remains in communion with the inclusive claims of Christianity to embrace all who believe; what is true for Christians and their seed is also true for Turks who believe in Christ. But in contrast to Tyndale's and Becon's views, the reformed sacramental theology that denied the miraculous power of baptism also provided theological justification for questioning the salvation of Jews, Turks, and Moors who underwent the rituals of Christian conversion. In the following chapters I will consider how the theology that stripped baptism of its miraculous power, as well as racial constructions of both Christian and infidel identities, mandated purposeful and self-conscious engagements with romance's infidel-conversion motif, one which could embody Christianity's claim to embrace individuals of every nation and race.

2.   *Ovidian Baptism in Book 2 of* The Faerie Queene

Critics have long disputed the meaning of baptism in the Nymph's well episode in Book 2 of *The Faerie Queene*, but none have explored the racial implications of Spenser's treatment of theological controversies.[1] As I illustrated in the previous chapter, the Church of England's theology of infant baptism and salvation encouraged English Protestants to conceive of Christianity as a racial identity, a hereditary or blood trait passed from parents to children. Book 2 of *The Faerie Queene* reflects this outlook in its epic project of national self-definition, rejecting the infidel-conversion motif and aligning religious identity with concepts of race that were gaining influence in Reformation England.

But to see how Spenser's poem aligns religious and racial identity, we must first understand the way in which Book 2 provides thematic and interpretive guidance to readers. In the proem to Book 2, the narrator highlights the elusive nature of the poem by drawing attention to the fact that readers may have difficulty locating Faeryland:

> Where is that happy land of Faery,
> Which I so vaunt, yet no where show,
> But vouch antiquities, which no body can know.

> But let that man with better sence advize,
>   That of the world least part to us is red:
>   And dayly how through hardy enterprize,
>   Many great Regions are discovered,
>   Which to late age were never mentioned.
> Who ever heard of th'Indian *Peru*?

> Or who in venturous vessell measured
> The *Amazons* huge river now found trew?
> Or fruitfullest *Virginia* who did ever vew?
>
> Of Faerie lond yet if he more inquire,
>   By certaine signes here set in sundry place
>   He may it find; ne let him then admire,
>   But yield his sence to be too blunt and bace,
>   That no'te without an hound fine footing trace.
>   And thou, O fairest Princesse unde sky,
>   In this fair mirrhour maist behold thy face,
>   And thine owne realms in lond of Faery,
>   And in this antique Image thy great auncestry.
>   (2.Proem.2–4)[2]

The inability to locate Faeryland does not consign it to an imaginary realm; rather, it points to the limits of human knowledge, understanding, and sensory perception. Understanding, or "better sence," comes through charting previously unknown and foreign territories—and here the narrator links Faeryland not with Englishness but with foreignness.[3] Although the narrator eventually tells us that it can be found if the reader "more inquire" into "certaine signes here set in sundry places," the word "certaine" exemplifies Spenser's characteristic duplicity. On the one hand, there are sure signs that will lead us to Faeryland, but on the other there are likely numerous signs in the poem that lack this surety, signs that may purposely lead a reader astray. Even so, the narrator provides an interpretive crutch for those with "sence . . . too blunt and bace." The attempt to understand Faeryland and Spenser's project is then likened to using a hunting hound that uses its sense of smell to locate a missing object that leaves a "trace" of its whereabouts.[4] The reader of *The Faerie Queene,* much like the hound, may often need to hunt for something that is absent and search for a "trace" that will lead to understanding.

Following this meditation, and within the same stanza, the poet apostrophizes Queen Elizabeth as the "fairest Princesse unde sky," claiming that the poem acts as a mirror for the queen to "behold [her] face, / . . . [her] owne realms in lond of Faery," and her "great ancestry." Yet the narrator has already suggested that Faeryland can be found only through difficult, diligent searching for traces; seeing the queen's image and ancestry requires a similar process.

The Proem, I believe, brings into focus *The Faerie Queene*'s poetics of absence and traces, a poetics that governs Spenser's self-conscious use of allegory and his disavowal of romance's power to transform racial and religious identities. Conspicuously absent from Spenser's poem are moments of infidel conversion. Despite Spenser's indebtedness to Ariosto and Tasso, especially in the 1590 *Faerie Queene,* in which there are so many traces of them, the conversion and incorporation of the infidel is noticeably absent. Not only that, Spenser explicitly rejects the infidel-conversion motif in Book 2, canto 8, when the Saracen knight Pyrochles refuses to "renounce [his] miscreaunce" (8.51.6). In addition to Pyrochles, Acrasia is left unredeemed at the end of Book 2; her fate is very different from that of her literary predecessor, Armida, who, in the final canto of *Gerusalemme liberata,* yields to Rinaldo's will and faith.[5] Through searching for traces of the absent infidel-conversion motif in Book 2, we find our way to seeing the image of Elizabeth, her kingdom, and her "great ancestry," a project that points to Spenser's indebtedness to Ariosto as well; he proposes to do for Queen Elizabeth just what Ariosto did for the Estes. But unlike the Este's genealogy, there is no converted Saracen in the queen's and England's imaginative ancestry, as the genealogies in Books 2 and 3 prove. This notable absence provides Elizabeth and England with racially and religiously pure origins.[6]

Although Spenser excludes the infidel-conversion motif, baptism—the sacrament featured so prominently in both Ariosto's and Tasso's infidel conversions—remains important to the poem's construction of Englishness and Christian identity. Yet baptism, as it is figured in the Nymph's well episode, is not linked to a Christianized, magical power that transforms and incorporates desirable Muslims like Ruggiero and Clorinda in Ariosto's and Tasso's poems, but to Ovidian metamorphosis and to Acrasia. The question then becomes, why does Spenser compare baptism to Ovidian metamorphosis? In *Metamorphoses,* metamorphosis often produces bodily change, announced by the poet at the beginning of the poem, when he "speaks now of forms changed / into new bodies" [*In nova fert animas mutatas dicere formas / corpora*] (1.1–2).[7] This is not to say that other types of change—epistemological or psychological, especially in the multiplicity of meanings for "*animas*"   do not occur as well, only that they remain in the body; as Leonard Barkan has taught us, "often the business of metamorphosis . . . is to make flesh of metaphors."[8] At the same time, individuals in *Metamorphoses* are seldom transformed into something completely new. Metamorphosis leaves intact a trace of the former identity, and it creates a correspondence between a character's internal state and his or her external form. In the comparison of baptism and metamorphosis in Book 2 of *The Faerie Queene,* then, Spenser points to the limited power of baptism, its inability to produce the bodily changes that would create the internal and external unity of Ovidian metamorphosis, and highlights the retention of original identity in both baptized and metamorphosed individuals. Through comparing baptism and metamorphosis, we also see why Spenser's *Faerie Queen* must reject romance telos, the itinerary from transformation to incorporation. The poem denies the magical transformations of romance and the infidel-conversion motif because baptism, Ovid, and even the allegorical mode prove unable to erase all traces of originary identity: racial, bodily, and literal.

Sacramental Theology and Sacramental Allegory

I am not the first to read *The Faerie Queene* as a poem that both thematizes and comments on its own poetics. Nor am I the first to establish links between Spenserian allegory and reformed sacramental theology.[9] But in line with these critical traditions, I suggest that the poem's self-referential quality is all the more appropriate in a book that explores theological questions surrounding baptismal theology, religious conversion, and racial identity. I also hope to draw attention to the importance of difference and disunity in reformed sacramental theology and the allegorical mode.

Spenser's poetics is undoubtedly informed by English Protestant sacramental theology, especially that which employed the authority of the early Church fathers who used linguistic and poetic theory to explain the sacraments. For example, John Jewel used Church fathers in extended discussions of sacraments, signs, and figures of speech. He emphasizes what he sees as the absurdity of Catholic sacramental theology and linguistic theory: "These men have sought to make up a kind of figure, such as neither grammarian, nor rhetorician, nor divine ever understood before." Using

Church fathers to bolster his argument, he writes in *A Defence of the Apologie of the Churche of Englande* (1567),

> How much better were it for those men to speak so as the old learned
> fathers were content to speak? St Augustine saith: *De signis disserenes hoc dico,*
> *ne quis in eis attendant, quod sunt, sed potius quod signa sunt, hoc est, quod*
> *significant:* "Reasoning of signs, I say thus: Let no man consider in them be,
> but rather that they be signs, that is to say, that they do signify." Again he
> saith: *Cavendum est, ne figuratam orationem ad literum accipias . . . Ad hoc . . .*
> *pertinet, quod apostolus ait, Litera occidit:* "We must beware that we take not a
> figure of speech according to the letter. For thereto it apperteineth that the
> apostle saith 'The letter killeth.'" St Hierome saith: *Quando dico tropicam*
> *[locutionem] doceo, verum non esse, quod dicitur, sed allegoriae nubile figurate.*
> "When I name a figure of speech, I mean, that the thing that is spoken is
> not true but under the cloud of allegory." Likewise Chrysostom: *Non*
> *alienum oportet esse et veritas ipsa foret:* "The figure may not be far off from
> the sign; otherwise it were no figure; neither may it be even, and one with
> the truth; otherwise it would be the truth itself," and so not a figure.[10]

The essence of Jewel's theology is expressed in his juxtaposition of Augustine, Jerome, and Chrysostom. Because sacraments are signs, they must signify and point toward something other than themselves. Moreover, although sacraments are figures of speech that are "not true but under the cloud of allegory," there still must remain a close connection between the sacrament or sign and the truth that it represents. At the moment a sign collapses into the truth, however, it ceases to operate through the principles of figurative language; Protestants characterized Catholic sacramental theology as enacting such a collapse. Protestant sacraments require *allegoresis*, an allegorical reading of signs that insists that they be viewed *"non verum esse."* Or, as Maureen Quilligan states it more emphatically, *"Allegoresis,* elder cousin to allegory, begins by saying that texts are, superficially, lies; they must be interpreted, or 'allegorized' into telling the truth."[11] Despite the inherent closeness of the sign and the truth, for Protestants like Jewel disunity between sign and truth is essential to their sacramental theology.[12]

Just as poetic theory helped to explain the Church of England's sacraments, so too the English Church's sacramental theology influenced English poets. Regina M. Schwartz has shown how sacramental theology, especially regarding the Eucharist, developed a theory of signs and signification that was adopted by post-Reformation English poets: "As sign-making characterizes the sacrament of the Eucharist, it also does poetry, which is similarly engaged in making present that which is absent— not just in figures of speech, like prosopopoeia, but in the very poetic enterprise."[13] Schwartz maintains that sacramental poetics—rather than Protestant sacraments themselves—can make present the absent, invisible, and unseen. Spenser's poem, however, is more ambivalent about sacramental poetics: *The Faerie Queene* thematizes the problematics of reading and interpreting "certaine signs."[14]

Spenser first exhibits concerns about signs and signification in the letter to Sir Walter Raleigh, acknowledging "how doubtfully all Allegories may be construed."[15] This doubtfulness may result from the fact that allegory, or "other speaking" as the Greek roots of the word suggest, is built upon principles of both sameness and difference between the literal image and the allegorical interpretation of that image.[16] George Puttenham, after all, labels allegory "the figure of false semblant or dissimulation" in *The Arte of English Poesy*.[17] Like the Protestant sacraments described by Jewel, allegory entails an equation between the literal and the figurative while also requiring discernible differences between the two.[18]

Consequently, allegory, as Angus Fletcher has observed, is a figure of inherent dualism and conflict: It produces and is indeed produced by "the radical opposition of two independent, mutually irreducible, mutually antagonistic substances."[19] Harry Berger has described a very similar conflict in Spenserian allegory:

> It seems inevitable that Spenser's allegorical method should create diversions from the poem's argument, from its fable and from its allegory. Though Image A is introduced into the fable to illustrate Idea B, the image has its own concrete character. The relationship between A and B is therefore one of similarity rather than identity, and it must include unlike elements; these differences between A and B constitute the body of irrelevance in the poem, the ornament which critics either praise or damn. Now clearly the irrelevance is in the poem and cannot be washed away. . . . In any analogical differences between Image A and Idea B, Spenser is likely to exploit the differences between the two.[20]

Berger goes on to explain that differences between "Image" and "Idea" necessitate holding the two side by side and considering their merits independently; in doing so we gain a better picture of the meaning Spenser intends to portray. The relation of Belphoebe to Elizabeth illustrates his point: Although there are instances of correspondence between Elizabeth and Belphoebe, whom Spenser's explicitly names as a figuration of the queen in the letter to Raleigh and the proem to Book 3, there is much in the description of Belphoebe—"certaine signes," if you will—that cannot or should not be read back into Elizabeth. There is not a perfect correspondence between the image, Belphoebe, and the idea, Elizabeth.[21] As Spenser's narrator tells Elizabeth, "In this faire mirrhour maist behold thy face"; Elizabeth's gaze into Spenser's mirror would reveal to her images of herself that, as allegorical dissimulations, are not entirely herself.[22] Allegory produces excess or waste material (and here we might recall Berger's language of allegorical irrelevance that "cannot be washed away") that inheres in the disunity between the literal image and the figurative meaning. Thus virginal Elizabeth, like Belphoebe, her chaste avatar, embodies absolute wholeness, a unity and purity of identity that contrasts with the doubled, veiled, or disguised selves who populate the poem. Both she and her image resist sacramental poetics that Schwartz describes—allegorical representation and interpretation that would transform them into other than who they are.[23] They prove unable to incorporate the kinds of disunity, difference, and otherness that allegories produce and require.

Despite the "darke conceit" that defines the occult nature of Spenser's allegory, copies need not be exact or literal reproductions of originals to harness their power. From the field of cultural anthropology, Michael Taussig provides another way to understand the power of mimesis. He notes that copies often gain their magic not through exact replication but rather through "contact" with the original. In its simplest form this contact is produced through the copy containing a piece of the original (hair, fingernail, bodily fluid, and so on). But it can also be obtained through a past physical contact that leaves its mark: Taussig gives the example a hoof print left in the mud by a horse.[24] This latter form of contact, in which the original (though now absent) leaves its mark or trace, is most relevant for this discussion of Spenser's poem; here we should recall the reader/hound who searches for traces of something now absent. (And certainly Spenser hopes that his poem will gain power from contact in the form of patronage from the queen.) Even if the poem proves unable to replicate the queen's image, in this construction of mimetic relationships contact with the original, the absent queen herself, gives the poem its political power and its power to "fashion a gentleman" and a nation. Allegory as a mode nevertheless attempts to occlude the original and the literal in order to promote figurative readings. The poem thus speaks out of both sides of its mouth, at once denying the usefulness of allegory because neither the queen nor her and England's ancestry can be figured through the otherness inherent to the allegorical mode, while upholding the power of figurative interpretation to point toward them.

My hope is that this brief consideration of sacramental theology and allegory clarifies the importance of considering literal images and absence in Spenser's poem, as well as its use of the literal and the absent to fashion Elizabeth and Englishness. Although there is nothing new in reading the presence of the absent Elizabeth in the poem, I wish to draw attention to a specific consideration of Book 2, where the poetics of the absent—one different from the kind that Schwartz describes—and the literal are prominent. Again, there are various absences that might be considered in Book 2, but the absence of the transformative power of baptism is most conspicuous in a poem that contains so many traces of Ariostean and Tassean sources. Spenser's poem gains artistic credibility and power through its mimetic relationship to its Italian sources, even as absences of Ariosto's and Tasso's infidel conversions in Book 2 point toward the poem's rejection of otherness in its attempts to fashion the queen, her ancestry, and Protestant England.

Rejecting Conversion: Race and Original Sin

Nowhere do Spenser's engagements with figurative language, allegorical transformation, and the theology of baptism converge more clearly and explicitly than in the Nymph's well at the beginning of Book 2. We first learn of the well's mysterious qualities in canto 2, when Guyon attempts to wash Ruddymane's hands:

> Then soft himself inclining on his knee
>   Downe to that well, did in that water weene
>   (So love doth loath disdainfull nicitee)
>   His guiltie hands from bloudie gore to cleene.
>   He washt them oft and oft, yet nought they beene

> For all his washing cleaner. Still he strove,
> Yet still the little hands were bloudie seene;
> The which him into great amaz'ment drove,
> And into diverse doubt his wavering wonder clove.
>
> He wist not whether blot of foule offence
>   Might not be purgd with water nor with bath;
>   Or that high God, in lieu of innocence,
>   Imprinted had that token of his wrath,
>   To shew how sore bloudguiltinesse he hat'th;
>   Or that the charme and venim, which they druncke,
>   Their bloud with secret filth infected hath,
>   Being diffused through the senselesse truncke,
> That through the great contagion direfull deadly stunck. (2.2.3–4)

Guyon's response and Spenser's image of a blood-guilty babe allude to numerous theological controversies surrounding the effectiveness and necessity of infant baptism. As the well "into diverse doubt his wavering wonder clove," the episode enacts in Guyon's own mind the kinds of theological "wavering" and divisions that "clove" English Protestant opinions about the sacrament. We see Guyon's divided opinion about what has (or has not) taken place when Ruddymanes is washed in the fountain, and he offers three possible explanations: one, that water cannot cleanse the "blot of foule offence"; two, that God will not allow the "token of his wrath" to be removed with water; and three, that the blood itself cannot be removed because his parents' blood was "infected" with "charme and venim." The first two questions speak to theological debates outside the poem, whereas the third looks ahead to the charms of the Circean enchantress and to the magic Guyon will confront in the Bower of Bliss.

The first two theological questions concern the efficacy of baptism and whether it erases original sin, questions that were answered explicitly by the Church of England in Article IX of the "Thirty-Nine Articles" (1563), "Of original or birth-sin":

> Original sin . . . is the fault and corruption of the nature of every man, that naturally is engendered of the offspring of Adam; whereby man is very far gone from original righteousness, and is of his own nature inclined to evil. . . . And this infection of nature doth remain, yea in

them that are regenerated. . . . And although there is not condemnation for them that believe and are baptized, yet the apostle doth confess, that concupiscence and lust hath of itself the nature of sin.[25]

The language of "original," "infection," "concupiscence," and "lust" will bear on Spenser's treatment of the Nymph's well, as we will see later. Here, however, Article IX makes clear that original sin, a kind of genealogical and racial characteristic that is passed down from Adam to all of humanity, persists after baptism. This theological position made sense given the explanation of baptism in the "Thirty-Nine Articles," in Article XXVII, "Of baptism": "Baptism is not only a sign of profession, and mark of difference, whereby Christian men are discerned from others that be not christened, but it is also a sign of regeneration or new birth, whereby, as by an instrument, they that receive baptism are rightly grafted into the church."[26] Although baptism is described as "an instrument," suggesting that the sacrament might have some power to create Christian identity, the insistence that baptism is a "sign" conversely indicates that the sacrament may only make visible—or "mark"—invisible election.

Summarizing the Church of England's view of baptism and its Calvinist underpinnings, David Cressy writes, "The baptismal water *signified* forgiveness and regeneration but did not automatically ensure it."[27] Baptism was most likely to be effective, then, when it was linked with correct belief in the sacrament and in Christ, and in being born into the race of Christians. This theological position was adduced by asking what would happen if Jews or infidels were baptized, as seen in John Frith's *A myrroure or lokynge glasse wherin you may beholde the sacramente of baptisme described* (1548):

> The signe in Baptisme is the ploungyng downe in the materiall water and lyftyng up agayne by the which as by an outward badge we are knowen to be of the number of them which professe Christe to be redeemer and Saviour.
>
> This outward signe doth neyther geve us the spirite of God; neyther yet grace that is the favoure of God. . . . That every man receyveth not thys treasure in baptisme is evident, for be it the case that the Jewe or an infidel should say that he dyd beleve and beleved not in ded, and upon his wordes were baptized in ded (for no man can judge what his herte is, but we must receive him into baptism if he confesse our fayth and with his

mouth al beit his herte is farre from thence) thys miscreant nowe thus baptized hath receyved this outwarde signe and Sacrament, as well as the mooste fayfuthfull man beleavyng. Howe be it he neyther receyveth the grace of God, neyther yet anye grace but rather condemnation.[28]

Again we find an emphasis on baptism as an "outward sign." Yet what is most telling here is the illustration Frith uses to support his position; the "Jew or an infidel," not an unbelieving Englishmen, provides what he seems to believe is the most obvious support for the idea that baptism is only a sign. This understanding contradicts the Catholic (and Lutheran) belief that baptism was efficacious in and of itself. In fact, baptism was held to have so much power in medieval Catholic belief that it was thought to be able to cleanse Jews of the *foetor judiacus,* an odor that Jews were said to emit.[29] Baptism was once believed to have miraculous effects on the body and even erase markers of racial difference. But what Frith implies here is a distrust of the sincerity of Jewish and infidel conversions, and Reformation theology concerning the inefficacy of baptism in effecting either spiritual or bodily transformation in no way assuaged this suspicion.[30]

   In light of the theological debates surrounding baptism, it is no wonder that the events of canto 2 send Guyon into "great amaz'ment." But unlike the first two questions Guyon poses, the third speaks directly to plot elements in the poem through the "cup thus charmed" (2.1.55) that Acrasia gives to Mordant. Before we are told of the well's magical quality, we learn about Ruddymane's parents, that "Their bloud with secret filth infected hath." This "secret filth" that infects his parents' blood can be better understood with the help of Patricia Crawford's analysis of blood in the early modern period. She argues that blood stood "symbolically for a line of descent," so well understood that it could also invoke a "'natural' kinship link" even where one did not exist.[31] If this is true, Spenser's image of filth that resides in blood has important resonances with the language of Article IX, recalling infection and filth as markers of kinship and the common fallenness of humankind. Additionally, the stanzas also recall the causal relationship between original sin and concupiscence that is expressed in Article IX—we must not forget that the whole episode is the result of Mordant's illicit escapades with Acrasia, who is associated with excessive concupiscence in canto 12.

Mordant's sexual liaison with Acrasia suggests that he is already infected with the concupiscence that is the result of original sin and that he has further been infected through having sex with her. The sexual contact leaves Mordant in an altered form, as noted by Amavia in canto 1 when she describes seeking him in the Bower of Bliss:

> Him so I sought, and so at last I found,
> Where him that witch had tralled to her will,
> In chaines of lust and lewd desires ybound,
> And transformed from his former skill,
> The me he knew not, neither his own ill. (2.1.54)

Sex with Acrasia has deprived Mordant of self-knowledge and autonomy: he is "tralled to her will" and ignorant of "his own ill." Amavia is able to recover Mordant temporarily, however: She "recured him to a better will, / Purged from drugs of foule intemperance" (2.1.53). Mordant's "infected will" (to borrow the famous phrase from Sidney's *Defense of Poetry* that implies spiritual depravity), is replaced with a "better will" through the purgation of "drugs of foule intemperance."[32] This language of purging and drugs points to the centrality of the body in Book 2 and the poem's equating of sexual relations with Acrasia with magic and "charms," infection and "venim." Amavia may temporarily recover Mordant, but the body remains susceptible to infection because, as she herself puts it, "all flesh doth frailtie breed" (2.1.52).

The body is indeed a problem in Spenser's poem. As Michael C. Schoenfeldt has shown, one of Book 2's primary investigations is "the relationship between physiology and morality, between matters of the body and conditions of the spirit," and in a book dedicated to temperance and the ability to manage bodily inclinations, "Spenser investigates the close relationship between bodies and souls."[33] I would add to Schoenfeldt's important insight that there are different types of bodies in Book 2, and specific bodies, like Acrasia's (and Pyrochles' and Cymochles'), are racially and religiously marked.

The language of infection used by Amavia also connotes racial and religious otherness. Racial markers in particular might be understood in terms of infection, as exhibited in Spain in its obsession with *limpieza de sangre,* and in England in George Best's description of the origins of blackness: "Blacknesse proceedeth of some naturall infection of the first inhabitants of that Countrey, and so all the whole progenie of them descended, all still poluted with the same blot of infection. Therefore it shal not be farre from our purpose, to examine the first originall of these blacke men, and how by lineall discente, they haue hiterto continued thus blacke."[34] Best then goes on to recount what had become a common argument, that God cursed Ham's son, Cush (Chus in Best's text), and his descendents with blackness.[35] He thus concludes, "And of this blacke & cursed Chus came al these blacke Moores which are in Africa . . . the cause of the Ethiopians blacknesse, is the curse & natural infection of bloud, & not the distemperature of the clymate."[36] Blackness is a bodily, genealogical, and spiritual condition. Moreover, that a racial marker like blackness is caused by "natural infection of bloud," a concept that was quite common in the medieval and early modern periods and not limited to Best, overlaps tellingly with Spenser's language and with early modern understandings of original sin as a genealogical trait that too is an infection of the blood. According to William Perkins, an Anglican clergyman often characterized as a moderate Puritan, original sin may be a symptom of the corrupted nature of the body: "The propagations of sin from parents to children is either because the soul is infected by the contagion of the body . . . or because God, in the very moment of creation and infusion of souls into infants, doth utterly forsake them."[37] Perkins was a proponent of double predestination, which explains the second part of this statement. As for the first part, we see again the language of contagion and the idea of hereditary sinfulness. Racial characteristics and original sin, indeed, work quite similarly.

Acrasia, Pyrochles, and Cymochles are also infected with racial and religious difference through literary imitation and romance. Not only is Acrasia modeled after Tasso's Muslim enchantress, Armida, but, as Benedict S. Robinson notes, Pyrochles and Cymochles are two of those "paynim" knights of romance.[38] I will say more about Acrasia below, but the importance of Pyrochles' and Cymochles' religious identities is highlighted in canto 8, in which they are associated thirteen times with non-Christian and at times Islamic identities: For example, they are called "Paynin," "Pagan," and "Sarazin," and they swear by "Termagaunt," "Mahoune," and their "Gods" (2.8.10, 22, 49, 30, 33, and 37). The brothers' religious identity is clear, but their racial identity is less so until we consider what is often considered their allegorical signification. Pyrochles and Cymochles are conventionally read, respectively, as allegorical representations of wrath and lust, the two character traits that were most closely associated with Turks and the Moors in early modern texts. If, in the early modern imagination, as Nabil Matar suggests, "The 'Turk' was cruel and tyrannical, deviant, and deceiving" and "the 'Moor' was sexually overdriven and emotionally uncontrollable, vengeful, and religiously superstitious," there is actually little need to read the brothers allegorically.[39] Pyrochles and Cymochles do not appear or act as other than the "paynims" that they are. Their literal characters are not transformed by the allegory into representations of wrath and lust; instead, they merely act out racialized character traits. That Spenser was invested in racial characterization is clear in *A View of the Present State of Ireland*, in which Irish behavior is presented as a consequence of Scythian ancestry.[40] As such, in *The Faerie Queene* the two brothers simply act out the dictates of their racialized bodies and wills. They should be read as beholden to the type of antiallegorical and antisacramental poetics and unity of character that I earlier attributed to Spenser's Elizabeth.

The Faerie Queene's project of unifying racial and religious identity does not allow characters that exist within antisacramental poetics to be transformed, either literally or figuratively. I am not suggesting that *The Faerie Queene* is largely nonallegorical, though there is a tradition of reading Spenser as rejecting allegory in later books of the poem.[41] The polysemy that allegory allows is certainly at times integral to a political project, and Spenser's "Letter to Raleigh" and explicit moments of allegory throughout the poem make it nearly impossible not to read everything in the poem as calling for *allegoresis*.[42] Additionally, *The Faerie Queene* operates on more than one level of allegory: The poem contains allegories within allegories. Thus, while there is no need to see the Saracen brothers as allegorical figurations of wrath and lust, their nonallegorical status as racialized subjects furthers the poem's allegorical project of anatomizing and racializing the English Protestant religious body. Consequently, there are instances in the poem where allegorical transformation would conflict with the poem's ideological and allegorical constructions of identity, namely in its attempt to create unity of identity by conjoining religion with race.

In Spenser's poem, then, race does not figure religion; race is religion. Arthur offers Pyrochles the opportunity to convert:

> Yet if wilt renounce thy miscreance,
> And my trew liegman yield thyself for ay,
> Life will I graunt thee for thy valiaunce,
> And all thy wrongs will wipe out of my souenaunce. (2.8.51)

But the Saracen must refuse: "he so willfully refused grace" (2.8.52). Although his refusal might be connected to the personal cost of conversion, yielding to a feudal servitude that inextricably links conversion to subjugation, Pyrochles' willful rejection of grace gains further significance when we recall Schoenfeldt's argument that Book 2 often locates spiritual conditions in the body. Pyrochles' embodied will—not explicitly connected to his body here, though one that we might consider as located in his body in light of Schoenfeldt's argument—leads to his destruction. Arguably, then, Pyrochles' will itself is racialized because it is embodied in a Saracen's body. Regardless, in this explicit rejection of the infidel-conversion motif, *The Faerie Queene* denies the possibility that characters can transform their embodied religious identities—and even more so because baptism, with its questionable power, is unable to assure that a Saracen like Pyrochles will become a Christian.

Ovidian Baptism, Originary Identity, and Figurative Unity

If baptism cannot produce real transformation within the epic's project of creating the English Protestant race, perhaps Ovidian metamorphosis can, especially if it is able to do what neither baptism nor allegory can by changing forms "into new bodies." Ovid enters the scene when the Palmer attempts to answer Guyon's third question. Before the Palmer provides details about this particular well, however, he has something to say about the very nature of water:

> Ye bene right hard amated, gratious Lord,
> And of your ignorance great maruell make,
> Whiles cause not well conceiued ye mistake.
> But know, that secrete vertues are infusd
> In euery fountaine, and in euery lake,

> Which who hath skill them rightly to haue chusd,
>   To proofe of passing wonders hath full often vsd. (2.2.5)

The Palmer first comments on Guyon's "ignorance" and "great maruell"; perhaps Guyon's struggle to understand correctly is similar to that of the readers whom the narrator describes in the proem. The Palmer provides a reading that stands in opposition to Guyon's, and, as Maurice Evans noted more than fifty years ago, he sets himself up as an interpretive guide who will help Guyon read and understand the world in which he travels.[43] Whether or not Guyon should follow his lead is another question, and various critics have questioned the fitness of the Palmer as reader and guide.[44] Nevertheless, the Palmer explains that Ruddymane's hands cannot be cleansed because of the virtue of the water itself, and he then relates that Guyon (and the reader) needs to "But know, that secrete vertues are infused / In euery fountaine, and in euery lake." In a surprising revelation, we learn that "euery" body of water seems to have some sort of magic.[45] Spenser could have drawn an understanding of the magical nature of water from several kinds of narratives, from travel narratives describing magical waters that were discovered in the New World, to folklore concerning the magical wells that dotted the English landscape.[46] Along with these, the *Metamorphoses* provided Spenser with numerous tales of water's magical power.

Whether it is Actaeon, who is splashed with water by Diana after encountering her bathing and then transformed into a stag, or Hermaphroditus, who is grasped by Salmacis in a fountain and then changed into the hermaphrodite, Ovid's many fountains and springs produce physical transformations that are memorialized on the poetic landscape. Spenser follows Ovid closely in this regard, in the Palmer's description of a well that has traces of multiple Ovidian tales:

> Such is this well, wrought by occasion straunge,
>   Which to her Nymph befell. Vpon a day,
>   As she the woods with bow and shafts did raunge,
>   The hartlesse Hind and Robucke to dismay,
>   *Dan Faunus* chaunst to meet her by the way,
>   And kindling fire at her faire burning eye,
>   Inflamed was to follow beauties chace,
>   And chaced her, that fast from him did fly;
> As Hind from her, so she fled from her enimy.

At last when fayling breath began to faint,
  And saw no meanes to scape, of shame affrayd,
  She set her downe to weepe for sore constraint,
  And to *Diana* calling lowd for ayde,
  Her deare besought, to let her dye a mayd.
  The goddesse heard, and suddeine where she sate,
  Welling out streames of teares, and quite dismayd
  With stony feare of that rude rustick mate,
Transformd her to a stone from stedfast virgins state.

Lo now she is that stone, from whose two heads,
  As from two weeping eyes, fresh streames do flow,
  Yet cold through feare, and old conceiued dreads;
  And yet the stone her semblance seemes to show,
  Shapt like a maid, that such ye may her know;
  And yet her vertues in her water byde:
  For it is chast and pure, as purest snow,
  Ne lets her waues with any filth be dyde,
But euer like her selfe vnstained hath beene tryde. (2.2.6–9)

Ovid's myths of Daphne and Apollo and Arethusa and Alpheus are invoked first and foremost. Daphne, Arethusa, and Spenser's Nymph are all imitative of Diana:

> Daphne calls it joy
> to roam within the forest's deep seclusion,
> where she in emulation of the chaste
> goddess Phoebe, devotes herself to hunting (1.658–61);

Arethusa "travers[ed] / the mountain pastures or setting out snares for small game" (5.779–80); and the Nymph "the woods with bows and shafts did range, / The hartless Hind and Robucke to dismay." It is Ovid's and Spenser's cruel irony that women who devote themselves to hunting and virginal chastity become hunted and chased by would-be rapists. In an epic simile, Ovid later writes that Apollo initially pursues Daphne "as a Gallic hound / chasing a rabbit through an open field; / the one seeks shelter and the other, prey" (1.736–38). Moreover, in Ovid's tale, Apollo then appropriates the metamorphosed object as the symbol of poetic triumph. Poetry and metamorphosis are linked in Ovid, for metamorphosis is both the subject and structuring principle of the poem, as one tale transforms into another through narrative entrelacement. Thus, both Ovid's and Spenser's readers, similar to Apollo, Alpheus, and Dan Faunus, are often pursuing that which is fleeing and on the verge of transforming itself in the hopes of escaping capture. Spenser's poem often purposefully eludes readers—as the proem to Book 2, I have suggested, makes clear—just as Ovid's chaste damsels attempt to escape those who would pollute them and use them to fulfill selfish desires.

More ironic still is the fact that metamorphosis becomes the means to maintain an originary identity, since metamorphosis keeps the women (and, perhaps, Spenser's poem) from being grasped and allows them to retain their chaste identities. For Ovid's nymphs who desire perpetual virginity, metamorphosis provides a potential solution. Daphne seeks the assistance of her father, the river god: "Help me, dear father! If your waters hold / divinity, transform me and destroy / that beauty by which I have too well pleased" (1.751–53); Arethusa cries to Diana, "Aid your armoress, Diana—to whom you have often / entrusted your bow, along with your quiver of arrows" (5.796–97); and Spenser's Nymph asks Diana "to let [her] dye a maid." These maidens find themselves in similar predicaments, but the means by which they are rescued are quite different. Daphne asks to be transformed by the power of her father's water, though the decision to transform her into the laurel appears to be her father's. Arethusa and Spenser's Nymph, in contrast, ask only for Diana's assistance; they simply find themselves being transformed into a fountain and a rock in a spring. Arethusa does not express her feelings about her metamorphosis, whereas Daphne, we might assume, is at least somewhat content because her father has followed her wishes—or perhaps the poem needs to silence her protest because she is to become the crown of poets.[47] We might even assume the same of Arethusa, even though her myth reveals that metamorphosis, paradoxically, only aggravates the problem. Diana attempts to conceal Arethusa by transforming her into a spring:

> Even so, [Alpeus] recognized me,
>   his darling there in the water, and promptly disregarded
>   the human form he had assumed for the occasion,
>   reverting to river, so that our fluids might mingle. (5.814–17)

Because Alpheus still recognizes Arethusa, Diana must intervene one more time; this metamorphosis would allow a more complete sexual mixing to occur between Arethusa and Alpeus in their watery forms. (Arethusa eventually falls into a hole in the ground that Diana produces.) Water may not have been the best solution, but it was a fitting one because it captures the moment of emotional distress.[48] Arethusa turns into a spring because, as she narrates it, "icy sweat thoroughly drenched the limbs that he looked for" (5.810). Although Barkan has taught us that Ovidian metamorphosis enacts the loss of the self, in this instance, and in many other instances in Ovid, metamorphosis does not produce a complete change.[49] Instead, metamorphosis allows the retention of an originary self.

Spenser's Nymph hopes to die in order to maintain her virginity, but she is instead "dismayd" by metamorphosis and a Spenserian pun—that is, her maiden state is seemingly undone because she finds herself in a state of dismay, suggesting that this metamorphosis enacts and then freezes in time what Dan Faunus could not.[50] In her reading of the scene, Susanne Wofford notes that "here to be 'saved' is to be petrified, in an Ovidian transformation that renders eternal the Nymph's grieving state: her fear is 'stony.' "[51] Moreover, as Carole V. Kaske notes, "Preservation is also the goal of the Nymph's metamorphosis."[52] Indeed, as both Wofford and Kaske suggest, metamorphosis indefinitely captures, perpetuates, and memorializes her fear of losing herself. In metamorphosis there is a correlation between interior feeling and external form.

This reading of metamorphosis, I hope, makes clear just how precisely the poem uses Ovid to engage theological questions about baptism. Spenser, in using Ovid to provide a pointed engagement with baptismal theology, does not merely echo theological controversies. He presents a theological statement about baptism and religious conversion: that both lack Ovidian power. Indeed, Ovidian metamorphosis is more powerful than baptism, but even it is unlikely to produce the kind of total transformation that would allow a Saracen's racialized body to become a Christian body. The limitations of Spenser's Ovidian baptismal font, moreover, raise questions about romance transformations. Spenser's baptism and his Ovid prove unable to alter blood-guilt or interiority, aspects of identity that persist after transformation.

Although Spenser uses Ovid to reveal the inefficacy of baptismal transformations, metamorphosis nevertheless may be preferable to baptism in projects of national, racial, and religious identity formation because it envisions a unity of interiority and physicality that baptism and religious conversion could never guarantee. To be sure, as scholars who work on literary representations of "turning Turk" have illustrated, economic and political interactions between European Christians and Muslim Turks and Moors in the early modern period fostered an awareness of diverse religious identities in differing political, economic, and geographical environments.[53] In this context, the religion individuals professed often had nothing to do with their religious convictions and inward beliefs—Frith, we should recall, raises specific concerns about the true beliefs of infidels who appear to convert to Christianity. Ovidian metamorphosis can produce an imaginative solution to this cultural anxiety by making interiority physical and visible.

Spenser's poem employs Ovid to illustrate the persistence of originary identity, for the *Metamorphoses* is also a poem about origins and causes. Ovid's waters thus provided Spenser with a topos for examining the problem of origins and sources. Discussing the connection between origin tales, literary sources, and poetic authority in the Nymph's well episode, John Guillory argues, "Fountains in *The Faerie Queene* are usually reservoirs of energy, sources of power."[54] Guillory goes on to note, however, that "the Nymph's fountain seems to be reduced to a negative image of a true source" because of the fountain's "secondariness"—that is, it is a source that itself draws from a more preeminent source, Dame Nature.[55] This reading of the Nymph's well opens up the possibility that the hunt for sources and origins leads to an infinite regress in which the narrative locates an original cause that only turns out to be another narrative, a literary source with its own origins. Originals too have their origins, which is perhaps why the Palmer eventually rejects the lengthy Ovidian tale— and Ovidianism itself, I would suggest—that he first used to explain Ruddymane's condition. In the end, his reading of Ruddymane's condition has very little to do with the Ovidian history he tells:

> From thence it comes, that this babes bloudy hand
>> May not be cleansed with water of this well:
>> Ne certes Sir striue you it to withstand,
>> But let them still be bloudy, as befell,
>> That they his mothers innocence may tell,
>> As she bequeathed in her last testament;

That as a sacred Symbole it may dwell
In her sonnes flesh, to minde reuengement,
And be for all chaste Dames an endless monument. (2.2.10)

Origins are just too difficult to locate, and thus the Palmer abandons this search altogether in favor of reading the babe's bloody hands in a way that calls for forward action—the regressive search for origins and Ovidian digression impede epic telos.

The Palmer attempts to privilege a very particular reading of the events, and Kaske has observed that the Palmer's reading conflicts with Guyon's more spiritual readings; she suggests that the Palmer's is an allegorical reading of a classical myth, whereas Guyon reads the scene as a theological allegory.[56] The Ovidian history describes causation and adequately explains why the hands remain stained, but the Palmer's "But" conflicts with his earlier Ovidian history. Through the Palmer the poem uses Ovid to criticize allegory, baptism, and romance, and afterwards rejects him. This rejection, however, does not negate the earlier critique of baptism through Ovid; rather, it highlights the incompatibility of all these transforming projects—allegorical, baptismal, romantic, and Ovidian—with the epic's project of racial and religious formation.

Instead of an Ovidian explanation, the Palmer chooses to read the bloody hands as a "Symbole." This decision to read symbolically is difficult to parse given the long critical debate about the differences between allegory and symbolism. Following the Romantics, however, the symbol has been understood as holding a greater figurative unity than allegory. Gordon Teskey describes this quite poetically: "The symbol is raised up out of the inhuman otherness of figurative language by means of schematic ordering, polysemy, that is based on the assumption of a single, underlying truth."[57] Also suggesting as much is the Greek etymology, as Jeremy Tambling notes: "From the Greek 'symballein,' 'to throw together, to bring together, to collect, to compare.'"[58] "Symbole" thus appears to differ from allegory because it may be able to forge the kind of unity between image and idea that Book 2 strives for. Nevertheless, Guyon accepts the Palmer's symbolic reading as truth and gives the child up to his reading: "He harkened to his reason, and the childe / Uptaking, to the Palmer gaue to beare" (2.2.11). In accepting the Palmer's reading, Guyon also accepts his call for "reuengement."

The Palmer may also reject Ovid because metamorphosis, in fostering ontological unity, also leads to figurative disunity. Wofford explains: "Ovid's method of detailing the stages of metamorphosis might be read as a literalizing of the method of metaphor: a natural simile would work by claiming that a character is like a tree, while a metaphor says that a given character is a tree."[59] If metaphor, as Judith H. Anderson remind us, "carries two terms which are and/or are not alike: X=Y and/or X does not =Y," then even Ovidian metamorphosis proves unable to confer the unity required for the poem's construction of religious identity.[60] Although metamorphosis can create unity of being by establishing correspondence between interior and exterior, it can also reveal, paradoxically, the kinds of transformations and losses that metaphorical and allegorical figuration necessarily entail in creating such correspondences; Ovid's nymphs may maintain their chaste identities, but they still lose their bodies. Even Ovidian metamorphosis proves too problematic because it simultaneously and paradoxically maintains and destroys.[61] Neither baptism nor Ovid are allowed to have complete transformative effects in the poem, but following the Palmer's interpretation of the infant's bloody hands and his rebuff of Ovid assures that Guyon will reject a romance narrative that could have had at least partially transformative and redemptive power.

We should not be surprised that Spenser turns to—but eventually rejects—Ovid in a book about the transformative power of romance. Syrith Pugh discusses the close affinities between Ovid and romance, and she notes that romance moments in *The Faerie Queene* often allude to the *Metamorphoses*.[62] Moreover, Daniel Javitch has illustrated that sixteenth-century Italian critics—Cinthio being the first—defended Ariosto's *Orlando Furioso* by linking it to the *Metamorphoses,* which provided a classical alternative to sixteenth-century neo-Aristotelianism; Ovid's poem became the classical model for romance's inclusion of multiple plots and digressions.[63] Javitch illustrates that Ovid was read as a type of romance, and indeed we find in the *Metamorphoses* tales imbedded within tales that seem to be digressions from the topic at hand.[64] Moreover, as a poem that defies Aristotelian unity, the *Metamorphoses* is commonly viewed as a counterpoint to the *Aeneid* and the Augustine imperial politics that are upheld in Virgil's epic.[65]

Although Ovid can be read as casting a critical gaze at both imperial and proto-imperial projects, it may not be possible to make this same generalization about early modern romance.[66] If romance has any affinity with Ovid's project, however, it resides in its ability to uncover digressive counternarratives that are just as important (or perhaps just as attractive) as the goals of epic; all errant knights have a primary goal, even if various adventures and erotic enticements are temporarily more appealing than the pursuit of that goal. Hence the incorporation of Ovid into a narrative that has transformed romance digression into epic telos (Rinaldo's romance-like digression with Armida in *Gerusalemme liberata* becomes the concluding quest for Guyon when he encounters Acrasia) may seem contradictory.[67] We might expect Spenser to use the similarities between romance and Ovid to provide an alternative to epic telos and to criticize an English imperial fantasy. Spenser does no such thing. Instead, he uses Ovid in the Nymph's well episode to criticize the transforming impulses of romance and allegory. Neither romance, because of its dependence on the sacrament of baptism, nor allegory, because of its stubborn persistence of the literal, prove able to alter indelible marks of originary identity.

Reading Literally in the Bower of Bliss

Numerous events occur between Guyon's departure for the Bower of Bliss and his arrival there. Even so, I would like to turn to the end of the book and consider the consequences of the Palmer's reading for Acrasia and the end of Book 2. Surprisingly, though the Nymph's well and Bower of Bliss have been discussed at great length and for a variety of purposes, critics have tended not to read the beginning (especially its engagement with theological issues) and end of Book 2 in relation to each other.[68] It is well known that Spenser draws from Homer, Ariosto, and Tasso to create his Acrasia, but I suggest that he also draws from Ovid's Circe in Book 14 of the *Metamorphoses,* which provides a potential backstory that would explain why the Palmer and Guyon feel the need to bind Acrasia and destroy her bower.

In Book 14 Macareus narrates the familiar Homeric tale of Circe's magic and her ability to transform men into animals. What is less familiar is the story that follows: Picus's metamorphosis into the woodpecker. The nymph tells Macareus to pay special attention to this tale: "'Listen to this, Macareus . . . / and learn how powerful my mistress is; / apply yourself to what I have to say'" (14.542–44). The tale that follows, though seemingly just another recounting of Circe's ability to transform men into beasts, yields a fresh insight into the true nature of Circe's power for both Macareus and Homer's readers. After Circe transforms Picus, his men demand that Circe return him to his human state:

> Instead, she sprinkled them
> with noxious drugs and poisonous concoctions,
> and summoning up Night and all his gods,
> that dwell below in Erebus and Chaos,
> she called upon the goddess Hecate
> with long-drawn ululations.
>   *Astonishing*
> *to say it,* but the woods leapt from their place,
> the earth shuddered, the nearby trees turned white,
> and clumps of grass were stained with blood;
> stones seemed to bellow and wild dogs to bay,
> the earth appeared to writhe with poisonous serpents,
> and ghostly forms flutter all around.
>   *Astounded* by these monstrous apparitions,
> his comrades turned into a fearful mob;
> she touched their faces—trembling, terrified—
> with the magic wand by which these youths were changed
> into a great variety of beasts;
> and not a one of them kept his old shape. (my emphasis, 14.570–87)

So that we do not miss what the tale has to teach us, the nymph draws our attention to the "Astonishing" nature of the tale (a "*dictum mirabile*" in the Latin [14.406]), and Picus's men are "Astounded" by Circe's magic as well, as she touches their "*mirantia virga*" (14.413). Acrasia's magic, like Circe's, comes from drugs and charms, but it is in her alteration of the landscape that she reveals the true depth of her power; the land reacts physically and affectively to her magic—it "shudders" [*ingemuitque solum*] (14.407) and is "stained with blood" [*sanguineis maduerant*] (14.408). Ovid's Circe can conjure fear and loathing from the earth.

Circe is especially troubling in her ability to produce affect; the affective responses of her victims (topographical and human) enact metamorphosis. Arthur Golding's 1567 translation of the tale illustrates this point clearly, as Golding translates Ovid's "*dictum mirabile*" as "a woondrous thing to tell."[69] He later translates the response of Picus's men and their transformations as "woonderous" as well:

> The folke were flayghted at theis syghts.
> And as they woondering stood amaazed, shee strokte her witching wand
> Uppon theyr faces. At the touche wherof, there out of hand
> Came woondrous shapes of savage beastes uppon them all. Not one
> Reteyned still his native shape.[70]

There are affinities among the wondrous nature of the tale, Circe's wondrous magic within the tale, their "woondering," and the "woondrous" shapes into which they are transformed. Their emotional transformation is replicated in their bodies, much in the manner of Arethusa and Spenser's Nymph. Again, metamorphosis produces a physical representation of emotional distress; it materializes and makes visible inward feelings.

Although Acrasia seems similar to Ovid's Circe because they both produce wondrous topographies, there are significant differences between Circe's magic and Acrasia's. They both turn men into beasts, but they have very different effects on the landscape. Both landscapes are dangerous in their power to summon affect, but Acrasia's is perhaps more dangerous because it is appealing and able to distract Guyon from his purpose. The Palmer, after all, rebukes Guyon for his "wandring eye" (2.12.69) when he catches him looking at the two "wanton Maidens" (2.12.66) bathing in a fountain. The significance of this visual wandering is heightened by this fountain's location at the center of the Bower of Bliss: "In the midst of all," the narrator tells us, "a fountaine stood, / Of richest substaunce, that on earth might bee, / So pure and shiny. . . ." (2.12.60). Surprisingly, Spenser portrays the fountain positively, emphasizing its purity and clarity: "through the waves one might the bottom see" (2.12.62). The language of clarity and purity highlights the fountain's transparency and thus links it to the Nymph's well in canto 2. As the maidens exhibit, the fountain leaves nothing to the imagination—there is nothing hidden, nothing to wonder at.

This is not to say that Acrasia's creations are benign, for they may lead epic and romance knights astray; Guillory has suggested that "the strongest temptation to which the heroes of *The Faerie Queene* are subject is denominated in the medieval system of vices as *accidie*, sloth. The temptation is simply to rest, in its most radical form, to give up."[71] Acrasia, then, like Duessa before her, leads knights away from both epic telos and romance wandering, for although she may be encountered through error, she then calls knights to stasis—to remain in a perpetual present in her *carpe diem* lyric in stanzas 74 and 75. And if she calls errant knights to stasis, she also calls them to get lost in a lyrical moment from *Gerusalemme liberata*; it is well known that Spenser's *carpe diem* lyric imitates the bird's song in Armida's *locus amoenus.*[72]

Guyon must reject this Italianate lyrical moment, and at the end of canto 12 Guyon and the Palmer not only destroy the location that produces such lyricism but they also attempt to restore those who have been seduced by it—the Palmer restores Acrasia's victims after Guyon destroys the Bower. These acts of restoration and destruction are undermined, however, by the emotional responses of the restored men and by Grill, who are all very unhappy with Guyon and the Palmer:

> Streight way he with his virtuous staffe them stroke,
>   And straight of beasts they comely men became;
>   Yet being men they did unmanly looke,
>   And stared ghastly, some for inward shame,
>   And some for wrath, to see their captive Dame:
>   But one above the rest in speciall,
>   That had an hog beene late, hight Grille by name,
>   Repinded greatly, and did him miscall,
> That had from hoggish forme him brought to naturall.
>
> Said *Guyon*, See the mind of beastly man,
>   That hath soone forgot the excellence
>   Of his creation, when he life began,
>   That now he chooseth, with vile difference,
>   To be a beast, and lack intelligence.
>   To whom the Palmer thus, The dongill kind
>   Delights in filth and foule incontinence:
>   Let *Grill* be *Grill,* and have his hoggish mind,
> But let us hence depart, whilest wether serves and wind. (2.12.86–87)

Quilligan notes, "here there are limits to the transforming powers of good. . . . The proper response to Grill's choice is not to force his conversion, however, but to let him be."[73] Although Quilligan is not interested in religious conversion, her reading of Grill and her use of the word "conversion" is worth considering. Conversion, of course, can never be forced officially in a Protestant context, especially because the emphasis placed on faith and race stripped baptism of its power to transform. Consequently, no act of will or force can transform Grill.

The inability to transform Grill has further spiritual implications if, as Darryl J. Gless suggests, the image has affinities with the Calvinist doctrine of predestination:

> . . . "the dunghill kind" suggests that some are "by kind" incorrigible. . . . A reader inclined to apply Protestant notions of causality to such reflections could easily . . . share the palmer's dismissive view because people who resist moral rectification. . . . provide more than usual evidence of their reprobation. As Reformed dogma insists, however, such people willingly "choose" the viciousness to which they are predestined, and are appropriately left to work out their own damnation.[74] (186)

I would add that in this episode reprobation is made visible through the incomplete transformations: though "they comely men became, / Yet being men they did unmanly look." Here there is a tension between what they "became" and how they "look" because the Palmer has rejected Ovid and the kinds of unity metamorphosis might have allowed. That said, because the poem has already used Ovid to suggest that metamorphosis creates unity between the internal and the external, it is likely that these men's initial transformations into beasts by Acrasia—who harbors Ovidian power—were the mere outward manifestation of an already-present internal unmanliness. The unmanly looks that remain are thus likely an expression of the very unmanliness they had before Acrasia transformed them, even if it is an unmanliness that she herself creates in her ability to inspire lust—in a manner similar to Circe's creation of affect in Ovid.

It is likely within the symbolic economy of Ovidian poetics that Grill, too, became a hog because he already had a "hoggish mind." Moreover, it is Grill who most explicitly manifests a resistance to redemptive transformation. The Palmer tells us Grill's name, but it is Guyon, not the Palmer, who, as the allegorist, tells us how to read Grill's resistance. At the same time, this reading, like the allegorical readings before it, hopes to obscure the more obvious fact that Grill and his comrades like being Acrasia's pets. In the end, all the Palmer can say is "Let *Grill* be *Grill*"; he urges Guyon to leave the island and to let Grill remain there. Grill represents transparency, like the well at the center of the Bower, and resistance to transformation through his transparency: Grill is simply Grill, embodying the stubborn persistence of the literal.[75]

The binding of Acrasia and the destruction of her bower, then, is on the one hand an attempt to bind the remaining element of Ovidian metamorphic power, and on the other a final rejection of romance transformation and elements of the poem's Italian sources. This is all the more true if, as John Watkins argues in reading Acrasia in relation to Dido, "Book II of *The Faerie Queene* reestablishes epic as a genre valorizing the surrender of whatever one holds most alluring and precious. Its cataclysmic denouement indicates the clemency of Italian romance as a deviation from the 'rigour pittilesse' with which Virgil exhorted his readers to self-denial."[76] Watkins's reading stems from his earlier observation that in Book 2 what is romance digression in Tasso is epic telos in Spenser (it also relies on a common reading that situates romance in opposition to epic).[77] It is true that Tasso's readers may sympathize with Armida after Rinaldo leaves her, but romance, like epic, is unwilling to leave its heroes stranded in love affairs that might divert from the ideological concerns of the poem—in Tasso's poem Rinaldo must initially leave Armida because he is a Christian knight and she is a Muslim, and their final reunion is predicated upon her implied conversion to Christianity. Moreover, Ovid and romance cannot be excised completely from Spenser's rewriting of Tasso's story of Armida and Rinaldo. In his unwillingness to allow for conversion, transformation, or restoration, and in his unwillingness to allow his hero to reconcile with Acrasia, Spenser explicitly rejects a moment of romance in Tasso's epic, but the effects of Acrasia's Ovidian magic persist beyond the conclusion of Book II, as Guyon and the Palmer leave Grill being Grill. Like the well at the center of her garden, Acrasia is fully sexualized, anti-Protestant, and nonallegorical. She and everything in her Bower appear exactly as they are; they resist any other use than simple, present pleasure.

The unwillingness to convert Acrasia at the end of the poem, moreover, cannot be separated from the racial and religious difference she inherited from her original, Armida, in Tasso's poem; her racialized and religiously marked body necessarily presents itself as a site of anxiety. Because racial and religious difference, marked as an "infection" just like original sin, persisted after baptism, we see the power of racial markers themselves to contaminate religious identity. From a different religious and national context, the Spanish terms *moriscos* and *conversos* illustrate this point; the pre-Christian identity is captured in the postconversion nomenclature, revealing either suspicion that these converts may not be fully Christian or at the very least that their non-Christian past remains part of their identities. Perhaps this is because racial markers, whether registered through skin color, social customs, or genealogy, have always been more conspicuous identifiers than inward faith. Spenser's theology only reifies this belief, maintaining that the transformed and converted necessarily retain a part of their original identity (original sin or race, both of which are passed down genealogically). Neither Spenser's poem nor baptism could ever assure that infidels become true Christians when they convert, and in *The Faerie Queene* we see a version of the theory of blood purity that appeared in Spain under a completely different set of theological and historical circumstances. Baptism, conversion, and romance prove unable to transform and cleanse the "bloud [that] secret filth infected hath."

Nevertheless, Spenser remembers that the British have not always been Christians. In the "Briton monuments," the narrator apostrophizes the queen and tells her of her "realme and race" (2.10.4).[78] Here she also learns about "good *Lucius* / That first received Christianitie, / The sacred pledge of Christes Euangely" (2.10.53). But this recollection is first encountered and then left behind in a "chamber [that] seemed ruinous and old," and is kept by "an old old man, halfe blind" (2.9.55 & 57). England's pre-Christian history is kept hidden away, scarcely visible, an archived and fading cultural memory. Even so, it is important that this history of Briton is located in the House of Alma, commonly read as the human body itself. The body retains this history of conversion, a history that Spenser acknowledges but one that proves secondary to present religious concerns about infidel conversion and racial and religious purity.

Race, Ovid, and Purity Beyond Book 2

Given the problems surrounding the allegorical, Ovidian, and baptismal transformations in Book 2, it is hardly surprising that metamorphosis is equally undesirable in Book 3, especially because Britomart manifests a poetic unity between herself and the virtue of chastity, of which she is the knightly champion. But Britomart, too, has to confront Ovidian challenges, which in Book 3 are connected to anxieties about racial and religious miscegenation. Anxiety that Britomart's desire may be tainted with a transformative Ovidianism is most explicitly addressed after her encounter with Merlin's mirror. Glauce hopes that Britomart's love "Be . . . worthy of [her] race and royal seed" (2.32.4). She fears, however, that Britomart may suffer from a desire that is "Of filthy lust, contrary to kind" (ii.40.4), that it may be similar to the transgressive desire typified by Ovidian heroines: "Not so th'Arabian Myrrhe did set her mind; / Nor so did Biblis spend her pining hart, / But loved their native flesh against all kind" (2.41.1–3).[79] Glauce expresses a concern that Britomart's desire be of the right "kind" and fitting of her "race." Her obsession with race and kind also points to a concern for the stability of categorical distinctions made problematic by incest and metamorphoses.[80]

But if incest blurs differences of "kind," the poem asserts other kinds of distinctions with Britomart's rejection of desires that are marked as foreign; she rejects the "Arabian" desire of Myrhha as contrary to kind as well.[81] The poem creates a distance between Britomart and Ovidianism that captures, Cora Fox argues, "pagan emotional states that lie outside the prescribed limits of Elizabethan and Protestant experience."[82] Instead, Britomart's desire is directed toward Artegall, and Merlin points to the fitting nature of the match:

> The man whom heavens have ordayne to be
> > The spouse of Britomart, is Artegall:
> > He wonneth in the land of Fayree,
> > Yet is no Fary borne, ne sib at all
> > To Elfes, but sprong of seed terrestiall,
> > And whilome by False Faries stolne away,
> > Whiles yet in infant cradle he did crall;
> > Ne other to himself is knowne this day,
> But that he by Elfe was gotten of a Fay.

> But soothe he is the sonne of Gorlios,
> > And brother unto Cador Cornish king,
> > And for his warlike feats renowmed is,
> > From where the day out of the sea doth spring,
> > Untill the closure of the Evening.
> > From thence, him firmly bound with faithfull band,
> > To this native soyle thou backe shalt bring,

Strongly to aid his countrey, to withstanad
The power of forrein Paynims, which invade thy land. (3.3.27–27)

Merlin has much to say about Artegall's lineage: First we learn that he is
not a fairy but a changeling; second we learn that he is Cornish. The fact
that Artegall is of "this native soyle" also gives rise to a difference between
Britomart's future desire for Artegall and that of Bradamante (her literary
progenitor) for Ruggiero in *Orlando Furioso*; it is a love that precedes his
conversion to Christianity but is consummated after it. Merlin attempts to
ground Britomart's desire locally, for although Britomart goes to Merlin
to see whether her love lies "beyond the Afrik Ismaell, / or th'Indian
Peru" (3.6.7–8), she learns that her lover is not from such foreign locations—
and in noting "Africk Ismaell," the poem forecloses the possibility that
Britomart would be in love with someone like Ruggiero. The poem acknowledges that Britomart's love could have been similar to that of Bradamante for the North African, Muslim Ruggiero, but it rejects this
possibility by insisting that her love interest springs from her and the
poem's native soil. The poem is quick to distance Britomart, and consequently Elizabeth as her descendent, from contaminative miscegenation,
thereby sparing Britomart the fate of desiring a foreigner, as Artegall may
be suspected of doing in his relationship with Radigund in Book V.[83]

Indeed, Book 3, canto 3, illustrates its own obsession with origins. Before Merlin reveals Britomart's genealogy to her, he says, "For so must all
things excellent begin" (3.3.2). Excellent progeny, in this case Elizabeth,
must have excellent genealogical origins. When the poem takes an interest in Elizabeth's purity, it again rejects allegory by insisting instead on a
racial or genealogical connection between image and idea, thus creating a
racial rather than an allegorical connection between Britomart and Artegall and Elizabeth.

The Faerie Queene's concern with racial and religious purity is fulfilled
in Britomart's desire for Artegall. His purity and the purity of his and
Britomart's lineage are connected to what canto 3 portrays as a continual
battle with non-Christian forces: Repeatedly in canto 3, Merlin notes
Britomart's and Artegall's progeny fighting "paynims." Artegall in particular will defeat the "forrein Paynims, which invade thy land." In the context of this Protestant and often anti-Spanish epic, it is likely that Spenser
is registering widespread fears of a Spanish invasion in the 1590s, as well as

a past anxiety about the Queen's marriage proposals from the Duke of Anjou and Phillip II (the latter allegorically portrayed as the Souldan in Book 5). These potential marriages were causes of concern because they would compromise English Protestant identity. Even so, we cannot ignore the racial and religious differences that reside in these figures of the paynims and the Souldan. By creating a literal conflict between Britomart and Guyon's progeny and paynims, the poem imagines an England and a Protestantism that are genealogically resistant to Islam.

3. Infidel Texts and Errant Sexuality

Translation, Reading, and Conversion in Harington's *Orlando Furioso*

Spenser's self-conscious uses and rejections of allegory in *The Faerie Queene* most likely reflect Protestant ambivalence about allegorical interpretation, which was usually associated with Catholic hermeneutics. Tyndale, for one, tells readers, "Beware of allegoryes for there is not a more handsome or apte a thing to begile withal than allegory," and, conversely, "there is not a better vehementer or myghtyer thing to make a man understand than allegory."[1] Contradictory as these two statements may seem, Tyndale is less concerned with allegory as an author-intended mode of figuration than he is with the Catholic hermeneutic penchant for imputing allegorical meanings to texts that should, in his opinion, be read literally. Tyndale is chiefly concerned with the misuses of allegory, evincing a common Protestant belief that Scripture should be read literally. One effect of Tyndale's insistence on the literal meaning of the Bible is, as Stephen Greenblatt has asserted, "an emphasis on the rhetorical nature of Scripture . . . The Bible is not a vast network of occult signs but a divine work of persuasion, designed to strengthen the reader's faith and to deter him from evil."[2]

Tyndale held that reading Scripture should bolster faith and that faith, in turn, is a prerequisite for correct interpretation of Scripture. In *The exposition of the fyrste, seconde, and thyrde canonical epistles of S. Jhon* (1538), Tyndale asserts that the reader risks misinterpretations if he or she does not "haue the profession of his baptysme in his harte, he can not understonde the scripture."[3] Tyndale's baptismal theology leads him to see a connection between the ability to interpret Scripture correctly and the baptism of the heart rather than of the body. Being truly baptized, with or without receiving the outward sacramental sign, not only assures salvation but also conduces to a correct reading of Scripture.[4]

The anxieties surrounding reading and interpretation expressed by Tyndale and so many others partially originate in the Reformation's commitment to vernacular religion—making services and Bibles available to the laity in native tongues. In article twenty-four of "The Thirty-Nine Articles," the English Church vehemently denies that Latin should be used in church services: "It is a thing plainly repugnant to the word of God, and the customs of the primitive church, to have public prayer in the church, or to mister sacraments in a tongue not understanded of the people."[5] In England, English is the language of spiritual edification; conversely, Romish Latin is repugnant to God and his word. But as Scripture itself was originally written in a language not understood by the laity, it needed to be translated and converted into the new language of the church. The English language played an integral part in the national conversion from Catholicism to Protestantism.

The sanctification of English had a literary corollary. English emerged not only as a spiritually edifying language but also, as Richard Helgerson argues, the language through which early modern English poets self-consciously created a nation and a national literature.[6] Helgerson demonstrates that the political and religious climate needed an English national epic like Spenser's *Faerie Queene*; this climate also ripened a desire for an English (and Protestant) version of Ludovico Ariosto's international bestseller, *Orlando Furioso*.[7] In this chapter I argue that Sir John Harington's translation of *Orlando Furioso* gained legitimacy by creating a reading experience that was similar to reading the Bible. Like early modern English Bibles, especially the Geneva Bible, it uses paratextual materials—in Harington, prefatory material, marginal glosses, "Moralls" and "Allegories"—in order to guide readers' interpretations and foster moral and spiritual transformation. Harington's translation demonstrates a Protestant commitment to translation, correct interpretation, and the spiritual transformation of the reader.

Translation preceded the Reformation in England, but it acquired an exalted purpose from Protestant discourse about Bible translation and a theology that asserted the necessity for the laity to read Scripture, notwithstanding the limited literacy in the period. Just as reading the Bible (alongside preaching, of course) was deemed necessary for spiritual transformation, Harington's translation and subsequent allegorizing of Ariosto's poem sought to transform and indeed convert readers. Moreover, Harington's translation is itself a convert: The formerly infidel text, a repugnant Romish romance, is transformed into an English Protestant poem. Harington thus likens the translation and allegorizing of *Orlando Furioso* to religious conversion.[8]

Even so, as we saw in Spenser, Harington's translation exhibits uneasiness with domesticating the foreign into the familiar, especially as regards the use of romance and religious conversion to transform infidels into Christians. This uneasiness is most clearly evident in the infidel-conversion motif, as exemplified in Harington's curious treatment of Ariosto's Ruggiero, the Saracen knight who converts to Christianity and marries the female Christian knight Bradamante at the end of the poem. In Harington's version, however, Rogero (Harington's translation of Ariosto's Saracen knight) is proleptically converted by the allegory into a figure of the Christian reader who must reject desires that are non-European and foreign to the Christian self.

There are thus important differences between Harington's Rogero and Ariosto's Ruggiero. Rogero becomes a figure of European Christian experience, but only through paratextual materials that continually deemphasize his racial and religious identity. Within the allegory, and thus in tension with the plot, Harington's Rogero appears to be Christian before his conversion. Because the translation repeatedly erases Rogero's preconversion identity and thus distances Rogero from his Italianate literary progenitor, Harington's *Orlando Furioso* repurposes the infidel-conversion motif: It becomes a parable of the Christian's attempt to defeat the concupiscence that persists after baptism. This repurposing also uncovers anxieties about Christian affection for things infidel: Ariosto's original poem, or its Saracen knight, Ruggiero.

Bible Translation, Interpretation, and Transformative Reading

In his monumental *Print and Protestantism in Early Modern England*, Ian Green asserts, "If there was one book that the English reformers, like their Continental counterparts, thought should be universally available, it was the Bible—in the vernacular."[9] Perhaps this conviction arose from the Reformation's roots in an act of reading: Martin Luther's encounter with the book of Romans. Luther's narrative of conversion through reading, like the one St. Augustine's described in his *Confessions*, indeed provided the justification for translating the Bible, the hope was that everyone—or, more precisely, every literate person—could read Scripture for him- or herself and undergo a similar act of spiritual conversion. Translating the Bible was thus essential to the Protestant mission. As Su Fang Ng suggests, "Translation for the early Protestants becomes a mode of piety and a means of evangelizing."[10] There could be no conversion from the old religion to the new without translation.

But as reading the Bible became necessary for the conversion from Catholicism to Protestantism, questions about what readers would do with the Bible—that is, how they would interpret it—necessarily came to the fore. Green goes on to note, "For while it was generally agreed among Protestants that the complete Bible should be made available to everyone, it was also recognized that while some passages were so clear and safe that even the youngest and most innocent reader could read them, others were so deep and dangerous that even great intellects could drown in them."[11] Consequently, those who commissioned English Bibles and their translators understood that providing vernacular Bibles was not enough. For the sake of evangelism and the propagation of Protestant religion, they also had to assure that readers would interpret the Bible correctly.

Paratextual materials (prefaces, annotations, and glosses) became important tools for assuring correct interpretation. In the preface to the new Protestant state's authorized Bible, the Great Bible (1539), Archbishop Cranmer records the types of concerns that many, Protestants included, had about the impact of vernacular Bible, among them the spread of heresy.[12] Cranmer begins his apology for the Great Bible by arguing that Bible translation is not the invention of the Reformation; he claims that the tradition of *not* reading the Bible in the vernacular is only about a hundred years old. He asserts that the Bible "was translated and read in the Saxon tongue, which at that time was our mother's tongue: whereof there remained yet divers copies found lately in old abbeys" (39).[13] Cranmer's pointing toward an older tradition of vernacular Bibles, as evidenced in the discovered Saxon Bibles, seeks to establish the vernacular Bible as part of a native Christian tradition. He counters the arguments of those who saw English Bibles as tools of Protestant propaganda.

Asserting that vernacular Bibles are part of a native Christian tradition is just the first argument in the preface. Cranmer goes on to use a bodily analogy that justifies English Bibles. He questions why "any man should be so mad as to refuse in darkness, light; in hunger, food; in cold, fire" (38–9). The body becomes a primary metaphor in the preface; he later calls reading scripture "the most healthful medicine" (44). The frail and sick body becomes a metaphor for the soul needing sanctification, a metaphor that Cranmer borrows from Chrysostom, whom Cranmer employs to support his argument: "I intend here to say nothing but that was spoken and written by the noble doctor and most moral divine, St. John Chrysostom, in his sermon *De Lazaro*" (40). Just as he does through drawing attention to the existence of Saxon Bibles, Cranmer argues that reading vernacular Bibles has long been a practice in the universal church.

Cranmer quotes Chrysostom at length; a major reason the "noble doctor" gives for reading the Bible is that it fortifies the spirit against inordinate lust:

> Where canst thou have armour or fortress against thine assaults? Where canst thou have salve for thy sores, but of holy scripture. Thy flesh must needs be prone and subject to fleshly lusts, which daily walkest and art conversant amongst women, seest their beauties set forth to the eye, hearest their nice and wanton words, smellest their balm, civet, and musk, with many other like provocations and stirrings, expect thou hast in a readiness wherein to suppress and avoid them, which cannot elsewhere be had, but only out of the Holy Scripture. Let us read and seek all the remedies that we can, and all shall be little enough. (41)

Harington, too, regards reading as a way to fight the concupiscence inspired by literary romance (more about that later). Chrysostom argues that Scripture is the body's chief defense against the effects of a dangerously sensual world. Cranmer, by way of Chrysostom, emphasizes the Pauline opposition between the pleasures of the body and the health of the spirit, but what is remarkable here is the sensuality of the description itself. The hypothetical male walker sees, hears, smells, and then is stirred sexually by his senses. The belief that reading can curb sexual desire thus mandates that the Bible be read by all who can read—though Chrysostom notes that even reading the Bible "shall be little enough" defense against human sexuality.

Human sexuality prompts the need for Bible translation, perhaps because reading was viewed as a brake on the concupiscence that remains after baptism. (As I mentioned in the previous chapter, the "Thirty-Nine Articles" of the Church of England asserted that baptism does not remove concupiscence, which humans inherit from their fallen forebearers Adam and Eve.) Cranmer's belief in the power of reading the Bible to transform individuals likely draws from early modern understandings of reading as a practice that affects the passions and the humoral body; Katharine A. Craik and Elizabeth Spiller, in tracing the development of this view, observe that concerns about the body's health figure prominently in both arguments for reading spiritually edifying texts and against reading poetry.[14] Spiller notes that early moderns understood the effects of reading as analogous to the effects of diet: "Humanist projects controlling reading in this period should be understood as fundamentally related to more familiar projects that sought to exert control over the humanist body through diet; both were aimed at subduing passion and achieving reason within the humoral body."[15] What one reads, just as what one eats, either positively or negatively affects the health of the body and the spirit. Early moderns surely would have seen the Bible—the divinely inspired word of God—as the healthiest of all texts: We should recall that Cranmer refers to the Bible as food and "the most healthful medicine."

The connection between Bible reading, spiritual transformation, and sexual restraint takes an unforeseen racialized turn when Cranmer quotes Chrysostom's description of the Ethiopian eunuch's conversion in Acts 8. Cranmer quotes Chyrsostom as writing, "Remember the eunuch of Candace, Queen of Ethiopia, which, albeit he was a man of a wild and barbarous country, and one occupied with worldly cares and businesses, yet riding in his chariot, yet he was reading Scripture, what thinkest though of like was he wont to do sitting at home?" (43). On the one hand, the reference to the Ethiopian eunuch reminds its reader of the universal mission of Christianity: to make disciples of every nation. On the other hand, it fosters racial shame. Why is an Ethiopian from a "wild and barbarous country" seemingly more devoted to Bible reading than the typical Englishman? Perhaps it is because this Ethiopian is a eunuch and thus less susceptible to—or, at least, less able to act upon—sexual desire that he is able to channel his energy into reading Scripture. Although less explicitly here than earlier in Cranmer's preface, reading the Bible is again counterposed to sexuality. Moreover, this eunuch is an African, who would have been associated with excessive sexuality were it not for his physical deficit. Mary Floyd-Wilson has shown in her study of race and geohumoralism that "sexuality became a central focus of the racializing process" and that northerners like the English were believed to be more sexually temperate than southern Europeans and Africans.[16] As such, the allusion to the Ethiopian eunuch may have shamed the Bible-ignoring Englishman by questioning his distinctly English virtues of sexual restraint and religious piety.

Alongside the various arguments he uses to justify the need for English Bibles, Cranmer also addresses the dangers of misreading. Cranmer asserts, however, that misreading is the fault of the reader, not the English Bible. Like Tyndale, he argues that misreading comes from the defective faith of the reader. To illustrate his point, he likens misreading the Bible to pagan idolatry. Pagans worship the sun, moon and stars, but God's creations are not responsible for that idolatry. Cranmer concludes this argument by writing, "to them that be evil of themselves everything setteth forward and increaseth their evil" (45). The Bible is no exception: "Therefore to conclude this latter part, every man that cometh to the reading of this holy book ought to bring with him first the fear of Almighty God, and then next a firm and stable purpose of reforming his own self according thereunto" (49).

Cranmer believes that correct interpretation of Scripture lies within the individual; it comes from the individual's fear of God and a desire to be reformed by what is read. Cranmer's position is a common one among Protestants, but this does not mean that English translators did not seek to reform the reader from the outside. The Geneva Bible (completed in 1560) was the most heavily glossed of the early modern English Bibles; it attempts to intervene where the fear of the Almighty might prove insufficient for producing correct interpretation. Unlike the Great Bible, the Geneva Bible acknowledges that understanding the Bible can be a difficult task. Its preface states,

> And considering how hard a thing it is to understand the holy Scriptures, and what errors, sects and heresies growe dailie for lack of the true knollage thereof, and how many are discouraged (as thei pretend) because thei can not ataine the true and simple meaning of the same, we haue also indeuored bothe by the diligent reading of commentaries, and also by the conference with godly and learned breathern, to gather brief annotations vpon the hard places, aswel for the vnderstanding of such wordes as are obscure, and for the declaration of the text, as for the application for the same as may moste apperteine to Gods glorie and the edification of his Churche. (sig.a1v)

Unlike Cranmer and the Great Bible, the Geneva Bible seeks to thwart heresy through its substantial annotations, which are, perhaps, its most distinctive feature.[17] Green notes that unlike other early modern English Bible translators and compilers, "the translators of the Geneva Bible had few inhibitions about moving from elucidation to interpretation and application."[18] The glosses guide the reader toward the compliers' Calvinist strain of Protestantism.

Although it is hardly surprising that translation and annotation affect how the Bible is read (and thus mark the confessional differences among Protestants, Catholics, and Protestant sects), Protestant translators were careful to distinguish their Old Testament from the Hebrew Bible. Ilona N. Rashkow's examination of differences between early modern English Bibles and the Hebrew Bible reveals that these differences reflected anxieties about "judaization," the reading of Scripture with singular attention to carnal and earthly concerns. Here we should remember Daniel Boyarin's correlation between hermeneutics and anthropology. Paratextual materials provided a way to protect the translator from accusations of judaizing: "Since the English Renaissance biblical translators were determined to avoid the stigma of judaization, the Hebrew Bible as narrative was to be read only as part of a larger unit including Christian marginalia, appendices, woodcuts, and even the New Testament."[19] According to Rashkow, English Bibles render the Hebrew Bible itself as no more than the prelude to the New Testament. To further distance themselves from being labeled judaizers, Rashkow observes, English translators, including the translators of the Geneva Bible, often resorted to more straightforward racialized anti-Semitism.[20] Rashkow's examination reveals how translation reflects not only religious difference but also the culture's emerging racial ideologies. Translations record the translators' desires to solidify racialized forms of religious difference.

Converting the Infidel Text and Erasing Race

In her reading of Harington's translation, Tiffany Jo Werth compares the textual apparatuses of the English *Orlando Furioso* and the Geneva Bible.[21] I would add to Werth's insight that we can see in the paratexts that accompany Harington's translation a concern for the effects of reading on human sexuality and for the ways in which interpretation engenders distinctions between races and religions. English Bibles are not the sole examples of how paratexts attempt to influence interpretations of texts (we might consider E. K.'s glosses to Spenser's *Shepherd's Calendar*, for example), but William W. E. Slights upholds biblical paratexts as "a pronounced instance of the marginal maneuvering that characterizes the texts of the day."[22] Harington's paratextual materials attempt to govern readers' interpretations and to help them mark differences between Protestants and Catholics and between Christians and Muslims. The work is thus caught between producing a distinctly Protestant poem and narrating a story that calls its readers to identify with Catholic France and universal Christendom's shared fears about an expanding Islamic empire. The poem faces the conundrum: Who is *more* different, the Catholic or the Muslim? Harington's translation thus engages the polemical Protestant/Catholic/Muslim triad that I discussed in chapter 1. Harington's paratextual materials—his preface, marginalia, "Allegories" and "Morralls"—helped English readers to negotiate the racial and religious differences in this conundrum.

To begin this consideration of Harington's *Furioso*, I start not with the translation's beginning but with its end: "A Briefe And Summarie Allegorie Of Orlando Furioso, Not Unpleasant Nor Unprofitable For Those Who Have Read The Former Poem," which immediately follows the final canto of the poem. I start here because Harington makes explicit both the aims of his translation and his anxieties about it. "A Briefe," therefore, provides a framework for understanding how individual moments in the poem support his goals of producing a moral Protestant poem and alleviating fears about a potentially dangerous infidel text. And most important, "A Briefe" demonstrates Harington's awareness of the Protestant linkage of translation, reading, and conversion.

"A Brief" begins with Harington describing a chance moment of reading:

> When I had finished this translation of *Orlando Furioso* and began almost proud in my own conceit that I had in these my younge years employed my idle hours to the good liking of many and those of the better sort, I happened to reade in a grave and godly book these words: *So devines do hold (for examples sake) that the glory of St. Paul is increased dayly in heaven and shall be to the worlds end by reason of them that dayly do profite by his writing and rare exampler life upon earth, as also on the contrarie part that the torments of* Arrius Sabellius *and other wicked heretikes are continually augmented by the numbers of them who from time to time are corrupted by their sedicous and pestilent*

writings. If it had stayed there, it would never have troubled me, but immediately followes: *The like they hold of dissolute Poets and other loose writers which have left behind them lascivious, wanton, and carnal devices, as also of negligent parents, masters, teachters, &c*. This saying (gentle Reader) was such a cooling card to me and did so cut the combe of that pleasing conceit of mine that I could not tell whether I should repent me or not of my former taken paine. (558)[23]

The godly text he happens to read—Robert Parsons's *The First Book of the Christian Excercize Apperytayning to Resolutions* (1582)—causes a spiritual crisis. Harington announces that he is concerned with the spiritual import of his translation of Ariosto's Italian, Catholic romance, and his own spiritual state after its completion. His "almost" sinful pride is curbed, however, by a chance act of reading—about Paul, no less—that results in a transformation of character. Indirectly, Harington audaciously compares his works to Paul's; perhaps he wonders whether he will achieve the same eternal glory as the apostle for writing spiritually edifying texts.

Even so, it is difficult to read this comparison as anything but facetious, a critique of puritanical attacks on poetry's and romance's supposed wantonness, and of translations of foreign texts into English. As Werth has shown, romance bred anxieties "under the banner of '*sola scriptura*,'" under which "texts became especially fraught catalysts for—or against—faith."[24] More than ever, secular and foreign books aroused concerns about their effects on readers. In the *Schoolmaster* (1570), for example, Roger Ascham rebukes the "English man Italianated" and condemns books "of late translated out of *Italian* into English, sold in euery shop in London, commended by honest titles the soner to corrupt honest manners."[25] Just a bit later, Ascham criticizes "bookes of Cheualrie" like *Morte d'Arthur*, but he then qualifies this critique: "And yet ten *Morte Arthures* do not the tenth part so much harm, as one of these books, made in *Italie*, and translated in England."[26] Ascham does not mention *Orlando Furioso*, but as an Italian book of chivalry, he likely would have seen its popularity in England as a great evil. He argues that Italian texts carry within them Popish ideas that might transform readers into monstrous Anglo-Italian hybrids. The telos of this hybrid identity is hybridized religion, which he regards as satanic: "he shall haue free libertie to embrace all Religiouns, and becum, if he lust at once, without any let or punishment, Iewish, Turkish, Papish, and Deuillish."[27]

Harington surely fits Ascham's description of the "English man Italianated": Harington not only expresses great admiration for *Orlando Furioso,* but at one time he also referred to himself as a "Protesting Catholic Puritan."[28] Harington refused to align himself with a specific confessional community, and his translation upholds Christian beliefs and values that cross confessional divides. As Jane E. Everson suggests, in his translation "Harington must also consider the ambivalent nature of the religious settlement in England, the shifting political alliances of his own day and country."[29] At the same time, despite his admiration for Ariosto's poem, Harington is aware of what materials might offend a Protestant reader. Everson also points out that Harington often deletes moments exhibiting Catholic forms of piety, such as Bradamante's prayer to the Virgin Mary at the beginning of canto 4.[30] When it comes to moments of plot that cannot be easily excised from the poem, however, Harington uses paratextual materials, like "A Brief," to strip those moments of nefarious Catholic content. Thus, as tongue-in-cheek as his comparison of his work and Paul's might be, and even as he makes fun of puritanical arguments, Harington reexplains the spiritual lessons that an allegorical reading of *Orlando Furioso* can offer. Rather than repent for the translation, as he suggests he should do, he rearticulates the allegorical and moral readings that he has offered throughout his version of the poem.

Nevertheless, we might also read Harington's insistence on an allegorical and moral reading of Ariosto's romance as itself a type of conversion and turning away from romance as a genre that was often viewed, in the early modern period, mainly as a vehicle for pleasure and entertainment; allegory will absolve the poem of implications of heresy and sexual wantonness and endow it with chastity and orthodoxy. That Harington would here mention Paul of all people points to the importance of conversion as a trope for understanding the type of moral Protestant poem he created. Paul (formerly Saul), of course, was created by a radical act of conversion that occurred on the road to Damascus. *Orlando Furioso* recalls this conversion when Rogero has his chance encounter with a hermit in canto 41. The hermit's first words to Rogero are those that Saul heard from the heavenly voice: "ô *Saule,* ô *Saule,* / Why persecutest though my people so?"(41.53). Ariosto asks his readers to consider the relation between Ruggiero's conversion and Paul's, but in "A Brief" Harington asks his English readers to make a connection between his allegorical project, itself a response to his encounter with Paul, and the moment of Rogero's conversion. Like Spenser, however, Harington appears uneasy with transforming a Saracen into a Christian. Although we see the infidel-conversion motif in Harington's translation—a plot element that cannot be removed from the poem—the allegorical Rogero (that is, what Rogero is to signify within his allegory) is a Christian and a European long before the literal Rogero converts to Christianity. In Harington's translation we thus see a reappropriation of the infidel-conversion motif; it now signifies the sanctification of the Protestant reader.

Harington's "A Brief" also resonates with an influential narrative of Christian conversion through reading, found in book 8 of Augustine's *Confessions*. In the well-known story, Augustine hears the voice of a child chanting "Pick up and read, pick up and read."[31] By chance or divine intervention Augustine opens the Bible to Romans 13:13–14: "So that we walke honestly, as in the day: not in glotonie, and dronkennes, nether in chambering and wantonnes, nor in strife and euying: But put ye on the Lord IESVS CHRIST, and take no thought for the flesh, to fulfil the lustes of it." The passage speaks to what Augustine characterizes throughout the *Confessions* as his own struggles with sexual lust: earlier in book 8 he recounts cheekily praying, "Grant me chastity and continence, but not yet."[32] As we saw in Cranmer's preface, sexual desire impedes faith; reading, however, has the power to tame the sexual appetite. Although I do not believe that there is a direct connection between Cranmer preface, Augustine's *Confessions*, and Harington's "A Brief," together they show that Christianity had long seen the reading of religious texts as a cure for lust. Harington seems well aware of this tradition, one that was revivified in the early modern period by the Reformation's newfound emphasis on the transformative power of reading.

Another connection between reading, conversion, and sexuality surfaces in the apocryphal explanation of Harington's motivation for translating the poem in its (almost) entirety.[33] The story goes that Queen Elizabeth found Harington circulating a translation of the bawdy and misogynist canto 28. As punishment the queen sentenced Harington to translate the entire poem. The story of the translation's origins cannot be verified, but it nevertheless demonstrates that Ariosto's Italian eroticism was a source of English anxiety.[34] If true, however, the story might also explain Harington's desire to allegorize and moralize the poem, as well as his desire to make sure that he is not one of those *"dissolute Poets and other loose writers which have left behind them lascivious, wanton, and carnal devices."* This desire may also explain why the translation, according to Colin Burrow, "does lack much of the amorous magic which keeps Ariosto's poem flowing delightfully from action to action."[35] The story also allows us to see a likeness between Augustine and Harington in their randy youth. Whereas Augustine's act of reading leads to his conversion, Harington's act of translation leads to a conversion of the text and its reception. Harington's translation attempts to sanctify the poem and its readers by purging it of errant eroticism, to restrain rather than excite the dangerous passions that romances were believed to inspire[36]

Harington's treatment of Rogero illustrates the translation's attempt to direct readers away from wayward desire. This intent is unmistakable in the translation's preface, in which Harington compares Rogero's rendezvous with the enchantress Alcina to Aeneas's with Dido. The preface, a defense of poetry in general and of *Orlando Furioso* in particular, seeks to justify the poem's mixture of Christian morality and sexual errancy (a characteristic of many romances), with the latter most apparent, according to Harington, in Ariosto's description of Ruggiero's relationship with Alcina: "But now it may be and is by some objection that although [Ariosto] writes Christianly in some places, yet in other some he is too lascivious, as in that of the baudy Frier, in *Alcinas* and *Rogeros* copulation . . . and some few places besides. . . . But as I say, if tis a fault, then *Vergill* committed the same fault in *Dido* and *Aeneas* intertainment" (11–12).

Although Harington seeks to elevate the status of *Orlando Furioso* by pointing out similarities between Ariosto's poem and Virgil's epic, he also elevates the status of Rogero; the comparison of Rogero and Aeneas is a significant one because Rogero, not the mad Orlando, becomes the father of a dynasty.[37] In being compared with *pius Aeneas*, Rogero is initially associated with a specific kind of romance errancy, that which thwarts both dynastic lineage and religious piety. In this formulation Alcina, like Virgil's Dido and Spenser's Acrasia, is the sexually enticing foreign woman who can corrupt proper uses of sexuality—namely, the sexuality that propagates a desirable race and its attendant modes of European piety.

Harington fully capitalizes on the comparisons of Rogero and Aeneas, creating a Rogero whose particular faults (not to mention his non-Christian identify) are forgiven because, as the reader knows, he will become the father of a noble Christian race: Merlin's prophecy to Bradamante in canto 3 makes this clear. But the comparison also disassociates Rogero from Africa, his ancestral homeland, and associates him instead with Europe. This disassociation is crucial to Harington's allegorical project of erasing Rogero's African Saracen identity in order to facilitate moral instruction. The most explicit allegorical erasure of Rogero's African identity occurs in "Allegorie" in canto 6, in which Rogero is carried away by the hippogriff to Alcina's island:

> First thereof is *Rogero* . . . we may understand the Griffeth horse that carried him to signifie the passion of the mind contrarie to reason that caries men in aire, that is, in the height of the imaginations, out of Europ, that is out of the compasse of the rules of Christian religion and feare of God, unto the Ile of *Alcyna*, which signifieth pleasure and vanities of this world. (79)

I am struck by Rogero's European origin; he is carried "out of Europ," whence he seems to originate within the "Allegorie." Rogero's migration, moreover, has religious significance; Christianity is securely grounded in Europe, while non-Christianity is located much more ethereally elsewhere. On the "Allegorie's" geo-religious map Rogero is already a Christian; the allegory converts an African Muslim into a European Christian before the actual moment of conversion in the poem.

Because it locates Christian experience in Europe, whither Rogero travels and to which he already seemingly belongs, the "Allegorie" also expresses concerns about "the passions of the mind" that have the potential to carry Europeans away from the geographically situated "rules of Christian religion." Harington's allegory of the Rogero and Alcina episode overlaps with religious arguments about the dangers of reading romance; Spiller and Werth have shown that a major charge against romance was that it could dangerously alter readers' passions.[38] The allegory thus encourages a recognition of a correspondence between Rogero's story and the Europeans who read the poem wrongly. Romance, as a mode concerned with romantic relationships and errant sexuality, is able to carry Christian readers outside of the realm of Christianity and incite them to imagine exotic, infidel mores and passions.

The romance passions are thus figured as the illegitimate offspring of illicit sexual contact and miscegenation. Perhaps this is why Rogero's affair with Alcina is one of the most heavily glossed episodes in the translation; Judith Lee suggests that this heavy glossing demonstrates that "Harington placed new emphasis on the ethical value of the Rogero-Alcina episode."[39] At the same time, the heavy glossing and the "Allegorie" unwittingly reveal anxieties about translating a scene that is likely to arouse the very passions of the mind that godly texts are supposed to suppress. But if a reader has, by chance, been caught up in his or her own passionate reading of and desire for the sexually enticing Alcina, the allegory seeks to bring that reader back down to Christian earth.

Rogero's rejection of Alcina is also allegorized as a conversion from romance to epic; like Aeneas, Rogero must reject romance sexuality in order to become the progenitor of a dynasty. In fact, the rejection of romance desire is Rogero's first conversion. In "A Brief" Harington describes Rogero's sexual relationship with Alcina as being "drowned and utterly overwhelmed in this gulfe of pleasure which mine author hath set downe so lively as it were the verie picture of the prodigal sonne spoken of in the Scripture" (560). The Prodigal Son story is one of repentance, after all, and of turning back to God. The comparison between Rogero and the Prodigal Son foreshadows the conversion that is to come, which, in "A Brief," is fulfilled not in Rogero's eventual baptism by the hermit but in his seeing Alcina for who she really is: "This is to be understood," Harington writes, "that a man besotted in the fond pleasures of the world, entering into godly consideration with himselfe of his owne estate, heareth *Melyssa*, which is to be understood the devine inspiration of the grace of God calling him from the damned course of life to an honest and virtuous course" (560). For Harington, Rogero's rejection of Alcina is the evidence of an inward response to "the grace of God calling" and conversion. Just a bit later in "A brief" Harington writes that one of the lessons Rogero's journey teaches is that "our concupiscence . . . with a perpetuall thirst still maketh us covet things hurtful to our selves" (561). The allegory in "A Brief," therefore, connects Rogero and the Christian "our" who are still susceptible to sexual desires that could impel them, through a misreading of the poem or intercourse with an infidel woman, to transgressions of acceptable Christian behavior.

Harington's opposition between Europe/Christian and non-Europe/non-Christian also recalls the "catholic" Charlemagne romances, born of a pre-Reformation united Christendom that had been a hallmark of the

romance.[40] Harington finds the symbolic geography of Christendom useful for his allegory, but he does not allow readers of his translation to accept
Christendom's theology, especially in matters of conversion. Surprisingly,
Harington seems to find little allegorical significance in Rogero's literal
conversion: He does not mention it in "A Brief." Moreover, in canto 41,
which details Rogero's literal conversion to Christianity, Harington does
not include an "Allegorie." There are other cantos in the poem that do not
include an "Allegorie": In canto 5, for example, under the "Allegorie"
heading, Harington writes, "Allegorie there is none in this booke at all,"
and in canto 3, as in canto 41, the heading does not appear at all. Perhaps
the scene of Roger's conversion is so clear that it requires no further explication. Or the lack of allegorizing suggests some intention to undermine
the significance of the literal conversion and actual turning point in Ariosto's plot. Highlighting the conversion would actually work against his
allegorical Rogero, who is already a Christian.

Harington does not allegorize the contents of canto 41, but in the
"Morrall" at the end of the book, he moralizes Rogero's prayer and vow
to convert if he should survive the shipwreck:

> In that *Rogero* in his extremity of daunger feeleth a remorse of conscience
> and straight hath recourse to God by prayer and vow, it is a good
> president for others to do the like, though indeede most men are apt to
> do so but all the matter is performed the effect of their vow and promise
> to God after; for that few care, according to that saying made a proverb
> in Italian
>
> *Scampato il pericolo giabbato il santo.*
> *When daunger is scaped, the said is—mocked.*
>
> But the example of *Rogero* may move us to more true devotion, and
> this speech of the good Old Hermit let everie one apply to him self that
> hath need of it, and it may do him as good as a sermon, for in deed it is
> most sweet and comfortable and very true doctrine. (479)

Rogero provides a model for the Christian reader to follow. The prayer
and vow are described as a "*re*course to God"; "recourse" can be read as
denoting that he changes his course, but it can also suggest, according to
one of *Oxford English Dictionary*'s definitions of the word, that this moment is a actually a "return" to God.[41] If this is the case, Rogero is similar
to Spenser's Redcrosse, whose identity as Christian knight persists de-

spite his moral failings. In the "Morrall," Rogero's prayer and vow are linked less to conversion than they are to a Christian reforming his bad behavior.

The "Morall" then suggests that this episode should "move us to more true devotion" through the hermit's "sermon." The "Morall" places the hermit's words within a Protestant framework in which words—spoken in the form of a sermon and then read in Harington's book—rather than sacraments inspire spiritual transformation. Nothing in the hermit's sermon would be offensive to the Protestant reader: The hermit tells Roger, "how to Christ he must impute / The pardon of his sinnes, yet near the later / He told him he must be baptized in water" (41.58.6–8). Although baptism remains a "must," the mandate to be baptized follows, as it would in the Church of England's baptismal service, explanation of Christ's (not baptism's) saving power. The sacrament is deemphasized to underscore the transformative power of the spoken and written word. Rogero provides a model for "us" to follow: Like him, the reader is to be spiritually moved and transformed by the power of the words rendered here by Harington, the translator.

Yet Rogero's transformation and new identity need to be firmly established, and, in conformity with the romance formula, marriage seals the deal. Harington, in "A Brief," attempts to present Rogero as a unified figure of "the verie Idea and perfect example of a true knight that will by no means break his faith and his honour" (567); hence Rogero must be purged of imputations of racial alterity. We can see this in Harington's discussion of Rogero's encounter with the Saracen Rodomont, who shows up uninvited to Rogero's and Bradamante's wedding and calls the new Christian a traitor and an apostate. This insult, of course, incites the two knights to a battle, and the now-Christian Rogero defeats and slays the Muslim Rodomont. The "Allegorie" states that the scene provides an example of killing youthful passions:

> In that mine author brings in for the conclusion of his whole work that
> *Rogero* immediately upon his marriage to *Bradamante* killeth *Rodomont,*
> this is the Allegorical sence thereof: that *Rodomont,* which is to be
> understood as the unbridled heat and courage of youth (for in all of
> *Rodomonts actions* you shall find him described ever most furious, hastie,
> and impatient), *Rodomont,* I say, is killed and quite vanquished and killed

by marriage, and how soever the unrulinesse of youth is excusable in
divers kind, yet after that holy state of matrimonie is entered into, all
youthful wildness of all kinds must be cast away. (557)

In killing Rodomont, Rogero also vanquishes any residual non-Christian
identity remaining in him; through marriage Rogero defeats his inner
infidel. Like Spenser's Pyrochles and Cymochles, Rodomont embodies
emotions like rage, fury and haste; like *The Faerie Queene*, Harington's
Orlando Furioso locates intemperate modes of being in the body of the
Saracen. Harington's link between marriage and the death of Rodomont
also draws most likely from the English Church's marriage ceremony,
which portrays marriage as "a remedy against sin," and a way "to avoid
fornication."[42] One might also read the killing of Rodomont as a killing
of the "youthful wildness" that so offended the queen that she commanded
Harington to translate and allegorize *Orlando Furioso*. Rogero's marriage,
then, is linked not with religious conversion but with maturation. The
poem ends with a married and chaste Rogero, purged of foreign, infidel,
and Italianate passions—a reformation of character that finds its analogue
in Harington the penitent translator.

Disrupting Interracial Affection

Perhaps Rogero's redemptive trajectory accounts for Harington's effort, in
the paratextual materials, to distance the hero from his ambiguous racial
and religious identity. His identity is complicated by the interreligious and
interracial relationship of his parents. In the second canto we are reminded
of a fact first mentioned in Matao Maria Boiardo's *Orlando Innamorato*
(1495), that Ruggiero's father is the Christian Ruggiero of Reggio and his
mother is Galaciella, daughter to Agramante, King of the Saracens. Ariosto's
poem, however, makes very little of Ruggiero's Christian ancestry, although
it does become important inasmuch as the poem suggests that his conversion, like Clorinda's in *Gerusalemme liberata,* is a recovery of a Christian
identity that is lost to him; after the death of his parents, the orphaned
Ruggiero is raised by the Saracen wizard Atlante. Ruggiero's Christian
and noble origins are important because they make him a fit spouse for
Bradamante and a fit progenitor for the Este family—he is also a descendent
of Trojan Hector. That said, it is impossible to ignore the Saracen blood in

his veins—the poem does not forget it—and his Saracen identity through-out the majority of the poem.

I now wish to consider the significance of Harington's locating Rog-ero's figurative conversion at the beginning of the poem. The difference between the literal and figurative conversion suggests that the translation attempts to disavow the affective bonds Ariosto's poem portrays between persons of different races and religions. Writing of such bonds in romance, Barbara Fuchs argues as follows:

> Individual chivalric encounters while the heroes are away from the front do not observe the same rules as collective battles, so that the Christian knights occasionally experience love or friendship for the "infidels" whom they are collectively fighting. Thus romance challenges the political mythmaking of epic, and its tight networks of obligation and belonging.[43]

From the beginning, Ariosto proves willing to ignore the epic signifi-cance of the religious conflict in order to explore the ways in which erotic desire can erase difference. In canto 1, when Rinaldo realizes that Angelica is fleeing while he and Ferrau fight to win her, he suggests to his competi-tor that they suspend their combat lest they both lose the object of their desire; the Christian knight proposes an alliance with the Saracen knight. Ferrau consents, and the two ride off on a single horse. The narrator praises them for this action:

> O auncient knights of true and noble hart:
> They rivals were, one faith they liv'd not under;
> Beside they felt their bodies shrewdly smart
> Of blowes late given, and yet (behold a wonder)
> Through thicke and thin, suspition set apart,
> Like frends they ride and parted not a sunder
> Untill the horse with double spurring drived
> Unto a way parted in two arrived. (1.22)

The narrator commends the two knights for putting religious and cultural differences aside in order to achieve a common purpose. Erotic desire, disguised as chivalry, becomes a great unifier: it is able to create allies across cultures and religions. This scene, at the same time, points to the extraordinariness of this event, distancing itself temporarily from the present in the characterization of these knights as "auncient," or in the Italian, *"cavallieri antiqui."* Ariosto's temporal distancing asks the poem's Italian reader to consider whether such a rapprochement is possible in the sixteenth century and beyond. As they digress from the seemingly more important religious conflict, Rinaldo and Ferrau ignore their differences and instead focus on their similarities as knights and men in order to pursue their object of desire, Angelica.

Harington also calls his English readers' attention to this action, inviting them to "behold a wonder"—this command to the reader is not in the Italian.[44] Harington's addition suggests that for him and his English readers, Rinaldo's and Ferrau's action is indeed a "wonder," the stuff of romance, and a digression that imagines alliances that transcend racial and religious conflict—all the more notable because Harington usually disallows the marvelous to be read as such: Lee writes, "Harington's translator describes the marvelous episodes from the point of view of a 'plain speaking' Englishman who never expresses surprise or wonder at the magical enchantments or at unexpected turns of events. . . . Harington used the marvelous as a way to reiterate the real historical and moral framework of the fiction."[45] The wonder inspired by the alliance between Rinaldo and Ferrau highlights its radical divergence from the poem's context of religious conflict.

Harington's version of *Orlando Furioso* attempts to impede such alliances, conciliations, and affections, especially with respect to readers' views of Rogero. Although Ariosto's readers know beginning with canto 3 that Ruggiero will eventually become a Christian, the preconversion Ruggiero is nevertheless appealing to both readers and Bradamante—long before he converts in canto 41. As Patricia Parker has observed, the lateness of the conversion may demonstrate that romance narratives are propelled by deferral and the impediment of narrative closure, but it is also true that the deferral of Ruggiero's conversion allows more time for a reader to be moved by the hapless adventures of a Saracen.[46]

Harington's "A Brief," "Allegories" and "Moralls," as well as interventions in the plot, keep English readers from making the same mistake Rinaldo does; together they seek to reform the reader's desires in order to frustrate bonds between Christian readers and infidels. I am not arguing that Harington's English *Orlando Furioso* is entirely successful in this task, especially since this reforming work primarily takes place in the paratexts rather than in the translation. Yet given the persuasive authority accorded to paratexts in early modern England, these notations are clearly a major component in Harington's main goal of shielding the reader from forms of desire deemed alien to Protestant identity. Unlike his source text, which according to Albert Russell Ascoli revels in errancy and often diverges from European cultural values, Harington's *Orlando Furioso* denies its readers the opportunity to be captivated by a Saracen by portraying Rogero as a Christian before his actual conversion.[47] Harington's English version seeks to prevent readers from being carried away—as Rogero is to Alcina's island—by their affection for a non-Christian character.

4.   Transformative and Restorative Romance

Re-"turning" *Othello* and Locating Christian Identity

Epic romances like Spenser's *Faerie Queene* and Harington's *Orlando Furioso* are mainly concerned with internal differences of genealogy, blood, and the spirit, but they do not provide imagery that prompts readers to visualize those differences. Early modern English drama, however, seeks to make difference spectacularly visible. Non-European and non-Christian characters populate English plays, in which the internal trait of religious belief is often externalized through the mechanisms of early modern theatrical production: Costumes, skin coloring, and caricatured foreign behavior enlivened the dramatic spectacle.[1] *Othello* is such a play, probing the interconnectedness of black skin, Moorishness, and infidel identity that might place Othello outside the bounds of Christian community. The play dramatizes the elusive interplay between Othello's Moorishness and his infidelity to Christianity.

Nevertheless, *Othello* criticism has often seen the "Moor of Venice" as an outsider, citing Roderigo's assertion that Othello is "an extravagant and wheeling stranger / Of here and everywhere" (1.1.134–35).[2] Critics have tended to concentrate on the language of extravagance and strangeness (such critics usually read "everywhere" as Africa or the Middle East.)[3] More recently, however, Emily C. Bartels has asked us to reconsider Othello's strangeness. Taking a cue from the play's subtitle, she asks, "is the Moor necessarily out of place in Venice?"[4] What is the import of that "of"? What are we to make of the mixed characterization of Othello as at once an "extravagant and wheeling stranger" but also "of Venice" and "of here" and "everywhere"? In this chapter I argue that we need to consider not only Othello's difference but also his belonging, even though the latter is often eclipsed by current interest in uncovering the emergence of racial ideologies in the early modern period and in exploring Western-European anxieties about Islamic imperial ambitions.[5] Even granting the importance of such investigations, considering Othello's belonging in Christian Venice complicates our understanding of skin color as a marker of insurmountable differences between Europeans and non-Europeans in the early modern period and shifts our attention toward the play's exploration of the power of Christianity and romance to transform difference into similarity.[6]

I do not deny that Christendom's claims to incorporate all who believe were far from realized in the early modern period (or in any other), nor do I deny the strength of European xenophobia and its manifestations in England, as evidenced in Elizabeth's call for the expulsion of blackamoors from England in 1596 and 1601.[7] Nevertheless, criticism of *Othello* has often overlooked or at least discounted Othello's Christian identity.[8] The play, in contrast, makes it very clear that Othello is a Christian: Iago tells us that Desdemona would be able to make Othello "renounce his baptism, / All seals and symbols of redeemed sin" (2.3.338–39).[9] Iago is not only cognizant of Othello's Christian identity but also harbors a fantasy of undermining it in order to highlight the Moor's otherness—witness Iago's racist language in act 1, scene 1. Nonetheless, the racial and bestial imagery that Iago deploys to rouse Brabantio from his slumber finds no receptive ears in the Venetian senate.[10]

Although Othello's difference cannot be ignored, the failure of Iago's imagery suggests that racial difference, especially when severed from religious difference, is not enough in itself to justify exclusion from a Christian state. The play thus reveals that both Othello's religious identity and romance conventions override nontheological forms of racial discourse in the construction of identity. *Othello* draws from Ludovico Ariosto's *Orlando Furioso* and includes various motifs associated with the romance mode, including a tale of adventure, mistaken identity, magic, and shipwreck. Othello is patterned after Ariosto's Ruggiero, a fellow convert to Christianity who also marries an Italian heroine. *Orlando Furioso* provided Shakespeare with an imaginative alternative to the exclusionary politics that predominated in the early modern period, and *Othello* employs the romance telos that transcends geographical and cultural difference through religious conversion.[11]

Yet *Othello* is a tragedy that kills the converted romance hero; Othello is transformed from insider to outsider, from Christian hero who plays a vital role in Venetian imperial politics to an Islamic rival. Othello uses the romance telos as a means of gaining access to Venetian society; Iago, realizing that his initial form of racist discourse has so little effect, turns to romance as well, for only romance will have the power to undo the identity that Othello creates for himself in Venice. In order to re-"turn" Othello to what is presumably his prior Muslim identity, Iago exploits the erotic desire/religious conversion nexus that had become a romance commonplace.[12] Yet Iago's desire to re-"turn" Othello not only counteracts the hero's transformative romance, but it also provides an example of what comes to define Shakespearean romance: the restoration of originary identities. Shakespeare's engagement with romance, like Spenser's, thus draws attention to the persistence of origins. *Othello* both reveals the work of genre and geography in the creation of religious identities and dramatizes a debate about the soteriological implications of the two competing ends of romance: the transformation and restoration of identity.

Rare Infidel Conversion: Race, Religion, and Geography

The Church of England's conflation of race and religion seemingly undermined the legitimacy of Othello's Christian identity. Nevertheless, even as they sought to conjoin race and religion in the construction of English Protestant Christianity, English theologians never asserted that it was impossible for non-Europeans and those without Christian parents to become Christians—they were barred from going that far by Christ's command to make converts of every nation in Matthew 28, popular concepts of Pauline universalism, knowledge of Christians in Africa and Asia, and the fact of black Christians residing in England. English theologians were also reluctant to say as much for rhetorical reasons. To further his argument that baptism is not necessary for salvation, William Tyndale asserts in *A brief declaration on the sacraments* (1548), "a Turk unbaptized (because he either knoweth not, that he ought to have it, or cannot for tyranny), if he believe in Christ, and love as Christ did and taught, then hath he his part in Christ's blood" (351). Thomas Becon concurs in *A New Catechism* (1564):

> And it is not to be doubted that, even among the Turks and the other heathen, there are many spiritually baptized, and so are saved, although their bodies want the water of baptism. For he is not a Christian only, which is washed with water; neither is that baptism only, which is outward in the flesh, but that is the very baptism which God alloweth, even to be baptized in heart through the Spirit of God. (221)

In these instances infidel conversion is used to illustrate the nonessentiality of the baptismal ceremony.

Turks and other so-called heathens may become Christians without being baptized, but they would never be baptized until they were able to convince a minister that they were already de facto Protestant Christians. The administration of the sacrament illustrated that there was a clear difference between the children of Christians, who received baptism during their infancy, and adult converts, who were baptized only after their faith and beliefs were scrutinized. The Elizabethan Archbishop of Canterbury, John Whitgift, upholds this position in *The Defense to the Answer to the Admonition* (1574), a response to the Puritan Thomas Cartwright's *Replye to an Answere of Dr Whitgifte* (1573). In asserting that baptism should be delayed until an individual can declare faith for him or herself, thereby denying the legitimacy of infant baptism, Cartwright presents the hypothetical case of Jews and Moors who might wish to convert. In Cartwright's analogy, just as the Church of England would examine the faith of would-be Jewish and Moorish converts before baptizing them, so too should English men and women (not infants) be examined before they are baptized. Whitgift quotes Cartwright and responds, "It may be indeed that 'there be Jews in England and Moors,' and Turks also, and that some of them, being converted to the faith, be afterward baptized: and I think sometimes it is so; but the case is very rare; and there is no man that doubteth that they ought to be examined in their faith before they be admitted to baptism."[13] Cartwright's use of Jewish and Moorish figures to present an Anabaptist argument suggests that there should be no difference between the baptisms of Jews and Moors and the English, but Whitgift maintains differences among these groups. He does not disagree with Cartwright's point that Jews and Moors, "and Turks also," should be baptized only after their faith is examined, but he upholds infant baptism for the children of Christians. Whitgift does not even address Cartwright's objection to pedobaptism, most likely because he has already gone to great lengths to justify it previously in *The Defense.* To Cartwright's objection, all he writes here is "Anabaptism being so crafty an heresy, that it dissembleth many things, until it have sufficient aid" (134). Whitgift's response to Cartwright reveals a clear difference between those who are born into the Christian faith—for whom baptism is merely a reaffirmation of a racially grounded Christianity—and those who convert to Christianity, for whom baptism is a seal of faith, a final mark of approval.

This difference obtained not only in Whitgift's thinking but also in the lives of Turks who converted to Christianity in Elizabethan England. Meredith Hanmer's *The baptizing of a Turke, A sermon preached at the Hospitall of Saint Katherin* (1586) recounts the conversion of a Turk named Chinano; it also reveals that such a conversion was bound to be viewed as an extraordinary event—indeed a miraculous one—because of links early moderns made not only between racial and religious identity but also between these and geographical origin. In *The baptizing of a Turke*'s dedicatory epistle, Hanmer informs Raphe Rokeby (to whom the book is dedicated) why he has chosen to record the circumstances of Chinano's conversion: "I have thought good to shew unto you the good newes here hapned through the mercy & goodness of our gratious God, which hath brought home to his folde an erring sheepe, by birth a *Turke,* borne at *Nigropontus,* heretofore by professio[n] a *Saracen,* addicted unto the superstitious lawe of *Mahomet.*"[14] The conversion is represented as an act of supernatural intervention that is all the more miraculous because there are at least four factors that would hinder this Turk's "publike confession of his true faith in Jesus Christ": First, he is "by birth a *Turke*"; second, he is "borne at *Nigropontus,*" a formerly Christian city that fell to the Turks in 1470; third, he is "by professio[n] a *Saracen*"; and fourth, he is "addicted unto the lawe of *Mahomet.*" Before his conversion, his being born a Turk and his place of birth constitute his Saracen "profession" and "addiction" to Islam, all of which are cast as hindrances to Christian faith.

This view of race, lineage, and geographical origin as constituents of religious identity is consistent with the early moderns' geo-religious and geo-racial map of the world. Hanmer laments in the dedicatory epistle,

> Wee have cause to sorrowe, when we beholde the face of the earth in manner all covered with heathens, idolatrers, and false worshippers, *Asia* in greatness half the world, (though of olde reckoned for the third part) with the governours of *Zambei* of *Arabia,* the king of *Narsinga, Cham* of *Tartaria,* and the *Indian* Ilands, (if we may credit *Marcus Paulus* Venetus) amounting to the number of twelve thousand & seve[n] hundred, all at this day (excepting a few Christians here & there scattered) are either Infidels, living as brute beastes, or followers of *Mahomet,* joining with the *Turke* in false worshippe . . . . *Affrike* (excepting there dominions of *Presbiter John* the great king of *Aethiopia,* who professeth the faith in Christ, though not so purely as it is to be wished) hath many infidels, the rest are *Moores, Saracens, Nigroes, Barbarians,* addicted to *Mahomet,* and obedient to the great *Turke.* (sig. 2v–3r)

He adds a bit later, "Christian religion is now couched in the North partes of the world, and so far that it seemeth (if we looke for fruits) all frozen. The professors (according unto the words of our Saviour) are now a little flock. It is high time wee should earnestlie pray unto God, that he will enlarge his kingdome, that hee will open the eyes of Infidels" (sig. 3v). Like Harington's *Orlando Furioso,* Hanmer's sermon locates Christianity in Europe and infidel identity everywhere else—though we also see Hanmer's prayer that God will disrupt the very geo-religious map that he draws here and elsewhere in *The baptizing of a Turke.* In drawing this map, Hanmer highlights the vastness of the non-Christian world and underestimates the Christian presence in Asia and Africa. On the one hand, Hanmer's description conforms to accounts by European travelers to the Near East and Africa who noted indigenous Christian populations, sparse and small though they might have seemed amid Muslim majorities. On the other hand, Hanmer's hyperbolic language—excepting Europe, "we beholde the face of the earth in manner all covered with heathens"—portrays Europeans as the sole bearers of the Christian faith; Europeans are now the chosen people who are to be, as Isaiah said of Israel, "a light unto the nations" (Isaiah 49:6). Hanmer hopes and prays for the very infidel conversions that are rendered unlikely by his geo-religious mapping; he forges a link between geography and religion that can be broken only through divine intervention, if God should choose to answer the prayers of English Christians.

There were alternatives to the map that Hanmer (and Harington) created, however. In Reformation England acknowledging non-European churches became a way to point to the universality of non–Roman Catholic forms of Christianity. John Jewel, for example, points to the Ethiopian church, which, like the Church of English, prays in a language that the people can understand.[15] Thomas Becon, too, cites the Ethiopian Church as having a practice similar to the Church of England's: Both churches gave the people both the bread and the wine in communion (258). But the most extensive comparisons between the Church of England and non-European churches occur in Ephraim Pagitt's *Christianographie, or The description of the multitude and sundry sorts of Christians in the world not subiect to the Pope. With their vnitie, and how they agree with us in the principall points of difference betweene us and the Church of Rome* (1635). The very title of the work describes its goals; Pagitt states explicitly that his purpose is

> to confute them that would empale the Church of God, within the limits
> of the *Roman* Church, and pretend that all the Christians of the world,
> are subiect to the Pope, but only a few Protestants in *Europe,* for here you
> may see, that the Church of God is not tied to *Rome* onely, but that it is
> Catholike, and vniversall, dispersed vpon the face of the whole earth.[16]

Like Jewel and Becon, Pagitt notes doctrinal similarities between the Church of England and various churches in Asia and Africa; he allows us to question the conflation of Asia and Africa with Islam and heathenism. And although it is somewhat later than Hanmer's sermon, Harington's *Orlando Furioso,* and Shakespeare's *Othello,* Pagitt's *Christianographie* allows us to interrogate the geo-religious maps that many, but not all, early moderns constructed.

In contrast to Hanmer, Pagitt sees Christianity as already a global religion. He makes the claim early in his book, "*Christianity* is not confined to one Country or Nation, but it is dispersed over the face of the Earth."[17] Perhaps most relevant for this discussion is his description of Christians in Turkey and their depletion in North Africa. About Turkey he writes, "There are in *Constantinople,* the very seate of the *Turkish* Empire, about 20 Churches of *Christians,* and in the Citie of *Thessalonica,* about 30

Map of Africa, from Ephraim Pagitt, *Christianographie or The description of the multitude and sundry sorts of Christians in the vvorld not subiect to the Pope . . .* (London, 1635), between G1v and G2r. By permission of the Folger Shakespeare Library.

Churches, where in the later, the *Mahometans,* have but three Temples, or meskites."[18] Pagitt's statement allows us to ask questions about the rhetorical and political intentions behind the early modern tendency to read "Turk" as a metonym for "Islam." Additionally, Pagitt provides literal maps throughout *Christianographie* that detail where Christians (believers in Christ who are not Roman Catholic), papists, and non-Christians reside on the planet; these maps, too, ask us to question those who locate Christianity solely in Europe. When we look at Pagitt's map of Africa, for example, we not only see that Christians are located in Egypt and Ethiopia (as well as some in Angola), but also that there is a small remnant of Christians in the land known as Barbary: "Christiantie In a maner lost for want of teachers here have bene some 100 of B[isho]ps and now 2 only left." As we will see, Pagitt, unlike Hanmer, provides a pragmatic rather than a racial explanation for the lack of Christians in North Africa, even as he acknowledges that Christianity had once flourished in the region. Pagitt's North Africa is not as monolithic as the one portrayed by many other early modern writers.[19] Moreover, confessional similarity between English and non-European Christians proves more important than racial difference in *Christianographie*—although Pagitt at times glosses over the fact that some of the non-European Christians he mentions are Roman Catholics.

Nonetheless, Pagitt's text differs from the more popular understandings of Africa and Asia, which were influenced by the writings of English captives and merchants who traveled to Africa and Asia, and by the stage plays set in these locations. Like these texts and plays, Hanmer's work—as well as Pagitt's, though in a much different manner—is part of an early-modern project to chart the world along axes of proximity and distance, similarity and difference. Both John Gillies and Valerie Traub have examined this project. Gillies suggests that what he calls a "poetic geography"—the early modern inheritance of classical models that link civility to proximity to the *polis*—"is much more valuable in providing us with a conceptual purchase on the construction of otherness . . . that is completely independent of the anachronistic terminology of 'race,' 'colour,' and 'prejudice.'" Traub, responding to Gillies and others who question the early modern conception of race, argues,

> the spatial plotting of cartographic bodies in the early seventeenth-century
> depended on and fostered a delineation of differences not wholly
> circumscribed by notions of true and false religion, civility and
> barbarism. . . . Ideas of lineage bleed into notions of nation; the ideas of
> nation evolve out of complexion and clime. Through such convergences,
> specifications of difference begin to take on an increasingly racialized
> cast.[20]

As we will see, Hanmer's narrative provides another example of how the world was divided not only along lines of "true and false religion, civility and barbarism," but also along lines of race.

Race plays a prominent role in Hanmer's sermon, especially in its prelude to describing the circumstances of Chinano's conversion. Before describing the conversion, Hanmer provides a history of the genealogical origins of Turks, Moors, and Saracens—and significantly, this history of their origins occupies approximately two-thirds of the entire text. Of the Moors in particular he writes,

> The *Moores* called *Mauri* inhabit *Mauritania* in *Affricke*, they are . . . of the progenie of *Cham*, whose posterity *Noe* accursed, and no marvail cursed people receive the cursed doctrine of *Mahomet*. These people inhabiting *Mauritania* in *Affricke*, are because of their hewe and colour of the *Latins* called *Nigritae*, in our vulgar speach *Nigros*, and of the *Grecians* in the same sense for their adust, and blacke colour called μαύροι and μαυρούσιο *Moores*. (sig. B3v–4r)

Here Hanmer suggests inextricable links among race, black skin, geography, and religion by proclaiming that adherence to Islam, like blackness, is the consequence of Noah's curse on Cham and his descendents; like constructions of blackness as a genealogically inherited marker of spiritual cursedness, Muslim faith becomes a racial marker that is inherited by the descendents of Cham because of their progenitor's spiritual depravity. This linkage, however, reveals an ignorance of African Christians; Hanmer's narrative cannot account for the generations of Christians who resided in Mauritania—or Barbary, as it was commonly called in early modern England—prior to the eighth century, when Muslim Arabs invaded the region.[21] North Africa's earlier Christian identity, as well as the remnant of Christianity that remained, undermine Hanmer's totalizing geo-racial and geo-religious narrative, which links both North Africans and blackness to infidel identity.[22]

Hanmer's extensive description of the racial origins of Moors (rather than of Turks) suggests that he deemed it relevant to his audience's understanding of Chinano's conversion. Although early moderns often recognized that Turks were different from Moors, the juxtaposition of his history of the Moors with his discussion of a Turk's conversion suggests that Hanmer regarded them as similar. Thus, if the statement "cursed people receive the cursed doctrine" is a racializing, anti-Islamic truism in Hanmer's narrative, it might not be a stretch to say that he understood Chinano's prior faith as proof that he too belonged to a cursed people.

Moreover, this understanding of Islam as a curse that is similar to the curse of blackness is relevant to a consideration of Othello's religious identity. Muslim faith is seen as a kind of blackness, perhaps similar to the blackness of the Ethiope that cannot be washed away. Nevertheless, Hanmer combines two conceptions of race: one defined by skin color and the other by the reception of a religious doctrine.

The placement of this genealogical history of Turks, Moors, and Saracens before the description of Chinano's conversion underscores the noteworthiness of this transformation: God has worked a miracle by turning a Turk, geographically and racially predisposed to Islam, into a Christian. Once this is understood, Chinano can finally be baptized:

> After the sermon ended, the *Turke* confessed in the *Spanish* tongue before the face of the congregation, the Preacher out of the Pulpit propounding the questions and receiving the answers by skillful Interpretors, in summe as followeth. 1. In Primis, that he was verie sorie for the sinful life which he had lead in times past, in ignorance and blindnes, and hoped to obteine pardon in *Jesus Christ*. 2. Secondly, he renounced Mahomet the false Prophet of the *Moores, Saracens* and *Turkes,* with al his abhomination, and blessed *GOD* which had opened his eyes to behold the truth in *Jesus Christ*. (sig. F2v–3r)

The narrative recounts three other confessions: that he believed in the Trinity, that Jesus is the son of God and savior of the world, and lastly that "he desired hee might be received as one of the faithfull Christians, & bee baptized in the faith of the blessed Trinitie" (sig. F4r). Only after these confessions, though mediated through the "skillful Interpretors," is he baptized.[23]

Although there are at least two layers of mediation between Chinano's confession and what we receive as readers of the account, the account nevertheless reveals a significant deviation from the standard English baptismal service. In addition to the fact that Chinano must speak for himself rather than have godparents speak as his proxy, Hanmer's description of the baptism suggests that this Turkish convert was required to say quite a bit more than infants did through their godparents. In the Church of England's baptism service, the ministers would ask the infant if he or she believed in the various tenants of the Apostles' Creed, to which the godparents would simply respond, "All this I steadily believe."[24] Hanmer's narrative suggests, in contrast, that the convert was asked to state specific beliefs and not just offer the customary response. We cannot be sure that this was the case, but Hanmer's narration might well prompt readers to imagine Chinano articulating the kinds of theological statements that would normally emanate from a minister. This might have actually been true at Chinano's baptism if, as Whitgift urged, Jewish, Moorish, and Turkish converts were examined before they were baptized.

Hanmer's *The baptizing of a Turke* insures that readers of the text, if not those who witnessed the ceremony, would recognize that Chinano is different; as Christian as he may be after his baptism, the baptismal service announces that there are different processes by which people—depending on their race, genealogy, geographical origin, and age—are incorporated into the Christian community. His sermon also raises questions about how early modern Londoners might have viewed the Christians of non-European origin living in their midst. Imtiaz Habib's invaluable work in English parish archives has shown that there were black Christians in early modern London: for example, "Georg Negro," baptized in St. Margaret's church in Westminster in 1585; "Marye Phyllis a Blackamore," baptized in St. Botolph's church in Aldgate in 1597; and "a man child named John borne of a blackamoor woman," baptized in 1606 at St. Benet Fink's church near Cheapside.[25] We cannot know whether their fellow parishioners viewed these people as full-fledged Christians; judging by Whitgift's statement and Hanmer's sermon, it is likely that they were seen as racial and religious curiosities. Conversion was always understood as a miracle by Catholics, and perhaps even more so by English Protestants because the conversion to their creed of a Turk or an African defied the geo-racial and geo-religious mapping of the world, the ways in which race and geography were thought to determine an individual's religious identity. Chinano and the baptized Africans residing in early modern England (and maybe even Othello) are exceptional because their religion belies their race.

Romance, Tragedy, and Anagnorisis

Othello's religious and racial identity invites not only questions about geography (Might he be a member of that Christian remnant in North Africa? Might he be similar to those baptized Africans living in early modern London?) but also about genre, especially concerning connections between romance and tragedy. (I will discuss Othello's geographical origins later.) Critics have often recognized the numerous romance motifs in *Othello*, but the play also reveals the confluence of romance and tragedy, a trend evident in the work of Giraldi Cinthio, the author of *Othello*'s source. As Bernard Weinberg has noted, Cinthio felt that "tragedy [did] not need to have a tragic ending; when, after turmoil and sadness, a happy ending ensues, the play may be called tragicomedy."[26] For Cinthio, the very elements that so often characterize Aristotelian tragedy—*peripeteia, anagnorisis,* and *catharsis*—need not be limited to tragedy itself. In his *On Romances* Cinthio notes a similarity between romance and tragedy that occurs in the moment of *anagnorisis*: "It would be fitting . . . to speak of the recognition [*anagnorisis*] of the terrible, of the pitiable, of the change from a happy to an unhappy state and vice versa, and of the marvelous, without which this kind of poem [the Romance] is no less excellent than tragedy."[27] Although Cinthio's chief goal in *On Romances* is to elevate the status of the romance genre, he does so through finding similarities between romance and tragedy. For Cinthio romance seems to be more akin to tragedy than to epic—and it is not surprising that Cinthian tragicomedies like *Euphimia* and *Arrenophia* drew directly from romances.[28]

More than *catharsis* and *peripeteia* (the latter being subsumed by *anagnorisis* as the "recognition . . . of the change from a happy to an unhappy state"), *anagnorisis* is a significant ingredient in the generic makeup of both tragedy and romance. Even in Aristotle's *Poetics, anagnorisis* is not limited to the domain of tragedy. It is akin to the moment of romance or epic recognition: "Recognition, as the word itself indicates, is a change from ignorance to knowledge, leading either to friendship or to hostility on the part of those persons who are marked for good fortune or bad."[29] To illustrate his point, Aristotle notes the recognition of Odysseus by Euryclea. The example makes clear that Aristotle saw the moment of *anagnorisis* as just as important to epic and romance—or "heroic poetry," the term that early modern English poets used to categorize them both—as it is to tragedy.[30] Nevertheless, because Aristotle points to the moment when Euryclea correctly recognizes Odysseus, *anagnorisis* can be read as encompassing the ability to correctly recognize the identity of another.[31]

In Shakespeare, recognition scenes figure prominently in the comedies, tragedies, and romances. Tragic recognition is fulfilled when the hero correctly identifies the self and his or her present predicament (as seen when Lear sheds his madness at the end of *King Lear* and when Hamlet recognizes his place within divine providence at the end of *Hamlet*, for example), whereas romance recognition is achieved when the hero correctly identifies another and then alters another's predicament (as seen, for instance, in the recognitions and restorations of Marina and Thaisa by Pericles in *Pericles*, Perdita and Hermione by Leontes in *The Winter's Tale*, and Innogen, Guiderius, and Arviragus by Cymbeline in *Cymbeline*). Romance recognitions, like their tragic counterparts, seek to reassert truths about identity, truths about which characters have been misled.

We need not presuppose a great divide between romance and tragedy, even in plays not commonly regarded as exemplifying Shakespeare's experimentation with the intersections between the two genres, such as *Hamlet* and *King Lear*. There is, of course, also the tradition of reading romance as the "solution" to tragedy.[32] But in *Othello* romance *anagnorisis* becomes especially important because the play manifests the tragic consequences of misidentification. The importance of misidentification has been discussed by Daniel Vitkus, who asserts that "Othello's loss of identity is caused by his misidentifications of Iago, Cassio, and Desdemona; the Moor fails to know Desdemona and she is converted in his mind from virgin to whore."[33] Because misrecognition is a major cause of Othello's tragic demise, the hero's *anagnorisis* seems to determine whether the play will end as tragedy or romance—for it is likely that Othello would have obtained a romance happy ending if he had seen Iago and Desdemona for who they really were.

The problem of misrecognition, however, has escaped the world of the play, leaving audience members and critics uncertain how to identify Othello. This uncertainty can be separated neither from Othello's status as a "Moor," a category of identity that had ambiguous racial and religious associations in the period, nor from questions concerning Othello's visual representation on Shakespeare's stage. Because European descriptions and maps of Africa noted varying complexions among Moors (in which case "Moor" becomes an inclusive category of identity that encompasses various ethnic groups in Africa), early modern English plays staged Moors with various complexions. For example, although Aaron in *Titus Andronicus* and Othello are usually identified has having black skin (Aaron's statement that he "will have his soul black like his face" and Othello's "haply, for I am black" [3.3.267] are commonly cited as evidence that these characters were imagined as having black skin), Morocco in *The Merchant of Venice* is identified as a "tawny Moor" in the stage direction preceding his entrance.[34] Additionally, in *The Battle of Alcazar* (1588) George Peele appears to distinguish tawny Moors from black Moors: The villainous Muly Mahamet is distinguished from the other Moors in the play with the label "The Negro Muly Hamet" and the description "black in his look."[35] These instances suggest that early modern English playwrights made deliberate choices about the skin color of their Moors; playwrights created dramatic spectacles that drew from, and sometimes challenged, the traditional iconography that associated white with good and black with evil. It is nearly impossible, then, to unambiguously classify Othello's ethnic identity, for several reasons: the racial and religious connotations of "Moor," the controversy over whether Othello is black or tawny, and questions concerning whether the makeup used at that time could fully conceal the whiteness of the early modern actor playing Othello.[36] Although a decision about skin color and costuming would have given an early modern English audience more direct access to Shakespeare's vision of Othello, it is the very ambiguity of Othello's identity that ought to command our attention. Iago takes advantage of Othello's identity as a Moor, first working with its racial and then with its religious inflections in order to see which will prove more effective in propagating Othello's alterity.

Othello (and Ruggiero): Religious Conversion and Transformative Romance

Aside from Othello's background as a soldier and a Moor, the audience knows little about the title character until he explains the "witchcraft" that he used to woo Desdemona (1.3.170).[37] In this explanation we first see how romance transforms Othello from one who is cast as an outsider by Iago and Brabantio into a character who belongs:

> Her father loved me, oft invited me,
> Still questioned me the story of my life
> From year to year—the battles, sieges, fortunes
> That I have passed.
> I ran it through, even from my boyish days
> To th' very moment that he bade me tell it,
> Wherein I spoke of disastrous chances,
> Of moving accidents by flood and field,

Of hair-breadth scapes i' th' imminent deadly breach,
Of being taken by the insolent foe
And sold into slavery; of my redemption thence
And portance in my travailous history.

(1.3.129–40)

Brabantio is the first to fall in love with Othello, and it appears that this love is tied to Othello's history "of disastrous chances, / Of moving accidents." Othello's narrative is undoubtedly a tale of romance adventure, as both "chance" and "accidents" so often characterize a romance knight's errancy.[38] Moreover, the anaphoric use of "of" highlights the importance of the adventure stories that Othello tells Brabantio. Although Roderigo seeks to demonize Othello by highlighting the diversity and uncertainty of his geographical origins—that he is "of here and everywhere"—Othello uses the fact that he is "of" so many different places to move himself from outsider to insider; his narrative provides him access first to Brabantio's house and then to Desdemona's ear.

There is also a connection here to *Orlando Furioso* if, as Michael L. Hays persuasively suggests, this speech borrows from Robert Greene's *Orlando Furioso* (1594), a play that takes characters from Ariosto's poem but departs from the original plot quite substantially.[39] Greene's play begins with various suitors describing themselves and their adventures in hopes that their stories will move Angelica to love them. Hays argues that Othello's speech is most similar to Orlando's speech, which successfully woos Angelica through, among other things, tales of anthropophagi and cannibals.[40] Desdemona is thus similar to Greene's Angelica; both of them respond lovingly to the tales of their errant knights.[41]

Desdemona's eager response to Othello's romance tale (Othello says that she "with a greedy ear devoured up my discourse") also suggests that romance acts upon the body (1.3.151). If, as Brabantio tells the senate, Othello was "what she feared to look on," then Othello's tale explicitly changes the way Desdemona sees him (1.3.99).[42] In her statement, "I saw Othello's visage in his mind," she simultaneously implies that she does not see his outward "visage" and insists that she sees in Othello that which is internal, his mind (1.3.253).[43] And to this point, what we have seen most prominently about Othello's mind (or at least how his mind works to confront Brabantio's accusations) is the way that he narrates himself. Romance proves to be Othello's best defense against Brabantio's charges of witch-craft and alterity; it alters his identity and others' view of him.

The limits of seeing Othello as a stark "other" also manifest themselves in his wooing of Desdemona through tales of cannibals and acephali: "These things to hear / Would Desdemona seriously incline" (1.3.147). Des-demona's "greedy ear" and her desire to "devour" at once link her to the cannibals in Othello's tale; Patricia Parker has suggested that the mention-ing of cannibals works "synecdochally by its reference to the 'greedy ear' of Desdemona that did 'devour up' this stranger's discourse, . . . linking this form of domestic consumption with the figure of the 'Cannibals.'"[44] Des-demona participates in a typical European consumption of other cultures through travel narratives, a practice that suggests similarity between Euro-peans and the exotic cannibals so often cited in such stories. At the same time the mention of cannibals in the passage makes Othello seem closer to the "civilized" world of Europe; when compared to cannibals and aceph-ali, Othello appears remarkably similar to Venetians, making his incorpo-ration into Venice through romance all the more acceptable.

Othello's romance narrative, then, makes problematic the bestial and racist language that opens the play and the relevance of such racial dis-course in general.[45] Iago's claims that Othello is an "old black ram," a "devil," and a "barbary horse" point to kinds of difference that are imagi-nary rather than ontological (1.1.87, 90, 110). Although these images do have some effect (they arouse Brabantio's anxiety), Iago's use of them has little potency when confronted with Othello's romance stories. The power of his romance is legitimized by the duke: "I think this tale would win my daughter too" (1.3.172). At this point, the duke is the character most likely to sympathize with Brabantio: He must realize what it would mean to place his own daughter in the position of Desdemona. Even so, the duke acknowledges the power of Othello's narrative, even its power to challenge the miscegenation taboo. Romance allows him, to borrow Ania Loomba's words, to focus on Othello's "political colour."[46] Venetian imperial inter-ests necessitate an Othello who is "more fair than black" (1.3.291).

Othello's fairness is all the more remarkable because, as Dympna Cal-laghan notes, "Black skin persisted as the most conspicuous marker of ra-cial difference" on Shakespeare's stage.[47] Since some form of blackface would have been used to mark Othello as visually different from the other characters in the play, it is noteworthy that the conjoining of visual and discursive markers of difference has very little power to accomplish Iago's goals. Additionally, though the audience surely sees Othello's skin color, perhaps black skin was not as strange to early modern English audiences as we previously might have assumed. Habib's archival work informs us that "the locations of black people in London are coterminous with those of the personnel of what is early modern London's media industry, its public theaters, so that the black presence is inextricably intimate with the metropolitan cultural production of the age."[48] It is thus likely that the London theater district became a place where black skin was not such an extraordinary sight. Nevertheless, the play's audience is invited to see the "fair" Othello that Desdemona and the duke see. And in light of the fact that Othello was first played by the well-known Richard Burbage, the audience may also be invited to see the hero's difference in skin color as superficial, as something that only resides on the surface.[49]

A "fair" identity is also available to Othello because he is "of Venice," and the geographical setting of act 1 is important to a consideration of why Othello belongs. As Michael Neill suggests, "The importance of Venice as the metropolitan centre of the play world is that it supplies, or offers to supply, each individual with a clearly defined and secure position within an established social order."[50] Neill's important insight makes a clear connection between geographical location and social identity, a connection that Roderigo and Iago seem to understand when they suggest that Othello is a stranger. What they fail to consider, however, is Venice's reputation as a cosmopolitan center full of strangers, a fact that became known in England through William Thomas's *History of Italy* (1549) and Lewes Lewkenor's *The Commonwealth and Government of Venice* (1599).[51] In both Venice is reported as being a space of inclusion (though surely of a commercial and imperial nature), a place where a characterization of Othello as an "extravagant and wheeling stranger" makes little sense. Moreover, if Othello is "of here and everywhere," his multiplicity of geographical origins simultaneously place him within a space of inclusion and outside the confines of Africa and the Middle East, locations that would subject him to the kind of geo-religious and geo-racial map that Hanmer produces. And if Shakespeare learned anything about Venice from Cinthio's *Hecatommithi*, it was that despite any objections to the marriage of Disdemona and the Moor, Venice was a place where a Moor could live happily with an Italian woman: Cinthio's narrator tells us,

"They lived together in such concord and tranquility while they remained in Venice."[52]

I am not suggesting that difference did not matter in Venice—it certainly matters to Disdemona's kinsmen in Cinthio's text and to Brabantio in *Othello*. My point is, rather, that Othello's black skin proves to be an insufficient reason for exclusion from either civic or married life in Venice. That said, Shakespeare's Venice necessitates a certain type of Othello, one whose identity as "more fair than black" becomes fixed as part of ducal prerogative, political expediency, and a colonial agenda. The duke's desire to regain Venetian control of Cyprus necessitates an Othello whose identity has been mitigated by romance telos. In fact, Venice needs romance to do what that genre does so well—transform and incorporate the other—in hopes of converting other lands into imperial outposts.

If act 1 of *Othello* reveals anything about racial ideology in the early modern period, it is that sole reliance on the kind of racial categorization that Iago employs in act 1 to solidify degrees of similarity or difference is destined to fail. This is especially true in Catholic epic romances like *Orlando Furioso*; even as they engage with Christian-Muslim conflict, they often contain interracial and interreligious love affairs and friendships. *Othello* emerges from this tradition. The efficacy of romance in forging an identity for Othello becomes even more evident as the conventions of Catholic romance and its fondness for converting Muslim heroes emerge in the play. At the moment that we learn that Othello has been baptized, he becomes part of the lineage of Ruggiero in *Orlando Furioso*, in which an interracial marriage is not merely tolerated but even celebrated and divinely sanctioned.

In both *Othello* and *Orlando Furioso*, baptism provides access to Christendom and to an Italian heroine, and in both baptism is linked to erotic desire. Iago brings this linkage to our attention in Shakespeare's play. According to him, Desdemona would be able to make Othello "renounce his baptism" because

His soul is so enfettered to her love
That she may make, unmake, do what she lists,
Even as her appetite shall play the god
With his weak function.

(2.3.340–43)

Iago questions Othello's religious conviction, suggesting that his allegiance to the Christian God is not as strong as his allegiance to the god that is Desdemona's "appetite."[53] But even in this respect Othello resembles Ruggiero, a model for Moors who hope to become part of Christendom and marry Italian women. Ruggiero initially sees baptism and conversion to Christianity as means to an erotic end. After Bradamante tells him that she will marry him only after he is baptized, the narrator gives Ruggiero's response:

> But he, that would not onely not refuse
> To chaunge his life for his beloveds sake
> But also if the choise where his to chuse
> To leese his life and all the world forsake,
> Did answer thus: my deere, what ear ensues
> I will performe what ere I undertake;
> To be baptis'd in water or in fire
> I will consent, if it be your desire.[54]

On their way to the abbey where Ruggiero is to be baptized and then married to Bradamante, the two lovers are diverted from their purpose: They are sent on a mission of mercy to save a young lover who is sentenced to die. Perhaps this delay is for the best, for Ruggiero desires baptism for all the wrong reasons. In telling Bradamante that he will be baptized "if it be [her] desire," Ruggiero reveals that he views the sacrament as little more than a pickup ploy, so much so that he juxtaposes his decision to be baptized with a host of amorous clichés: In addition to baptism, he is willing to risk his life and undergo trial by fire.

Baptism, however, as the sacrament through which one gains entrance into the Church, is too important to the poem to be treated so flippantly by one of its heroes. In spite of his use of the sacrament to woo Bradamante, Ruggiero will take baptism more seriously nearer the poem's end. On his way to Africa, Ruggiero finds himself in the midst of a shipwreck,

> And calls to God for mercie, and is token
> Of true contrition voweth out of hand
> To be baptisd if eare he come to land.
>
> And that he would renownce all Turkish Lawes
> Nor gains a Christen Prince once weapon carrie

> But serve king *Charles* and ayd the Churches cause
> And from the same hereafter not to varie
> And never seeke delay or farther pause
> His virtuous spouse Dame *Bradamant* to marrie.
> (Twas strange) no sooner he this vow had ended
> But that his strength increast and swimming mended.[55]

Ruggiero's desire to be baptized is not completely divorced from the love plot, nor should it be, because we know from Merlin's prophecy that his desire for Bradamante is divinely sanctioned; but its sincerity is reinforced by his "guiltie conscience" and "true contrition." Because so much hinges upon the authenticity of Ruggiero's conversion, it is essential that Ruggiero has "true contrition"—hence his conversion to Christianity becomes a metaphorical defeat of Islam. The sincerity of Ruggiero's conversion also assures his political allegiance, that he will "serve king *Charles* and ayd the Churches cause."

The depth of Ruggiero's conversion is further corroborated by the hermit he meets when he finally reaches the shore. The hermit cries, "ô *Saule*, ô *Saule*, / Why persecutest though my people so?"[56] Like Saul on the road to Damascus, Ruggiero had found himself fighting for the wrong side. But with the help of divine intervention, both are baptized and converted. The allusion to Saul's conversion to Paul suggests that Ruggiero's baptism and conversion can erase both prior wrongs and prior identity; the efficacy of Paul's conversion is made clear not only in his name change but also in his own words: "If any man be in Christ, he is an new creature: old things are passed away; behold, all things are become new" (2 Cor. 5:17, AV). Ruggiero's baptism too makes him new, creating for him a new religious identity that erases, or at least distances him from, his erstwhile alterity. This theme is borne out in *Orlando Furioso*; as Ruggiero becomes the progenitor of the Este family, the poet evinces no anxiety about any possible umbrage from the Estes about a converted Saracen joining their family's lineage. Ruggiero's conversion and repentance enact a strategic forgetting that enables his embrace of new identities as Christian, husband, and father. Through baptism and religious conversion, the romance obscures difference and suggest that Ruggiero's religion, not his race, was the primary obstacle to the love plot and dynastic teleology. Romance demonstrates the principles of

Pauline universalism (which, as I discussed in chapter 1, were not easily reconciled with English Protestant attempts conjoin racial and religious identities) in an attempt to demonstrate that at least within the genre, there is neither Moor nor Italian, for all are the same after conversion.

Orlando Furioso insists that it is the Moorish hero's religious identity that is most important, and the same is initially true in *Othello*. Although we learn of Othello's Christian identity only through Iago's passing reference to the baptism, Nabil Matar notes that the reference itself created a new kind of staged Moor: "[Shakespeare] made it very clear that Othello was a Christian Moor. No previous Moor on stage had ever been presented as anything but pagan or areligious."[57] Moreover, it is likely that *Othello's* early modern audience would have assumed that Othello was Muslim, especially if they had seen plays like *The Battle of Alcazar* (1589) and *Lust's Dominion* (1600); in these plays and others, Moorish characters are repeatedly portrayed as Muslims and enemies of Christendom. The reference to the baptism, then, as Jane Hwang Degenhardt contends, "suggested a radical act of conversion that both epitomized the ideal of Pauline fellowship and performed an inversion of deep-rooted cultural association."[58] By conferring the status of "Christian," the sacrament of baptism transforms the audience's preconceptions as surely as it transforms the identity of Ruggiero and Othello.

Iago: Reversion and Restorative Romance

Although a romance like *Orlando Furioso* transforms identity in order to incorporate individuals who are different but desirable, Shakespeare's romances—from *Pericles* to *The Tempest*—move toward the restoration of originary identities.[59] This trajectory of romance did not originate with Shakespeare, however: it has its origins in the Greek romance, in Chariclea's recovery of her Ethiopian heritage at the end of *Aethiopica*.[60] Nonetheless, Iago is a participant in the Shakespearean romance tradition that often uses the magic of the stage as a means to restore identity—Paulina's staging of events at the end of *The Winter's Tale* and Prospero's use of spectacle and magic in *The Tempest* are perhaps the most famous examples. Like Paulina and Prospero, Iago too is often noted for his ability to stage spectacle: his creation of "ocular proof" and his direction of characters, especially in the metatheatricality of the scene he stages for Othello in act 4, scene 1, all become part of his plot to restore Othello to his presumably prior Muslim identity (3.3.363).

Iago's restorative romance must first confront the fair identity that the duke and romance have declared for Othello in Venice. Luckily for Iago, the change of setting to the island of Cyprus—a location with an identity conflict of its own, caught between Venetian and Turkish control—facilitates the contestation of Othello's Venetian identity. In his reading of *Othello* and *The Tempest*, Jonathan Bate argues that Shakespeare was interested in islands because "they constitute a special enclosed space within a larger environment of geopolitics. . . . An island is an experimental place where opposing forces are brought together in dramatic confrontation."[61] For Iago Cyprus is just such a laboratory of psychodrama, a place where he can wreak havoc with Othello's romance identity.

The change of setting to Cyprus also signals a move into—or, conversely, the play's continued occupation of—a romance landscape via shipwreck, one of those quintessential romance motifs. In *Othello* this shipwreck becomes a convenient solution to the Islamic threat. It is well known that both the shipwreck and the Turkish threat are entirely Shakespeare's invention: There are no Turks in *Hecatommithi*, and in Cinthio's tale the Moor and Disdemona "with a sea of the utmost tranquility arrived safely in Cyprus."[62] The conspicuously added shipwreck, however, is not only a miraculous solution to the Turkish fleet; it also provides the occasion for identity transformation. So often in the literature of the period, and always in Shakespearean drama, a shipwreck dislocates individuals, either requiring or allowing for the creation of new social identities (consider, for example, Pyrocles and Musidorus in Sidney's *Arcadia*, Viola in *Twelfth Night*, Pericles in *Pericles*, and the Italian nobles—as well as their parodic inversions, Stephano and Trinculo—in *The Tempest*). As a gentleman recounts that Cassio "prays the Moor be safe, for they were parted / With foul and violent tempest," it first appears that Othello will be subjected to the fate of many romance heroes who suffer shipwreck (2.1.33–34). But Othello had no desire to alter an identity that worked so well for him in Venice. Still, Iago takes advantage of the new setting and the shipwreck—which acts as a type of *deus ex machina*—that eliminates Islamic threats. As a Christian, however, Othello is safe for the time being.

Very soon after arriving in Cyprus, even while it is feared that Othello might be shipwrecked, Iago begins to alter perceptions about skin color through his praise of the black and witty woman: "If she be black, and thereto have a wit, / She'll find a white that shall her blackness fit" (2.1.132–33). "Black," though commonly glossed as brunette, is certainly implicated in the racial politics of the play, and Lara Bovilsky reads these lines as an inverted image of Desdemona and Othello's relationship.[63] Surprisingly, Iago now attempts to alter the prevailing view of blackness—perhaps because it did not signify what he hoped it would in act 1. Like Desdemona, he now seems to espouse the sentiment of Shakespeare's sonnet 127: "In the old age black was not counted fair," "But now is black beauty's successive heir."[64] Iago suggests that a "white" indeed may find pleasure in black, transforming this black and witty woman from a thing of scorn into a person to be desired. Desdemona's response to Iago's joke, "Worse and worse," however, bespeaks an uneasiness about Iago's sentiment, no doubt because of its blatant misogyny (2.1.134). At the same time, both sonnet 127 and Iago's joke suggest an alternative to cultural readings of blackness as evil and unattractive—and Desdemona has already chosen such an alternative.

From this point forward, the play signals a sustained engagement with "crueller comic traditions, such as the cuckold joke and charivari," as Frances E. Dolan notes.[65] Several elements conduce to Iago's plan to use Othello's marriage to sabotage the Moor's Christian identity: the connections that the play makes among its change of location, an engagement with romance through the shipwreck motif, a differing perspective on blackness, and traditions that attack married women in particular. (I will say more about this later). The play seems to shift from racial to misogynist discourse in the gradual undoing of Othello. Iago has very little to do with a racialized discourse of blackness after he arrives in Cyprus. In the remaining acts of the play, Iago refers to Othello's skin color only one more time, questioning how Desdemona could choose Othello over "matches / Of her own clime, complexion and degree" (3.3.233–34). But even here skin color by itself proves an insufficient reason for Desdemona's supposed infidelity: Iago also draws attention to differences between their geographical origins ("clime") and social status ("degree"). In trying to understand why his wife would be unfaithful, Othello too links his skin color to other factors: "Haply for I am black / And have not those soft parts of conversation / That chamberers have" (3.3.267–69). He thus expresses his own sense that black skin alone would not cause his wife to see him as undesirable.

Convincing Othello of Desdemona's infidelity, however, remains part of Iago's attempt to convert Othello. Iago seeks to turn Othello away from Desdemona and toward himself in order to disrupt the marriage bond. His racist discourse having failed to achieve the desired effect—to dehumanize and engender alterity—Iago seeks to manipulate Othello's religion through his marriage to Desdemona. Iago suggests that Desdemona has the power to make Othello "renounce his baptism," and to "make, unmake, do what she lists." This is Iago's desire, however, not Desdemona's. Nevertheless, the religious significance of Iago's statement is all the more pronounced because earlier in the same scene, after he is awakened by the commotion between Cassio and Mantano, Othello asks, "Are we turned Turks?" (2.3.166). Othello's question and Iago's statement about Othello's religious conviction raise questions about the sustainability of Christian identity. It appears to be easy to lose in Cyprus.[66]

Iago's notion that Othello would change his religion because of his love for Desdemona exemplifies a plot device that was common in early modern romances: love (and sometimes lust) as the reason for religious conversion. Before Ward in *A Christian Turned Turk* (1612) and Donusa in *The Renegado* (1623), Jessica in *The Merchant of Venice* evinces love, not spiritual conviction, as the motivation for conversion: "O Lorenzo, / If thou keep promise I shall end this strife, / Become a Christian and thy loving wife."[67] Jessica desires to convert in order to marry Lorenzo, but on the condition that Lorenzo keeps his promise. It is Lorenzo's and Jessica's desires (concerning love and marriage) that determine Jessica's religious identity.[68] Although Othello's Christian identity presumably precedes his acquaintance with Desdemona, Iago's language of "making" suggests that Othello's identity is malleable and vulnerable to external pressures. Whether it is alterable by Desdemona or Iago, or even by the duke, Othello's identity is at the mercy of the desires of Venetians.

Iago begins to undo Othello's Christian identity by turning Othello's desire away from Desdemona and toward himself. It can be no coincidence that the word "faith" appears six times in act 4, scene 1, in which Iago convinces Othello that his wife has been unfaithful by staging a conversation with Cassio. Othello's reversion to an infidel identity is triggered by Iago's ability to convince him of Desdemona's infidelity, a task made easier by the credence Othello gives to Iago's misogynist discourse: He believes, as he tells Lodovico, that "[Desdemona] can turn, and turn, and yet go on / And turn again" (4.1.253–54). Othello's use of the word "turn" to describe sexual impropriety clearly links sexual turning with religious turning, but perhaps these types of turning are connected to the play's turn from Othello's transformative romance to Iago's restorative romance.[69] This genre turn to Iago's romance thrusts Othello into domestic tragedy. According to Rebecca Ann Bach, domestic tragedy does not so much gesture toward the notion of "compassionate marriage" as it works to "praise men who value male-male alliances above relations with women."[70] This value of domestic tragedy seems to manifest itself in the mock marriage between Othello and Iago, when Othello kneels and vows, "Now are thou my lieutenant," and Iago responds, "I am your own for ever" (3.3.481–82). But because the tragedy of *Othello* is the result of imagined rather than actual female infidelity, the play demonstrates the dangers of the genre's misogyny.

The genre of domestic tragedy is especially significant given what marriage to Desdemona signifies for Othello. The now long-familiar words of the "The Form of Solemnization of Matrimony" from *The Book of Common Prayer* state, "Holy matrimony . . . is an honorable estate, instituted by God in paradise in the time of man's innocency, signifying unto us the mystical union between Christ and his church."[71] Although marriage was no longer an official sacrament in Reformation England, the religious significance of marriage remained a subject of debate; moreover, Christine Peters argues that we should not assume that marriage did not retain sacramental status for the laity.[72] At the very least, marriage remained a sign of salvation. Othello's vows to Iago, as well as the domestic tragedy that ensues from them, disrupt the marriage that is one of the "seals and symbols of redeemed sin." In rejecting his wife, Othello rejects the very institution that signifies Christian salvation.[73]

Despite the tragic consequences, perhaps Othello has some reason to reject his marriage to Desdemona, especially since he reads her loss of the handkerchief as a rejection of the romance narrative that unites them. The handkerchief is, after all, the stuff of romance. Othello's handkerchief draws from the description of the marriage pavilion that Melissa provides for Ruggiero and Bradamante in canto 46 of *Orlando Furioso*. The handkerchief is woven in a "prophetic fury" and the pavilion is woven in " *furor profetico*," and both the handkerchief and the pavilion have exotic, Egyptian histories (3.4.74).[74] Moreover, Roger Prior has noted what appear to be direct translations of canto 46 throughout this scene in the play.[75] The handkerchief is also burdened with images of conservation and constancy, from the handkerchief's ability to keep Othello's father "Entirely to [his mother's] love," to the silk "dyed in mummy. . . . / Conserved of maidens' hearts" (3.4.62, 76–77). This imagery suggests that the handkerchief has the power to preserve Othello and Desdemona's relationship.

Although the loss of the handkerchief provides Othello with "ocular proof" of his wife's infidelity, it is Desdemona's response to his narrative of the handkerchief that Othello reads as her ultimate rejection:

> DESDEMONA   Then would to God that I had never seen't!
> OTHELLO   Ha? wherefore?
> DESDEMONA   Why do you speak so startlingly and rash?
>
> (3.4.79–81)

Desdemona's question tells us that Othello's questions ("Ha? wherefore?") are asked with a great agitation over the meaning of his wife's rejection of his gift. As she wishes that she had never seen the handkerchief, she appears to reject the romance narrative that creates Othello's belonging. In other words, because the handkerchief not only is laden with images of fidelity and constancy but also alludes to the fulfillment of the romance between Ruggiero and Bradamante, Desdemona's rejection of the handkerchief is an unwitting dismissal of romance's ability to transform and incorporate a Muslim knight, the very romance narrative that establishes Othello's place within Christendom.

In killing his wife, Othello both departs drastically from the actions of Ariosto's converted Moor and ceases to participate in transformative romance. After Emilia's assertion that the murder makes Othello a "blacker devil," it is likely that he reverts into the stereotype of the barbarous Moor in the minds of at least some of the audience members, re-creating for them the alignment of Moorishness, blackness, and non-Christian identity (5.2.129). Othello is then thrust into the older dramatic tradition of the medieval morality play in which, as Anthony Gerard Barthelemy argues, "the black faces of the fallen angles signify their fall from grace and make visible the color of their damned souls."[76] As Jonathan Burton asserts, "The ideological incompatibility of his dark skin and Christian faith makes Othello susceptible to a vision of himself as that tainted other."[77]

Only when blackness is figuratively reunited with non-Christian identity does the "Moor of Venice" become an outsider. Othello's words at the
end of the play, however, may be a final attempt to reclaim part of his
initial romance identity:

> Speak *of* me as I am. Nothing extenuate,
> Nor set down aught in malice. Then must you speak
> *Of* one that loved not wisely, but too well,
> *Of* one not easily jealous, but, being wrought,
> Perplexed in the extreme; *of* one whose hand,
> Like the base Indian, threw a pearl away
> Richer than all his tribe; *of* one whose subdued eyes,
> Albeit unused to the melting mood,
> Drop tears as fast as the Arabian trees
> Their medicinal gum. Set you down this,
> And say besides, that in Aleppo once,
> Where a malignant and a turbanned Turk
> Beat a Venetian and traduced the state,
> I took by th' throat the circumcised dog
> And smote him—thus!
>
> (5.2.340–54, emphasis added)

Othello is most concerned with how the witnesses to the tragedy—both
on and off the stage—will speak *of* him. Again we see the importance of
storytelling in the construction of Othello's identity, though now the
power to speak of Othello belongs to others and not to Othello himself.
Although we may question Othello's characterization of himself when he
states that he is "one not easily jealous," he suggests that he is "wrought"
into being jealous—and here we should recall the desire that Iago pro-
jected onto Desdemona, "to make, unmake, do what she lists." We should
also note that Othello is now like "the base Indian" and "the Arabian
trees." These similes point to kinds of difference that may not be native to
Othello (the images are connected to places other than Venice and the
North African location from which Othello presumably originates); they
can remind us that Othello's identity is the product of multiple locations.
In the similes, Othello simultaneously embraces his diversity of origins
and upholds a view that the incorporation of the foreign can be desirable,
a view that *Orlando Furioso* itself embraces.

This final effort to embrace a romance identity, however, appears less than successful when it is positioned against the final five lines of this speech. The problem is the lack of specificity with which Othello speaks, the broadness of the terms "turbanned Turk," the "Venetian," and the "circumcised dog." This lack of specificity has implications for the themes of identity and identification throughout the play: from Iago, who says, "I am not what I am," to Othello's inability to identify the character of Iago and his wife correctly, and finally to our inability to fix Othello's identity amid shifting geographies, genres, and religious categories (1.1.64). These final words undoubtedly have shaped our own critical impasse. We might identify the "turbanned Turk" with Iago since he ironically announced his own "Turkishness" to Desdemona when he first arrived at Cyprus: "Nay, it is true, or else I am a Turk" (2.1.114). Moreover, as Bate notes, it is "Iago who does the Turkish work of destroying Christian community."[78] We might identify Othello as the Venetian since he is sent by the Venetian senate to protect Venetian interests. But Othello says that he "took by the throat" and "smote" the "circumcised dog," referring to his own suicide. Because circumcision was often equated with Muslim identity in the period, we might perceive Othello as the Turk who believes that his reversion to Islam has "traduced the state."[79] If this reading is true, the play upholds the efficacy of Iago's restorative romance.

We venture all these interpretations in groping for fixed identifications in *Othello*. The play, however, thwarts our quest for certainty. The ending enacts the crisis of Othello's and *Othello*'s oscillating religious and genre identities, a byproduct of the tragic collision of two modes of romance with competing projects of identity formation. G. W. F. Hegel asserts that tragedy is the manifestation of the collision of or conflict between old and new gods, between competing social or ethical systems.[80] A. C. Bradley nicely synthesizes Hegel's theory: "The essentially tragic fact is the self-division and intestinal warfare of the ethical substance, not so much the war of good with evil as the war of good with good."[81] Such is the case in *Othello*, with its collision of two types of romance, each a part of the formation of Christian identity and community, each embodying a different version of the "good" by the lights of that era. Romance's ability to convert and incorporate the Moor into Christendom could be used to uphold Christianity's claim to embrace all who believe. Conversely, the genre's ability to restore originary identities could generate an imaginative justification for the exclusion of converted Moors (and Jews), thus asserting the stability of a religious identity founded on the unity of racial and religious categories.

These two ends of romance, good as they both may be, help to define the opposition between the tragic hero and the villain. Consequently, these ends of romance participate in the moral order that Bradley believed is inherent to tragedy and that Chintio believed is inherent to romance.[82] Tragedy may stage a conflict within the "ethical substance," but Bradley also taught us that "the ultimate power in the tragic world is a moral order. . . . Let us understand that statement that the ultimate power or order is 'moral' to mean that it does not show itself indifferent to good and evil, or equally favorable to both, but shows itself akin to good and alien from evil."[83] Othello's romance of transformation is defeated; Iago's romance, which masks a racialist and racist logic, is triumphant. The triumph and tragic consequences of Iago's romance, moreover, raise questions about the ability of tragedy and romance to maintain the distinction between good and evil, and about the compatibility of the romance of transformation with Protestant theology: The romance of transformation is usually upheld by a Roman Catholic understanding of baptism and universal Christianity. With baptism no longer a guarantor of Christian identity, the romance of transformation can never be fully verified or sustained, leaving open the possibility that any type of religious transformation may be just an outward show, just as sacraments signify things that they inherently are not.

Just as *Othello* exemplifies competing modes of romance, so it reflects the competing forms of racial discourse in early modern culture—forms that sought to assert differences between kinds of people based on biological or animal nature or a geo-religious mapping of the world.[84] Iago employs both forms, first unsuccessfully asserting that Othello is different because is he animallike, but later stoking difference through religious conversion and Othello's lineage and putative geographical origins, all fueling doubts about the Moor's Christian identity. Although religion and geographical origin still seems to have more power than assertions of biological difference to foster a sense of alterity, Iago represents the nexus of both. He stands in the historical convergence of the past—in which religion asserted its power to construct all aspects of a subject's identity—and the future, which would turn to biological categories rather than religious theologies to construct racial difference.

5. Reproducing Christians

Salvation, Race, and Gender on the Early Modern English Stage

Behind the racial and religious themes of *Othello* there lurks an uneasiness about romantic relationships between non-European men and European women.[1] Early modern English comedies and tragicomedies, however, suggest that the English had less of a problem with romantic relationships between European men and infidel women. These types of relationships were staged often, in plays such as Greene's *Orlando Furioso* (circa 1590) and *The Comical History of Alphonsus, King of Aragon* (circa 1590); Shakespeare's *The Merchant of Venice*; Fletcher's *The Island Princess* (1621); and Massinger's *The Renegado* (1623/4) and *The Emperor of the East* (1632). In these plays there is either an implicit understanding of or an explicit reference to the infidel woman's conversion to Christianity. The frequency of interreligious and interracial relationships in early modern English comedy gains greater significance when we realize that no English comedy (to my knowledge) staged a relationship between a non-European man and a European woman.[2] Moreover, whereas numerous infidel women convert to Christianity on the early modern English stage, relatively few infidel men convert—only (again, to my knowledge) Corcut in Greene's *Selimus, Emperor of the Turks* and Joffer in part 2 of Thomas Heywood's *Fair Maid of the West* (and possibly, though less certainly, Shakespeare's Shylock in *The Merchant of Venice*).

This chapter considers the dynamic interplay of race, gender, and romance's infidel-conversion motif in early modern English tragicomedy. On the one hand, the frequent appearance of the infidel-conversion motif in comedies demonstrates the English stage's adaptation of Catholic romance's union of baptism and marriage as sacraments that work in tandem to confer Christian identity. On the other hand, the persistent gendering of eligibility for conversion—women far more than men—and the tendency of these comedies to veer toward tragedy register concerns about the reproduction of Christian identity. The stage's dictates concerning what kinds of relationships can achieve comedic resolutions reflects the confluence of early modern medical understandings of human reproduction and a Protestant view of marriage and child-rearing as the chief means of reproducing Christian identity; in both cases the female body was a critical site of investigation as early moderns attempted to understand what a mother contributed both biologically and spiritually to her children.

Protestant theology and early modern understandings of sexual reproduction converged in three ways: one, in describing the role of the male seed in creating a child's identity; two, in articulating a belief that women could be redeemed through childbirth; and three, in asserting that marriage and sexual reproduction were the chief means of producing Christian identity. This triad reinforced the developing system of racialized religious identity in England and delimited the kinds of romantic relationships that early modern English comedy could acceptably accommodate. The triad further demonstrates, as Joyce Green MacDonald has shown, that in early modern England the "raced body [is] a sexual body, so that the social aspects of sexual behavior—including but not limited to procreation, monogamy, infidelity, and the inheritance of property and goods—have been simultaneously racialized."[3] In this chapter I examine the theological significance of race and sex.

Although there are numerous English plays that feature relationships between European Christian men and infidel women, I focus on Shakespeare's *The Merchant of Venice,* John Fletcher's *The Island Princess*, and Philip Massinger's *The Renegado.* I examine these three plays not only because each incorporates numerous romance motifs and revises romance sources, but also because the conversion of the infidel woman is an important element in each plot. These plays use the infidel-conversion motif self-consciously and ask playgoers to consider the authenticity of the conversions.[4] Additionally, these three plays are designated (either by critics or the playwrights themselves) as that genre cousin of romance, tragicomedy. As I mentioned in the last chapter, Cinthio saw overlaps between tragedy, tragicomedy, and romance, most notably in their plot trajectories from happiness to unhappiness (or vice versa), and in their concern with *anagnorisis* and the recognition of identity. Both romances and tragicomedies move from the unhappy to the happy—thus the structures of these modes run parallel to the Christian narrative of redemption.[5] Tragicomedies featuring the infidel-conversion motif link their concerns about the confirmation and establishment of identity to the redemptive resolutions of texts. More than *The Merchant of Venice,* however, in which Jessica's religious identity is left ambiguous, *The Island Princess* and *The Renegado* attempt to verify the women's conversions by persuading the audience that the infidel heroines acquire Christian faith. Quisara in *The Island Princess* and Donusa in *The Renegado* embrace Christian martyrdom, demonstrating their willingness to die for their newly acquired Christian beliefs. Employing a discourse of martyrdom in which bodily death leads to the heavenly union with Christ, the tragicomic form provides a structure for plotting a narrative of transformation from tragic (tragic in the sense that they are damned within a system that links false faith with race and biology), racialized object to redeemed Christian.

These plays also reveal that infidels prove unfit for the typical comedy that reflects Protestant ideas about marriage and its purposes; their racialized bodies signify death. The ideological work of comedy can go largely unnoticed in plays featuring romantic relationships between people who share the same racial and religious background; the religious ideology of comedy most clearly surfaces at its potential breaking point, as playwrights feature interreligious and interracial relationships. Comedy sans tragedy is unable to incorporate infidels into a theological system and a dramatic tradition in which blackness and Jewish, Moorish, Turkish, and pagan identity all signify evil—irrespective of a character's actual religious state and moral character. As is the case in *Othello,* such characters' racialized bodies and costumes signify death.[6] In tragicomedy, however, tragically racialized subjects are transformed and saved through the embrace of death. Testing the limits of comedy through tragicomedy, these plays intertwine romance conventions with theology and biology; they thereby explore, in John Smyth's words, the possibilities and limits of "continu[ing] a Church by succession of a carnall line." These plays marry the theological and the biological, asking whether the infidel woman can be a legitimate sexual partner, and whether the infidel woman's racial identity impedes comedy's ideological reproduction of the Christian race.[7]

Salvation and Paternity

After Jessica offers her farewell to Lancelot, she explicitly links her marriage and conversion in an apostrophe to her future husband: "O, Lorenzo, / If thou keep promise I shall end this strife, / Become a Christian, and thy loving wife" (2.3.19–21). In typical romance mode, religious conversion and marriage work hand-in-hand to produce Christian identity. In the previous chapter I briefly mentioned that Jessica's religious identity, much like Othello's, is determined by the desire of Europeans; it seems that Jessica will not become a Christian if Lorenzo refuses to marry her. But now I wish to consider more fully whether Jessica can truly become a Christian through marriage—whether marriage can alter a racially determined religious identity. Janet Adelman, M. Lindsay Kaplan, and Julia Reinhard Lupton have already provided persuasive answers to this question. In this chapter I build upon their insights and more fully consider connections between theology and early modern "biology."[8] Moreover, I probe the extent to which Jessica's religious identity is determined by her biological relationship to her father, Shylock.

The notion that Lorenzo can turn Jessica into a Christian is reiterated later in the play, in the scene in which Lancelot questions if she can be saved:

> CLOWN   Yes, truly, for, look you, the sins of the father are to be laid upon the children; therefore, I promise you, I fear you. I was always plain with you, and so now I speak my agitation of the matter. Therefore be of good cheer, for, truly, I think you are damned. There is but one hope in it that can do you any good: and that is but a kind of bastard hope neither.
>
> JESSICA   And what hope is that, I pray thee?
>
> CLOWN   Marry, you may partly hope that your father got you not, that you are not the Jew's daughter.
>
> JESSICA   That were a kind of bastard hope indeed, so the sins of my mother should be visited upon me.
>
> CLOWN   Truly, then, I fear you are damned both by father and mother: thus, when I shun Scylla your father, I fall into Charybdis your mother; well, you are gone both ways.
>
> JESSICA   I shall be saved by my husband; he hath made me a Christian!
>
> CLOWN   Truly, the more to blame he; We were Christians enough before, e'en as many as could well live one by another. This making

Christians will raise the price of hogs; if grow all to be pork-eaters, we
shall not shortly have a rasher on the coals for money. (3.5.1–33)

Salvation and damnation are hardly laughing matters, and the tension between Lancelot's statements and the comedic language exemplifies the
play's use of tragicomedy to explore the relationship between racial damnation and salvation. Lancelot's comment adumbrates the theological connections among race, lineage, and religious identity that I have been
exploring throughout this book. His belief that "the sins of the father are
to be laid upon the children" also suggests that he believes fathers, more
than mothers, dictate a child's religious identity and the child's status as
saved or damned.

Lancelot has scriptural justification for his belief: He alludes to a passage in Exodus 20, in which Moses relates the law God has given to the
people. It is worth recalling the context of the passage, a context that
Lancelot ignores: "Thou shalt not bowe down thyself to [graven images]
neither serue them: for I the Lord thy God, am a iealous God, visiting
the iniquitie of the fathers vpon the children, vpon the third *generacion*
and vpon the fourth of them that hate me: And shewing mercie vnto
thousandes of them that loue me and kepe my commandments" (Exodus
20:5–6). Lancelot's decontextualization of the passage reinforces a racialized understanding of damnation; Jessica is damned because her father is
a Jew and therefore, in Lancelot's view, an idolatrous sinner. It may also
be significant that Lancelot (or Shakespeare) excludes what follows in
verse 6: God's equal willingness to show mercy. Doing so allows the
play to uphold what some critics have seen as an oversimplified version
of the Pauline dichotomy between Christianity as a religion of mercy
and Judaism as a religion of the law.[9] Lancelot's belief that Jessica is
damned by her father also raises questions about the extent to which a
biological father contributes to his child's racial/fleshly and religious/
spiritual identity.[10]

Concerns about race and lineage in *The Merchant of Venice* may also reflect a confluence of medical theories about human reproduction and a
Protestant theology that yoked the spirit to the flesh. Medicine and theology were interwoven in Reformation England. Attention to the convergence of these discourses, therefore, can help us understand Lancelot's
position that Jessica is damned because she is Shylock's daughter. English

Protestant interpretations of the Genesis 17 covenant illustrate the belief that salvation could come through lineage; the importance of "seed" in these readings gives rise to a correlation between human reproduction and religious reproduction, a correlation between sex and conversion. The Genesis covenant, which was used to justify infant baptism and to assert that Christian offspring (or "seed") are saved without the sacrament, is sealed through circumcision. "Circumcision," James Shapiro argues, "was an extraordinarily powerful signifier, one that not only touches on issues of identity that ranged from the sexual to the theological but, often enough, on the intersections of the two."[11] Moreover, according to Lupton, the ritual marking of the male organ of sexual generation was read in Jewish contexts, not only Christian ones, as signifying the genealogical nature of the covenant.[12]

Circumcision thus linked the sexual and the spiritual and made sexuality spiritually significant. The spiritual consequence of male sexuality, namely the consequence of begetting children, also registers the gendered nature of the Genesis covenant and its English appropriations: The promise is made to Abraham and his "seed." In early modern England, the word *seed,* which appears so often in English Protestant discussions of baptism, connoted both generation or progeny and semen.[13] As such, the language used in Protestant discussions of Genesis 17 could also have implied that the promises of God were transmitted through male semen, and that semen determines a child's religious identity.

Aristotelian understandings of sexual reproduction that circulated in medieval and early modern Europe would have made such a belief plausible. In *Generation of Animals,* Aristotle asserts, "Surely what the female contributes to the semen of the male will be not semen but material. And this is in fact what we find happening; for the natural substance of the menstrual fluid is to be classed 'prime matter.'"[14] The female's matter is then acted upon by the male's seed: "The male provides the 'form' and the 'principle of the movement,' the female provides the body, in other words, the material."[15] The form/matter distinction is certainly an important Aristotelian concept, but in *Generation of Animals* it is explicitly gendered. The creation of life—the shaping of matter necessary for life and the soul—is a masculine principle in Aristotle: "It is clear that semen possesses Soul, and that it is Soul, *potentially.*"[16] Although Aristotle's concept of the soul (mortal and unable to exist apart from the body) contrasts with the immortal soul of Christian theology, the theory of reproduction described in *Generation of Animals* nevertheless provided medieval and early modern Europeans with a way to privilege the role of the father in creating a child's identity.

The power attributed to male seed could allow the infidel woman to be a legitimate sexual partner, even within a culture that asserted that Christian parents unequivocally produce Christian infants. In her reading of *The Merchant of Venice*, Kaplan argues that medieval and early modern neo-Aristotelian theories were used to render the Jewish female body as matter that could be re-formed by Christian masculinity; through procreation, male seed was believed able to convert Jewish matter into Christian identity.[17] I would add that what is true of Jewish women in particular is true of infidel women in general, but Kaplan's argument explains why Jessica may be an acceptable marriage partner. If, as a Christian man, Lorenzo has the power to re-form Jessica, then, as she says, her husband has made her a Christian. Even if Jessica has not truly been converted—Gratiano refers to Jessica as an "infidel" even after her conversion and marriage (3.2.217)—the importance of seed in both the Church of England's baptismal theology and the Aristotelian theory of reproduction suggests that her religious and racial identity does not matter because she will still be able to produce Christian offspring. The Aristotelian theories Kaplan examines also provide an explanation for the problematic nature of relationships between infidel men and Christian women on the English stage; Aristotelian theories offer another way of understanding why a work like *Othello* (if Othello is an infidel and not a Christian) rejects what Susan Snyder recognized as the "comic matrix" operating in the play.[18]

Shylock's story, then, is very different from Jessica's. According to Aristotelian reproductive theory, his stubborn male Jewishness might be congenital.[19] Although we know that Shylock will be baptized following the conclusion of the staged action, the Protestant distinction between sacramental sign and grace received—and here we should recall Frith's statement about the baptized unbelieving Jew—would make it difficult for audiences to believe that Shylock experiences a true conversion; early modern audiences would have viewed Shylock's conversion—partially, at least—through the lenses of their personal understandings of the efficacy of the baptism. Moreover, as scholars who have examined the trial and execution of Elizabeth's doctor Roderigo Lopez have shown, no matter how much Lopez insisted that he loved Christ, he was condemned as a Jew and a traitor.[20] Shylock's gender, Protestant theology, and a distrust of Jews in early modern England would all conduce to the view that Shylock remains a Jew at the end of the play. Shylock is thus bracketed from the comedic ending of the play. If, as Northrop Frye suggests, "Unlikely conversions, miraculous transformations, and providential assistance are inseparable from comedy," racialized male bodies resist the transforming impulses of not only comedy but also of romance.[21] *The Merchant of Venice* seems to fulfill comedy's genre obligations through Shylock's forced acceptance of the sacrament that signifies the death of his infidel identity, his rebirth as a Christian, and his incorporation into Christian community; but his exclusion from that community at the end of the play raises questions about the authenticity of his Christian identity.

Shylock's body may also remain untransformed in order to uphold what critics like Barbara Lewalski have observed as the play's development of an allegorical relationship between Jews and Christians.[22] Suzanne Penuel and Adelman, moreover, have suggested that the play produces an allegory in which the fraught relationships between fathers and children signify pervasive Christian anxieties about the relationship between Judaism and Christianity. According to Penuel, the play "imagines the connection between Judaism and Christianity as a parent-child tie burdened by uncomfortable debt in an analogy that both feeds on and fuels early modern anxiety about the authenticity and genealogy of Christianity."[23] Penuel and Adelman also posit an allegorical relationship between the plot of the play and Christian history: Jessica's (and potentially Shylock's) conversions at the end of the play, problematic as they may be, may signal a belief in the eventual conversion of all Jews to Christianity.[24] Boyarin's assertion that "hermeneutics becomes anthropology" is certainly useful for understanding the allegorical structure in the play. Moreover, a biologically constructed Jewish male body supplies a biological surety necessary for signifying a stable Christian racial identity.[25] If *The Merchant of Venice* is an allegory for Christian history, it forges a link between the biological and the spiritual; the biological parent-child relationship has spiritual implications. The Church of England also created this link in a theology that racialized religious identities and allegorized Abraham's seed.

Salvation and Maternity

Indeed, the racialized father created particular anxieties for the English. In addition to Shylock, we should consider George Best's account of an "Ethiopian black as cole brought into England, who taking a faire English woman to wife, begat a sonne in all respects as blacke as the father was . . . whereby it seemeth this blackness proceedeth rather of some naturall infection of that man, which was so strong, that neyther the nature of Clime, neyther the good complexion of the Mother concurring, could anything alter."[26] Lancelot and Best emphasize worries about fathers, but *The Merchant of Venice* and early moderns were no less worried about the role of mothers in shaping their children's identities (cuckold jokes raise questions about the ability to verify paternity). Observing that mothers—Leah and the Moorish woman pregnant with Lancelot's child—are mentioned in close proximity to discussions of Jessica's conversion, Adelman provocatively asks, "But why should Jessica's mother turn up in the conversation about the efficacy of her conversion?"[27] For Adelman, the answer resides in an understanding that Jewish identity is transferred from mothers to children—a point evidently lost on Lancelot, however. I would like to take Adelman's question in another direction: Perhaps the play connects motherhood to Jessica's conversion precisely because it is through becoming a mother—which is, to be sure, the female telos of Christian marriage—that she might be saved. Although Kaplan's exploration of Aristotelian theory provides one way of understanding how Jessica might be saved by becoming a mother, Aristotle was not the only authority on human reproduction in the early modern period.[28] Early moderns also turned to Hippocrates and Galen to understand human procreation, and their theories, unlike Aristotle's, asserted that women, too, contributed seed that formed children. Moreover, discussions of reproduction in early modern England usually reflect Christian views of marriage and redemption; women's writings on childbirth and child-rearing often linked motherhood with Christian redemption as well.

Jessica's belief that she will be saved by her husband may be based on Paul's statement in 1 Corinthians 7:14: "For the unbelieving husband is sanctified by the wife, and the unbelieving wife is sanctified by the husband: else were your children unclean." For Paul belief is not a requirement for this sanctification. As I noted in chapter 1, this Pauline assertion was used to deny the necessity of baptism for the infant's salvation. But Paul's primary concern is saving children of interfaith marriages from being "unclean"; he sanctifies the unbelieving parent out of seeming necessity. The nature of this sanctification, however, is the source of a long-standing theological conundrum because it does not seem to require the conversion of the nonbelieving parent. Protestant commentators did their best to make sense of it, however. Calvin, for example, asserts that "thys Sanctification doth nothing at all profite the unbeeleuing spouse: only it serveth this farre, that his faythfull mate be not defyled, and Matrinonye it self prophaned."[29] The gloss for this passage in the Geneva Bible ignores the issue of what it means to sanctify the unbelieving spouse altogether: It merely states, "They that are born of either of the Christian parents faithful, are also counted members of Christ's church."[30] The gloss makes no mention of sanctifying the "unbelieving" wife or husband, but it still imbues the children of interfaith marriages with Christian identity, just as Jewel does in *Apologia Ecclesiae Anglicanae* (1562).[31] Thus, although Jessica, or any other infidel women who marries and begets the child of a Christian, may or may not be made a Christian through the telos of Christian marriage, from Paul forward the chief concern has always been the spiritual state of the child.

What is also striking is that Paul and the Geneva gloss are gender-neutral. If both Paul and the glossers wish to assert that certain children are born as Christians, linking as they do sexual and spiritual reproduction, they usually do not insist upon a gendered hierarchy or a particular understanding of religious identity as passed exclusively through either the male or female parent. Paul and the Geneva Bible may be gender-neutral in this instance, but early modern English culture surely was not (Calvin and early modern English drama imagine relationships between Christian men and an infidel women), especially in the religious and medical discourses on women. Moreover, Paul's argument resides uneasily next to Protestant appropriations of the gendered covenant of Genesis 17, which is passed down through male seed. It is here that Protestant readings of Genesis 17, when placed next to Paul's argument that a child of an infidel father and Christian mother would be sanctified as well, confront Hippocratic and Galenic understandings of human reproduction and Protestant discourses on marriage.[32]

Hippocratic and Galenic understandings of reproduction and Protestant views of marriage and motherhood can provide an alternative understanding of how and why the infidel woman could be redeemed through childbirth. According to Mary Lindmann, "More influential than the Aristotelian tradition . . . was the Hippocratic/Galenic theory in which both sexes contributed in equal measure to conception. Now the two sexes became complementary in that both produce seed."[33] Galen's theory was based on a "one sex" model, in which, as Thomas Laqueur's influential *Making Sex* has taught us, "*man* is the measure of all things, and woman does not exist as an ontologically distinct category."[34]

Although women were understood to be unperfected men, this imperfection was indeed seen as necessary for reproduction. In Helkiah Crooke's *Mikrokosmographia* (1615), for instance, the Galenic theory of reproduction is explained in terms of a redemptive telos:

> A woman is so much less perfect then a man by how much her heate is lesse and weaker than his; yet as I saide is this imperfection turned vnto perfection, because without the woman, mankinde could not haue beene perfected by the perfected sexe. The Maister workman therefore of set purpose, one made the one halfe of mankinde imperfect for the instauration of the whole kinde, making the woman as a receptacke of the seede of which a new man was to be created.[35]

The Galenic theory—though here bearing some marks of Aristotelianism—is rendered completely compatible with the "purpose" of the "Maister workman." The language of transformation is palpable here; as "imperfection [is] turned vnto perfection," the unperfected female body becomes a kind of *felix culpa* for the "instauration" of the whole human race.

Crooke's discussion demonstrates how religious concepts informed medical understandings of the female body. Indeed, as Patricia Crawford has argued, "Medical understandings of the female body reflected Biblical ideas about the female as a contingent being."[36] The importance of the "imperfect" female body for the propagation of the race is given a more explicit religious context when Crooke moves to his discussion of Hippocrates, in which he discusses reproduction in the context of Christian marriage:

> The man therefore and the woman together in holy wedlocke, and desirous to raise a posterity for the honour of God and propagation of their family; in their mutual imbracements doe either of them yeeld seed the mans leaping with greater violence. The woman at the same instant doeth not only eiacultе seede into her self, but also her womb snatcheth as it were and catcheth the seede of the man, and hideth it in the bottom and busome thereof.[37]

The primary desire—in Crooke's sentence—is to produce Christian posterity. Here, Crooke's medical explanation echoes the Church of England's *The Form of Solemnization of Matrimony,* which places the propagation of God-fearing children first in the list of reasons for the creation of holy matrimony: "One was the procreation of children, to be brought up in the fear and nurture of the Lord and praise of God."[38] This echoing, too, demonstrates that even the medical theories of sexual reproduction were governed by understandings of Christian truth. In fact, to understand human reproduction was to understand the mysteries of God. In the often-published *The Englishemans treasure: with the true anatomie of mans bodie* (first published in 1587), for example, Thomas Vicary writes, "And for as much as it hath pleased the Almightie God to giue knowledge of these his misteries & works unto his Creatures in this present world, here I propose to declare what thing Embreon is, and his creation . . . of which is made by the might and power of God in the mothers wombe a child."[39] Crooke, Vicary, and other early modern doctors and anatomists collapse the distinctions between biological knowledge and religious truth.

Crooke's theo-biological explanations correspond with Protestant discussions of the redemptive power of motherhood. Although pregnancy and the accompanying pains of childbirth had long been viewed as evidence of woman's fallen nature, it is equally true that in Christian belief, as Julie Crawford notes, "it was through a woman, Mary, and a birth, the incarnation of Christ, that humanity was redeemed. While the Reformation displaced the Virgin Mary from her central role in Christian worship, it nonetheless understood women in marriage and the household as key to the implementation of the Protestant faith."[40] In Protestant England the figure of Mary remained a foundation of Christian belief in childbirth and child-rearing as central to redemption, and at least one early modern English mother made an explicit comparison between her motherhood and Mary's; in *The Mother's Blessing* (1616), Dorothy Leigh interprets her own pregnancy and maternal care for her children in relation to the incarnation of Christ:

> My dear children, have I not cause to fear? The Holy Ghost saith by the prophet, *Can a mother forget the child of her womb?* As if he should say, is it possible, that she that carried her childe within her so near her heart and brought it forth into this world with so much bitter pain, so many groans and cries forget it? Nay rather, will she not labor till Christ be formed in it? Will she not bless it every time it sucks from her breasts, when she feeleth the blood come from her heart to nouristh it? . . . And can any man blame a mother (who indeed brought forth her child with much paine) though she labor till Christ be formed in them?[41]

In *The Mother's Blessing* the travail of childbirth is not a consequence of Eve's curse but rather that which produces Christ in the child. Leigh in fact conflates the labor of childbirth with the labor of child-rearing: Both are mainly the mother's duty, and both found Christian identity.[42] The pregnant female body, then, reenacts a kind of Marian fiat ("let there be") every time a child is conceived. Crooke's assertion, "The woman at the same instant doeth not only eiaculte seede into her self," reflects a common early seventeenth-century belief that female orgasm was necessary for reproduction.[43] Consequently, the sexually desiring female body, chaste within the bounds of Protestant marriage, becomes essential for the propagation of Christians. In spite of widespread anxieties about uncontrollable female sexual desire, religious and medical discourses on motherhood sublimate that desire for religious purposes.[44]

Leigh's argument concerning the primacy of the mother's influence on her children also corresponds to the Galenic view of motherhood. The volition of the male seed in the Galenic model did not undermine the influence of the female seed and the womb—the womb Crooke describes actively "snatcheth." In Thomas Raynalde's translation of Eucharius Rösslin's *The byrth of mankynde* (1540), moreover, the mother has more influence on the child than the father: "And although that man, be as princypall moovar and cause of the generation yet (no displeasure to men) the woman doth confer and contribute much more what to the encresement of the child in her womb, & what to the nourysshment therof after the byrth, then doth the man."[45] Despite the male's role as "princypall moover," the female womb and breast are believed to have greater power to shape the child and his or her race. Mothers shape their children in the womb and after their birth through breastfeeding.

Scholarship on breastfeeding in early modern England has shown that racial identity was believed to pass through the milk of the mother or the wet nurse; mothers were therefore encouraged to nurse their own children. The Galenic model viewed mother's milk as a product of the mother's blood; as Rachel Trubowitz has shown, the centrality of debates about breast-feeding responded to "anxieties about England's cultural and racial (in)coherence. . . . One key medical/moral concern was that breast-milk physically transmitted the moral and bodily character of the nurse to her charge, ideally complementing, but more often compromising or even eradicating the familial identity the child had inherited from its parents."[46] The biological mother's milk, however, allayed fears about racial/moral contamination for it was believed to nurture the child and maintains its racial purity.[47] I see neither implicit nor explicit references to breastfeeding in the plays discussed in this chapter; nevertheless, this scholarship on early modern breastfeeding is germane to our analysis because it demonstrates the link between anxieties about maternal influence and concerns about racial identity and purity. Early modern English discussions of breastfeeding provide another example of the view that a child's racial, religious, and moral identity might be influence more by a mother than by a father.

The harnessing of sexual reproduction to the propagation of the Christian race suggests another way to think about the spiritual consequences of sexual desire in early modern culture: Improper desire—especially the sexual desire that commingles people of different races and faiths instead of reproducing Christians—can damn the soul and sever the link between desire and redemption. The early modern English stage attempted to police desire in plays featuring the dangerous consequences of "turning Turk"—an inversion of the infidel-conversion motif. In contrast to the numerous romance tales in which interfaith desire leads to a conversion to Christianity, a play like *A Christian Turned Turk* equates desire for the infidel with the loss of Christian identity and death: At the end of the play,

Ward, an English pirate, laments his love affair with a Turkish woman and his conversion to Islam; here sex leads to death, not reproduction. The same minatory, policing themes pervaded tragicomedies of the time that featured interfaith and interracial relationships. Yet these plays remained tragicomedies rather than tragedies because of the conversion of the infidel woman through sexual or other means.

Notwithstanding Pauline theology and the various theories of pregnancy and character/cultural/racial transmission, the plot of *The Merchant of Venice* leaves Jessica's religious identity ambiguous; Jessica's final line in the play, "I am never merry when I hear sweet music" (5.1.69), suggests that she cannot be fully incorporated into the harmonious reunion of friends and lovers at the end of the play.[48] The play's ending may reveal lingering uneasiness about Jessica's marriage to Lorenzo, but this union is portrayed as less problematic than the potential pairing of Portia and Morocco—perhaps because it was the Jewish and Moorish men, more than the women, who posed the most serious threat to the reproduction of Christian identity. In *The Merchant of Venice*, there is no shortage of anxiety about economic and sexual commingling—and hence miscegenation—among people of different races and religions, but the degree of anxiety varies with gender.[49]

Martyrdom and Recuperating Romance

Unsure as Shakespeare's play may be about the ability of romance to produce true Christians, the imaginative and ideological work of the infidel-conversion motif was too useful to abandon completely. Romance had found ways to sublimate desire and to transform the foreign but desirable into the acceptable. I would now like to turn to *The Island Princess* and *The Renegado,* in which Fletcher and Massinger similarly attempt to revise and recuperate the infidel-conversion motif.[50] Although the love/conversion/marriage romance trajectory may seem the same as that found in Catholic romances, these plays introduce two critical steps in the process: erotic detachment and the acquisition of belief. Unlike Jessica, who may or may not become a Christian through her husband, Quisara and Donusa become verifiably Christian not through marriage but through their imitation of Christian men who prove willing to die for their faiths. Armusia's and Vitelli's willingness to die rather than "turn Turk" persuades the two women that they too should become Christians and martyrs; indeed, Quisara's and Donusa's willingness to die as Christian martyrs is used as proof that they have acquired Christian faith. It is only after the women's conversions that the romantic relationships are restored and lead to marriage. The plays make it clear, however, that the women do not convert merely for love; by verifying that the two women acquire faith, the plays seek to allay anxieties about the religious identity of the children of interfaith relationships; the plays produce two Christian parents.

The Island Princess asserts that its heroine experiences a true conversion as it explores the connections between sex and conversion that I discussed in the preceding section. This becomes clear in the words spoken by Pyniero, a Portuguese captain, to an "Indian" waiting woman, Panura: "If thou wilt give me leave, Ile get thee with a Christian, / The best way to convert thee" (5.4.14–15).[51] Pyniero states outright what theological discussions seemed to imply but could never say explicitly: Having sex with a Christian has the power to convert the unbeliever. Moreover, this proposal suggests that sex with a Christian and begetting a Christian child are the "best" means of religious conversion, with even greater power than the sacrament of Christian initiation to produce Christian identity. If *The Island Princess* advances a cultural ideology in which the infidel women can be redeemed through motherhood, it simultaneously features the power of Christian masculine desire to redeem female sexuality. Even so, the play also stages an infidel conversion that is based on faith rather than sex or sacrament.

In her reading of *The Island Princess,* a play dramatizing the Portuguese mercantile activities in the East Indies, Claire Jowitt suggests that "conversion—particularly of the woman to Christianity—was an accepted part of Christian patriarchy from the Crusades onward. . . . Hence Quisara's conversion to Christianity in order to marry Armusia at the end of *The Island Princess* is an example of a literary staple."[52] Jowitt rightfully notes the literary tradition with which Fletcher engages, but the play's participation in romance tradition, I suggest, is mediated by the Protestant emphasis on *sola fides* and the theological understandings of racial and religious identity that I have been describing throughout this book. The princess of Tidore, Quisara, is portrayed as a desirable object, and thus ripe for conversion, from the very beginning of *The Island Princess*. Moreover, although the tragicomic form, Valerie Forman argues, provides a structure for redeeming European mercantile endeavors, I read the form as structuring the play's recuperation of the infidel-conversion motif and a more literal story of redemption.[53] Quisara is first described in the play as "the faire and great *Quisara*" (1.1.29), signifying her desirability to Europeans. Moreover, she is part of a familiar romance storyline: She will marry whoever frees her brother, the king of Tidore, from captivity.[54] Quisara wishes to marry the Portuguese Captain Ruy Dias, but the Portuguese nobleman Armusia proves victorious. The play aligns the infidel princess with a nobleman rather than a captain, thus betraying a proclivity to pair characters according to social status. Jean Feerick argues that the play's interest in social status is not divorced from its engagement with national and racial difference: "The logic of social difference thus interanimates the play's representation of national and religious difference, urging us to consider how the spatial displacement that lies at the center of this and other tragicomic plays might be a tool for reconfiguring the laws of difference structuring England from within."[55]

Although the play represents Portuguese activities in the East Indies, Feerick shows that its concerns are resolutely English. Feerick is most interested in the play's negotiation of social difference, but her analysis suggests a connection between that theme and the integrity of national and religious identity. At the moment that Quisara redirects her desire from Ruy Dias to Armusia (she despises Ruy Dias's cowardice and falls in love with Arumsia because of his bravery) the play resolves an anxiety about a particular kind of mixed relationship: that between individuals from different social statuses. I would add to Feerick's reading that the play also resolves the remaining religious difference between Armusia and Quisara.[56]

The religious difference between Armusia and Quisara bears the seeds of tragedy. This becomes evident when the Governor of Ternata (an enemy of Tidore who disguises himself as a "Moorish priest" in order to wreak havoc on the island) convinces Quisara that she should ask Armusia to convert to their religion. Quisara does just that: She tells Armusia, "Worship our Gods, renounce that faith ye are bred in; / 'Tis easily done, I'll teach ye suddenly; And humbly on your knees" (4.5.36). Here the play introduces the fear of "turning Turk," which we will see in *The Renegado* as well. Quisara's words also show that changing religion is not only a matter of belief but also a rejection of one's breeding. For Armusia, rejecting Christianity would mean renouncing "the faith [he] was bred in." Vitelli expresses a similar sentiment in *The Renegado*; he fears that his captured sister, Paulina, may have "turn[ed] apostata to the faith / That she was bred in" (1.1.138–9). Moreover, later in *The Renegado,* the pirate Grimaldi repents for rejecting "the Faith, / that [he] was borne in" (4.4.96–7).[57] Because the verb "breed" denotes generation, engendering, and the like, these sentiments express the plays' explorations of the interconnectedness of race, reproduction, and religious identity.[58] In the early modern context, rejecting one's religion seems equivalent to rejecting one's race.

But Armusia cannot reject either his race or his religion if, as it is commonly argued, *The Island Princess* is to legitimize proto-imperial and mercantile projects by demonstrating that Europeans can remain unaltered by contact with the East. He must reject Quisara's proposal. "Ha? I'll be hang'd first" (4.5.36), Armusia responds, and he makes it clear that he had hoped that their love would lead Quisara to convert to Christianity—an outcome that is common in the romance tradition. Nonetheless, Quisara initially believes that Armusia is merely playing hard to get, and she reads the rejection as a kind of foreplay to his conversion; she simply replies, "Come, come, I know ye love me" (4.5.50). Quisara's various attempts to use her romantic relationship with Armusia to convert him illustrate what critics like Vitkus, Burton, and Degenhardt have identified as the seductive allure of Islam and the East. Non-Christian women like Quisara (and Donusa) who hope to use romantic ties to coax religious conversion are thus part of a tradition that carries a stigma after the Reformation; the conversion motif of Catholic romances is now demonized, a portent of the dangers of the East.

Armusia does not deny that he loves Quisara, but he notes at length—fifty-eight interspersed lines—all the reasons he will never convert. Images of death permeate his speeches, culminating in his most violent response:

> Now I contemn ye, and I hate my self
> For looking on that face lasciviously,
> And it looks ugly now me thinks.
> It looks like death it self, to which 'twou'd lead me;
> Your eyes resemble pale despair, they fright me,
> And in their rounds, a thousand horrid ruins,
> Methinks I see; and in your tongue hear fearfully
> The hideous murmurs of weak souls have suffer'd,
> Get from me, I despise ye; and know woman,

That for all this trap you have laid to catch my life in,
To catch my immortal life, I hate and curse ye,
Contemn your Deities, spurn at their powers,
And where I meet your Mahumet gods, I'll swing 'em
Thus o'r my head, and kick 'em into puddles,
Nay, I will out of vengeance search your Temples.
And with those hearts that serve my God, demolish
Your shambles of wild worships. (4.5.105–18)

Armusia's love is converted to hate; as Michael Neill asserts, "at the point when Quisara urges her lover to forsake his faith, her beauty is ultimately transformed to a black ugliness that 'looks like death itself.'"[59] Quisara becomes a deathly blazon, a racialized figure of death and damnation: Her face now "looks like death it self," her "eyes resemble pale despair," and her voice sounds like "hideous murmurs of weak souls." On the stage, however, it is likely that Quisara looks just as she always has: a boy actor wearing white pancake makeup and a costume that makes him appear exotically foreign and female. What has changed is Armusia's and the audience's perception of Quisara. At this moment he and the audience turn from seeing her as "faire and great" to seeing her as a casualty of the forsaking of Christianity. The play's insistence on maintaining (and also reproducing) Christian identity requires that Armusia and the audience now view her non-Christian body as disfigured by sin and damnation. The maintenance of male Christian identity mandates that her outward beauty fall victim to the less tangible ugliness of racial and religious otherness.

Armusia's blasphemy—to kick and swing Quisara's Mahumet gods over his head and throw them into puddles—cannot go unpunished; he is sentenced to die by the very king he freed from prison. The play, at first, seems ready to punish Armusia and veer toward tragedy because of Armusia's misrecognition of Quisara and his misreading of her body. Her outer fairness conceals her inner wickedness. Quisara, like Crashaw's baptized Ethiopian, tests the limits of color-coded religion. In *The Island Princess* fair skin, indeed whiteness, does not necessarily signify spiritual purity—though it cannot be denied that her fairness makes her a desirable convert. At the same time, Armusia's punishment for misreading Quisara's body is a prerequisite of the tragicomic genre; there can be no tragicomedy without the threat of death.

The play more fully exemplifies tragicomedy as literary mode patterned after the Christian redemption story by connecting death with redemption. Armusia willingly accepts his death and chooses to become a martyr, believing that in dying a faithful Christian he will receive a heavenly reward. Consequently, martyrdom itself is tragicomic in its structure, for the suffering of the body gives way to spiritual union and celebration. The English theologian John Bradford, for example, writes in a 1555 letter, "When the fire doth his appointed office, thou shalt be received, as a sweet, burnt offering, into heaven where thou shalt joyfully remain in God's presence forever."[60] In the theology of martyrdom, the death and destruction of the body are joyful.

Armusia's willingness to die for his faith leads Quisara to forsake her religion and embrace tragicomic martyrdom as well. She is a "virgin won by [Armusia's] faire constancy" (5.2.109), and she states more fully just a few lines later that his constancy convinces her to become a Christian:

QUISARA Your Faith, and your Religion must be like ye,
    They that can shew you these, must be pure mirrors,
    When the streams flow clear and fair, what are the fountains?
    I do embrace your faith, Sir, and your fortune;
    Go on, I will assist ye, I feel a sparkle here,
    A lively spark that kindles my affection,
    And tells me it will rise to flames of glory:
    Let 'em put on their angers, suffer nobly,
    Shew me the way, and when I faint, instruct me;
    And if I follow not—
ARMUSIA   Oh blessed Lady,
    Since thou art won, let me begin my triumph,
    Come clap your terrors on.
QUISARA   All your fell tortures.
    For there is nothing he shall suffer brother,
    I sweare by my new faith which is most sacred,
    And I will keepe it so, but I will follow in,
    In spight of all your Gods without prevention.

              (5.2.118–34)

Armusia's faith inspires a faith in Quisara that is authenticated by her willingness to die for it; she embraces the faith and flames, their angers, and the suffering. Significantly, rather that embracing Armusia, she embraces his faith and his path—"Shew me the way"—to martyrdom.[61] The willingness to undergo bodily torture rather than baptism (though the "streams . . . clear and free" certainly invoke baptismal imagery), initiate her into the Christian faith; her willingness to forsake her body will allow her to "rise to flames of glory."

Armusia joyfully responds to Quisara's desire to endure torture; here the play turns from tragedy to comedy, for her willingness to "clap her terrors on" demonstrates that Quisara willingly accepts the death of her flesh in order to become Christian in spirit. Luckily for Armusia and Quisara, the Portuguese wage war on Tidore when they learn that Armusia has been taken prisoner. The Portuguese are successful, and the Moorish priest is revealed to be the scheming governor of Ternata. Armusia and Quisara are eventually married, but not before the play tests her faith. The tragi-comic form redeems the infidel woman (who possesses great wealth to boot) whose Christian faith is verified in the end.[62]

At the end of the play, male faith shows power to transform racial and religious others into Christians. Armusia's faith not only transforms Quisara but also nearly transforms the king of Tidore: The king tells Armusia, "You have halfe perswaded me to be a Christian" (5.5.76). That the king is only "halfe perswaded," however, suggests the influence of the view that women are more alterable than men.[63] With the social and religious status of Armusia and Quisara now fully aligned, they can reproduce the ideo-logical imperatives of early modern comedy. At the play's end, Quisara's former suitor, Ruy Dias, celebrates the union and wishes the couple "Chil-dren as sweet and noble as their Parents" (5.5.70). Ruy Dias's statement re-minds us that comedy's end is to reproduce children—in this case children whose parents are of the same social and religious status.

The Island Princess mostly avoids a number of important issues of the era: theological questions about the sanctification of infidel parents, the belief in the redemptive nature of motherhood, and biological theories about paternal and maternal influence on children. Moreover, although *The Island Princess* represents two models of conversion, Panura's through sex and Quisara's through rejecting the infidel faith that she was "bred in," the play ends with the celebration of the marriage of two Christians.

Massinger's *The Renegado* follows *The Island Princess* closely, both in its explorations of race, gender, and religious conversion, and in its investigation of the relationships among martyrdom, redemption, conversion, and the tragicomic form (the words "martyr" and "martyrdom" appear four times in the play).[64] The play also matches characters of the same social status and religion: Although Donusa's love interest, Vitelli, is disguised as a merchant, we learn that he is really a Venetian gentleman. In addition, the willingness to become a martyr is the test of true Christian faith.

The scene in which Vitelli denounces Donusa for asking him to convert to Islam is strikingly similar to the scene featuring Armusia and Quisara: Both are marked by strong hatred and violence. Donusa, however, is associated not with death but with Satan himself:

> The Devil, thy tutor, fills each part about thee,
> And that I cannot play the exorcist
> To dispossess thee—unless I should tear
> The body limb from limb, and throw it to
> The Furies that expect it—I would now
> Pluck out that wicked tongue that hath blasphemed
> That great Omnipotency at whose nod
> The fabric of the world shakes. (4.3.107–14)

Vitelli goes on at length in this vein, but what is significant here is that at the moment when Donusa attempts to turn him, she becomes an embodiment of spiritual evil—so much so that Vitelli now imagines it impossible to disconnect spirit from body. The only way to exorcise her is to destroy her body, the very body that he enjoyed sexually earlier in the play. Although the scene surely betrays European anxieties about "turning Turk," it also exemplifies the play's investment in embodied forms of religious identity.[65]

At the same time, Vitelli's rhetorically powerful language can exorcise Donusa without his having to resort to the kinds of physical violence he mentions. Donusa is moved by the power of Vitelli's speech, an act of preaching that persuades her to become a Christian. Unlike Quisara, who converts after witnessing how nobly Armusia endures his torture, Donusa desires to convert immediately after hearing Vitelli's sermon, which exhorts to martyrdom: "Can there be strength in that / Religion that suffers us to tremble / At that which every day—nay hour—we hasten to?" (4.3.135–7). For Vitelli true religion requires the embrace of death, a conviction that leads Donusa to question her own religion: "This is

unanswerable and there's something/Tells me I err in my opinion"
(4.3.138–9). Vitelli's question plants the seed that later grows into her
conversion.

From this point forward, the play employs a revised form of the infidel-
conversion motif's yoking of conversion to marriage: In *The Renegado*
conversion and marriage are simultaneously linked to death. This link,
reiterated throughout the rest of the play, first emerges soon after Donusa
expresses that she might convert. Vitelli tells her,

> Oh Donusa!
> Die in my faith like me and 'tis a marriage
> At which celestial angels shall be waiters,
> And such as have sainted welcome us. (4.3.150–3)

Vitelli's marriage to Donusa and their deaths are conflated both in
his speech and in the plot—they will occur in the same ceremony. The
earthly marriage between Donusa and Vitelli is to be superseded by
their heavenly union with Christ. Vitelli's language draws from the understanding that marriage signifies the union between Christ and his
church, a union that can be consummated only in the world to come.
Massinger thus revises romance's traditional yoking of conversion and
marriage by linking them with death. The play thereby asks the audience to reconsider the spiritual significance of the staged rituals; baptism
and marriage both signify and will literally lead to—without the intervention of tragicomic providence—death and union with Christ after
death.

Like Quisara, Donusa must prove her faith. She does so through an act
of blasphemy that demonstrates her full rejection of Islam and her willingness to die a Christian. After Vitelli assures her that she will be baptized,
she responds, "Then thus I spit at Mahomet" (4.3.156). The Viceroy of
Tunis, Asambag, is outraged and responds, "Stop her mouth!/ In death to
turn apostata" (4.3.158–9). That she must die because of her blasphemy is
not surprising; Asambag's words are surprising: "in death to turn
apostata"—they suggest that in death she will become an apostate and a
Christian convert.

The play is so invested in exploring the signifying power and spiritual
efficacy of baptism and marriage that these rituals are staged as part of
the action of the play. But before the play stages the conjoined baptism,

marriage, and execution ceremony, it asks the audience to consider the power of baptism. Vitelli asks the Jesuit priest, Francisco, about the efficacy of baptism performed by the laity. Francisco gives the traditional Catholic position:

> Midwives upon necessity perform it,
> And knights that in Holy Land fought for
> The freedom of Jerusalem, when full
> Of sweat and enemies's blood, have made their helmets
> The font out of which with their holy hands
> They drew that heavenly liquor. 'Twas approved then
> By Holy Church, nor must I think it now
> In you a work less pious. (5.2.34–41)

Benedict Robinson has astutely observed that Francisco describes "a scene virtually right out of Tasso . . . with the water drawn out of a helmet by Tancred to a dying Clorinda."[66] Francisco's speech, then, justifies baptism through romance literary tradition. An earlier generation of critics interpreted moments such as this as evidence of Massinger's Catholic faith, but I am not so sure that we can read the play, or the audience, as fully embracing Francisco's theology.[67] This theology of "Holy Church," to be sure, is at odds with the theology I discussed in chapter 1, especially as regards the English Church's rejection of lay baptism. Francisco's belief that " 'Twas approved" is associated with a past theological position, one that Francisco assumes to be still true but that conflicts with religious beliefs that the Church of England insisted on every time an infant was baptized.

At the end of their discussion of baptism, Francisco tells Vitelli, "And though now fall, / Rise a blest martyr" (5.2.45–6), signaling the play's consideration of the salvific powers of baptism, marriage, and martyrdom. This consideration culminates in act 5, scene 3, when Dounsa is to be baptized, married to Vitelli, and then executed with her new husband. The scene has the trappings of tragedy: The impending deaths are signaled by the "*dreadful music*" described in the stage direction. Vitelli, however, like Armusia, responds joyfully to death:

> A joyful preparation! To whose bounty
> Owe we our thanks for gracing our Hymen?

> The notes, though dreadful to the ear, sound here
> As our epithalamium were sung
> By a celestial choir, and a full chorus
> Assured us future happiness. (5.3.47–52)

Again Vitelli sees earthly marriage as a prelude to spiritual union with Christ. He continues to connect the earthly to the spiritual in his ability to hear a "celestial choir" in the "notes . . . dreadful to the ear" that signify "future happiness." The relationship between the music and what it signifies is similar to the figurative disunity that Jewel argued is inherent to Protestant sacraments; Vitelli's speech thus suggests that the marriage, death, and music require the type of *allegoresis* that Maureen Quilligan describes; it implies a distinctly Protestant sacramental relationship between the tragic and the comedic, between earthly death and spiritual union with Christ.[68]

Vitelli's speech at the beginning of the combined baptism/marriage/execution ceremony helps us understand the significance of various instances of figurative disunity in the scene. Vitelli asks Asambeg and Mustafa, Pasha of Allepo, to be allowed to perform a rite that prepares Christians for death. Vitelli is making a veiled reference to baptism:

MUSTAPHA   What's the mystery
      Of this? Discover it!
VITELLI   Great sir, I'll tell you.
      Each country hath its own peculiar rites:
      Some, when they are to die, drink store of wine,
      Which, poured in liberally, does oft beget
      A bastard valor, with which armed they hear
      The not to be declined charge of death
      With less fear and astonishment. Others take
      Drugs to procure heavy sleep, that so
      They may insensibly receive the means
      That casts them in an everlasting slumber;
      Others—
                Enter Gazet, with water.
                O welcome!
ASAMBAG   Now, the use of yours?

VITELLI   The clearness of this is a perfect sign
          Of innocence, and as this washes off
          Staines and pollutions from the things we wear,
          Thrown thus upon the forehead, it hath power
          To purge those spots that cleave upon the mind,
          If thankfully received.
                                Throws it on her face.
ASAMBAG   'Tis a strange custom.

                                            (5.3.100–16)

Vitelli does not fully "discover" the "strange custom" of baptism; instead he conceals it in a number of ways. First, Vitelli characterizes baptism as an example of the "peculiar rites" of specific countries, hence as a national custom, not a religious ritual. Second, although baptism might be a way to ease fear in the face of death, he places it side by side with wine and drugs, which either dull or alter the perception of death. Vitelli thus undermines the spiritual significance of the sacrament; his explanation suggests that the impending rite is different from what it appears to be to Asambeg and Mustafa. It also suggests to the audience that what they see on stage is not necessarily the thing that it signifies.

The way in which Donusa's baptism is enacted also undermines the audience's ability to take it seriously: The stage direction informs us that Vitelli throws water on Donusa's face. What the stage directions denotes may be ambiguous, but it has a comic potential that could have been realized in performance—one might imagine Vitelli doing exactly what the stage direction denotes, throwing water in Donusa's face. Moreover, Paulina, steadfast in her religious beliefs throughout the play, finds the scene comical. She laughs on stage, noting the foolishness of the presentation of religious ritual:

PAULINA   Ha! ha! ha!
ASAMBAG   What means my mistress?
PAULINA   Who can hold her spleen,
          When such ridiculous follies are presented,
          The scene, too, made religious?

                                            (5.3.139–42)

Her metatheatrical language asks the audience to pay special attention to "the scene" it has just seen. On the one hand, according to Degenhardt, "Paulina calls attention to the very discrepancy between performance and religion that threatens to evacuate drama [and romance as well, I would add] of its religious significance."[69] On the other hand, the audience, like Paulina, may find the scene worthy of laughter. In his study of Turk plays, Burton notes that playwrights often treat Muslim-to-Christian conversion comically, as a way of producing "a source of anxiety-dispelling laughter."[70] We may see something similar here. If the "turning Turk" motif is an inversion of the infidel-conversion motif, Paulina's laughter may seek to alleviate anxieties about conversion in general; it may also function as a skewering of romances' conversion scenes. Paulina's response to the baptism allows us to ask if religious conversion in romance has ever truly been about religion. Infidel conversions in romance may attempt to cover with a thin veil of religion other forms of desire: sexual, mercantile, and imperial. The audience is left to wonder whether the staged ritual they have just witnessed is actually baptism, a skepticism that might prompt larger theological questions about the capacity of religious ritual to achieve its claimed results.

Massinger's treatment of the infidel-conversion motif reflects Protestant debates about the efficacy of baptism. Although Robinson, Degenhardt, and Neill suggest that Donusa's baptism reflects the rise of Arminianism and anti-Calvinism in the early seventeenth century, the theology of Jacob Arminius was not universally accepted in the Church of England.[71] A number of printed works indicate that Arminianism was controversial, among them an English translation of a Dutch text entitled *A proclamation giuen by the discreet lords and states, against the slanders laid vpon the euangelicall and reformed religion, by the Arminians and separatists containing all the points, accusations, declarations and confessions, taken out of the last prouinciall synode holden at Arnhem* (1618); William Prynne's *The Church of Englands old antithesis to new Arminianisme. Where in 7. anti-Arminian orthodox tenents, are euidently proued* (1629); and Francis Rous's *The truth of three things, viz, the doctrine of predestination, free-will, and certainty of saluation. As it is maintayned by the Church of England, Wherein the grounds of Arminianisme is discouered, and confuted* (1633). Moreover, although sacraments may have played a more prominent role in some English churches, Arminian theology did not radically alter the efficacy of sacraments. According to Arminius himself,

> The sacraments of the New Testament have not the *ratio* of the sacraments beyond the very use for the sake of which they were instituted, nor do they profit those who use them without faith and repentance; that is, those persons who are of adult age, and of whom faith and repentance are required. Respecting infants, the judgment is different; to whom it is sufficient that they are the offspring of believing parents, that they may be reckoned in the covenant.[72]

Arminius argues that sacraments have different effects on different people: in adults they work only when they are accompanied by faith and repentance; in children, however, the efficacy of the sacraments depends on the child's genealogy. The efficacy of the sacraments is racially hedged. Arminius's theology may have altered the Church of England's views of free will and predestination, but it did not alter its view of the sacraments.

I do not deny that English Arminianism provides a context for understanding this scene; nor do I deny the major role played by Catholic characters and Catholic magic in leading to the comic resolution. I do, however, question the assumption that the rise of religious ceremonialism in the Church of England means that sacraments recovered the miraculous power they had lost under Calvinism's influence. That said, regardless of Massinger's intention or how audience members (who undoubtedly held a variety of religious views and had varying degrees of competence in theology) might have viewed Donusa's baptism, her Christian identity is not solely dependent upon it. The confirmation of her Christian identity is so integral to the reproductive ideology of comedy that it cannot rest solely on something as controversial as baptism.

Although disagreements about the efficacy of baptism persisted, both Catholics and various Protestants sects embraced the idea that suffering and martyrdom had a cleansing power that exceeded that of baptism.[73] Of the early church fathers, Origen most emphatically asserted that martyrdom, which he characterized as "baptism of blood," was superior to baptism by water.[74] In early modern England, the English Jesuit Robert Southwell argued in *An epistle of comfort*,

> Martidome seemeth to haue a prerogatyue aboue baptisme. For though baptisme perfectlye clense the soule, and release not onley the offense, but also the temporal punishment due vnto the same: Yet sticketh the roote of sinne in the flesh, & partye baptysed retaynet in him, the badge and cognizance . . . of a sinner. But Martidomes virtue is such, that it not onley workth the same effect of baptism, but purchaseth also to the soule, forth with a perfect radiance of all concupiscence and inclination to sinne.[75]

Martyrdom resolved a multitude of problems that baptism never did, especially those pertaining to the concupiscence that arises from "the roote of sinne in the flesh." From the Protestant side, in Thomas Becon's *A New Catechism* the son explains that there are three types of baptism: "baptism of water"; martyrdom or "baptism of blood"; and the inward death of the sinful nature, "the baptism of the Holy Ghost" (222). He believes, like Origen, that martyrdom is superior to water baptism: "of all these three the baptism of water is the most inferior" (222). Martyrdom could also be understood as a sign of election. The bishop of London Thomas Ridley wrote concerning his impending execution, "[martyrdom] is an inestimable and honourable gift of GOD, given only to the true elects and dearly beloved of GOD."[76]

Attention to martyrdom in *The Renegado* allows us to put aside questions about Massinger's confessional identity. Martyrdom was truly a universal Christian precept, and both *The Island Princess* and *The Renegado* make use of its cultural prominence to recuperate the infidel-conversion motif. Perhaps the use of martyrdom to authenticate Quisara's and Donusa's conversion reflects anxieties about the inconstancy of women. Scholars who have studied early women martyrs have suggested that martyrdom became a way for women to prove their depth of knowledge in theological matters, the strength of their religious character, and indeed their religious autonomy.[77] If this scholarship illustrates the importance of martyrdom for constructing women as religious subjects, Quisara's and Donusa's willingness to become martyrs helps to portray them as true Christians. I do not wish to suggest that these plays are chiefly concerned with the religious convictions of real women at home or abroad; I suggest, rather, that the desire to recuperate the infidel-conversion motif requires a discourse as powerful as that surrounding martyrdom in order to confirm Quisara's and Donusa's Christian identity. The discourse of martyrdom is powerful for purging the infidel-conversion motif of the concupiscence so closely associated with romance.

Armusia, Quisara, Vitelli, and Donusa do not literally die for their faiths. Nonetheless, their willingness to become martyrs demonstrates the depth of their spiritual commitment and their transcendence of the desires of the body. The infidel-conversion motif thus emerges in sharp relief from the plays' romantic plots. As with Armusia and Quisara, the tragicomic form comes to the rescue: The born-again former pirate Grimaldi and the priest have a boat waiting for the newlyweds' escape, which will allow Vitelli and Donusa to have "future happiness" beyond the confines of the play. Just as the tragicomic form structures the plot's movement from the spiritual death of the infidel to the resurrection of the Christian convert, so the play's plot stages and literalizes the spiritual significance of the romance rites of baptism (death) and marriage (spiritual union with Christ).

Even given the recuperation of the infidel-conversion motif in the works of Massinger, Fletcher, and Shakespeare (albeit with more ambiguity), it is important to note the dynamic interplay of race and gender in these plays. Not only do these plays imply that the religious identities of women are more malleable than those of men, but they also insist that the women who do convert are racial anomalies. Ania Loomba has noted that each of these plays emphatically characterize these woman as phenotypically different from others of their race.[78] In *The Merchant of Venice*, for instance, Salarino insists that Jessica's flesh and her blood are different from Shylock's: "There *is more* difference between thy flesh and hers than between jet and ivory; *more* between your bloods than there is between red wine and rhenish" (3.1.34–36, my emphasis). We cannot know whether Shakespeare imagined Jessica's skin color to be different from Shylock's. Did Shakespeare's theater give Shylock tawny skin like Morocco? Yet the language of color, especially as it is applied to flesh, suggests that for Jessica to be incorporated into the Christian community, she must be more different from her father than black is different from white—yet if there is nothing more different than black is from white, how do the Venetians understand Jessica's relationship to her father?[79] Color also marks Quisara and Donusa as different from others of their race. Loomba observes, "Unlike Shakespeare's Cleopatra, who is 'with Phoebus amorous pinches black', 'the very sun', the Portuguese solider Christophero tells us, dares not dye Quisara 'Into his tauny Livery.' "[80] And unlike Mustapha, who has a "grim aspect or toad-like complexion" (3.1.50), Donusa is associated with whiteness. Vitelli says to Donusa after their sexual encounter, "the sating of your lust hath sullied / The immaculate whiteness of your virgin beauties, / Too fair for me to look on" (3.5.46). Vitelli's language implies that Donusa's sexual whiteness or purity previously manifested itself visually. Although Vitelli no longer sees her immaculate whiteness, her physical appearance has not actually changed. Donusa's servant, Manto, assures her in act 3, scene 1 that no one will be able to detect visually that she is no longer a virgin. Thus her conversion works to cleanse her whiteness; as Degenhardt observes, her conversion enacts a process of "re-virgination."[81]

By early modern standards of beauty, Jessica, Quisara, and Donusa are fit objects of desire for European men. At the same time, these plays lay bare the connection between conversion and desire in romance. Although the infidel-conversion motif has its origins in Christianity's claim to embrace all who believe, the motif's past tendency to yoke conversion to sexual desire limits the kinds of difference that can be transformed and then incorporated in Christendom. Romance has often asserted that not all infidels are desirable as converts.

Afterword

A Political Afterlife of a Theology of Race and Conversion

Not all infidels are desirable converts to Christianity; the conversion of non-Christians to Christianity can have unwelcome repercussions. Brabantio certainly found this to be true; he could not have known that welcoming a converted Moor into his home would lead to the loss of his daughter, his property. Iago and Roderigo suggest that Othello's marriage to Desdemona is a kind of home-invasion robbery. Othello has crossed boundaries he should not have; he has disturbed the sanctity of home. Brabantio later amplifies the consequences of this invasion when he states, "For if such actions may have passage free, / Bond-slaves and pagans shall our statesmen be" (1.2.98-99). But why should Brabantio speak of bond-slaves and pagans? Othello is neither at the moment he marries Desdemona. And what does any of this have to do with the state?

The panic Iago and Roderigo inspire in Brabantio through the language of thievery resonates with that expressed by Thomas Newton in *A notable historie of the Saracens* (1575), which deals with an invading Ottoman empire: "They were (indeede) at the first very far off from our Clyme & Region, and therefore the lesse to be feared, but now they are even at our doores and ready to come into our Houses."[1] Newton's panic is conveyed through an image of decreasing distance between Christians and infidels: a movement from far away to right outside the door to inside the house. He fears the effects of this decreasing distance; he worries that it will lead to forced conversion to Islam. This fear is brought home by the questions raised about what happens once Muslims are inside the house.

Through metaphor both Brabantio and Newton collapse differences between the home and the nation, between the personal and the political. Newton is concerned with actual Muslims who might invade England

and force English men and women to forsake Christianity. Brabantio, in contrast, resorts to racializing religious difference in a moment of parental crisis. He excludes Othello from the baptized race at the point at which he recognizes the full consequences of the infidel-conversion motif—political chaos seems to be a stretch, though. Brabantio's dismissal of Othello's Christian identity brings to the fore that a refusal to believe in conversion is not always theologically motivated.

The infidel-conversion motif, if one puts his or her faith in it, generates a potentially troubling narrative of boundary crossing and inversion of perceived social hierarchies. Perhaps it is because I began writing these words in the spring of 2012, with a U.S. presidential election gaining momentum, that I find myself pondering the connections between Shakespeare's Othello and America's forty-fourth president, Barack Hussein Obama. The first person I heard make this comparison was Emily C. Bartels, in brief remakes she made while chairing the panel "Un-Mooring the Moor across Cultural Borders" at the 2010 meeting of the Shakespeare Association of America. But as I now think about the fears Obama's origins and "travels' history" (*Othello*, 1.3.141) have aroused in the political imaginary, I find the similarities between Othello and Obama just too striking to ignore: Both figures' Christian identity seems to be gainsaid by their genealogy and geographic origin.

A 2008 poll conducted by the Pew Research Center stated that 12 percent of Americas believed that Obama is Muslim, a belief shared in equal percentages by Republicans and Democrats; 11 percent of Independents held this belief. A quarter of those polled were unsure of his religious faith. Some 37 percent of Democrats who believed that Obama is Muslim stated that they would still vote for him. Although these Democrats were still willing to vote for a supposedly Muslim candidate, the poll revealed that Obama's supposed Muslim faith was actually a more important factor for Democrats than for Republicans; the latter were unlikely to vote for him even when they believed he is Christian.[2]

Although poll statistics can seldom be taken at face value, the Pew report raises important questions about our contemporary feelings about the connections between race, genealogy, geographical origins, and religious identity. The question must be asked: Where did the 12 percent get the idea that Obama is Muslim? Although President Obama writes of his conversion to Christianity in his memoir, *Dreams from My Father: A Story of Race and Inheritance*, the veracity of that conversion, as well as his birth within U.S. borders, have aroused continued scrutiny and skepticism in some quarters; those who wish—to use the phrase popularized by Republican primary candidate Michele Bachmann—to "take back America" have often questioned both his geographical origins (whether he was born in America) and his religious faith. In this political context few have asked whether Obama is a "good" Christian whose beliefs and political views are compatible with Christian orthodoxy—there are, and have always been, numerous Christian orthodoxies.

In *Dreams from My Father*, Obama explores what he inherited from his father. Although Obama inherited his father's name and a phenotype that marks him as black within American constructions of race, a portion of the population on both the left and the right seems to believe that he also inherited his father's religion despite his paucity of contact with his father after the age of two and despite his descent from Kansans on his mother's side. Those who believe that the President is Muslim unwittingly embrace a theology of race that, as I have been arguing, emerged in Reformation England. Today, as then, religious identity is understood to pass from father to child. Muslim identity—like dark skin, dark hair, and brown eyes—seems to be a kind of dominant genetic trait. For some it seems to operate through the principle of the "one-drop" rule that in many ways continues to construct racial identity to this day. Obama's "black" skin betrays his genealogical ties to his father and Muslim Africa.

I am not arguing that Obama's political antagonists, or those who believe that he is Muslim, are racist. Rather I hope to highlight that we are still living with two major consequences of the Reformation: its redefinition of the origins of religious identity and its theological skepticism about the conversion of non-Christians to Christianity. Moreover, because skepticism about Obama's religious identity is as common among Democrats as it is among Republicans, we can see that belief in race and geographical origin as indicators of religious affiliation has crossed political-confessional divides. Constructions of race and religion are intimately tied to questions of political legitimacy, both locally and globally. To acknowledge the possibility of any sort of conversion—from one religion to another or, through naturalization, from one national-ity to another—is to acknowledge the permeability of both ideological and material borders and hence to recognize the value of inclusiveness in cultural and political life. To affirm the reality of conversion is to deny the reality of rigid, unalterable identity, whether racial, religious, or national.

Notes

Introduction: Not Turning the Ethiope White

1. Richard Crashaw, *Steps to the Temple* (London, 1646), sig. B4v.

2. Geffrey Whitney, *A choice of emblemes* (Leiden, 1586). Unless otherwise noted, all biblical passages are from *The Geneva Bible* (1560).

3. In fact, "Ethiope" is the more common translation. See the King James Version, for example, and the Vulgate's *"Aethiops."* On "black" Jews, see M. Lindsay Kaplan, "Jessica's Mother: Medieval Constructions of Jewish Race and Gender in *The Merchant of Venice,*" *Shakespeare Quarterly* 58 (2007): esp. 3–10; and Janet Adelman, *Blood Relations: Christian and Jew in* The Merchant of Venice (Chicago: University of Chicago Press, 2008), 83–84.

4. Ania Loomba and Jonathan Burton, "Aesop, *Fables,*" in *Race in Early Modern Europe: A Documentary Companion,* eds. Ania Loomba and Jonathan Burton (New York: Palgrave, 2007), 39. On the varied appearances of this proverb and its ubiquity in early modern England, see Carolyn Prager, " 'If I be Devil': English Renaissance Responses to the Proverbial and Ecumenical Ethiopian," *Journal of Medieval and Renaissance Studies* 17 (1987): 257–79; and Anu Korhone, "Washing the Ethiope White: Conceptualizing Black Skin in Renaissance England," in *Black Africans in Renaissance Europe,* eds. T. F. Earle and K. J. P. Lowe (Cambridge: Cambridge University Press, 2005), 94–112.

5. As Ania Loomba notes, "Conversion thus creates a living contradiction, a person who is black outside and white inside." *Shakespeare, Race, and Colonialism* (Oxford: Oxford University Press, 2002), 56.

6. On the importance of Crashaw's conversion for understanding his poetics, see Molly Murray, *The Poetics of Conversion in Early Modern English Literature* (Cambridge: Cambridge University Press, 2009, 105–37).

7. Romance is commonly understood as a mode characterized by wandering, deferral, and dilation, particularly after Patricia Parker's *Inescapable Romance: Studies in the Poetics of a Mode* (Princeton: Princeton University Press, 1979), and David Quint's essay, "The Boat of Romance," which was later incorporated into

chapter 6 of *Epic and Empire: Politics and Generic Form from Virgil to Milton* (Princeton: Princeton University Press, 1993).

8. Although conversion is a much-discussed topic, it is often understood primarily as a trope of empire and less as a doctrinal concern; critics who look at conversion are usually more interested in empire than they are in confessional identities and religious belief. Elizabeth Spiller's "From Imagination to Miscegenation: Race and Romance in Shakespeare's *The Merchant of Venice*," *Renaissance Drama* 29 (1998): 137–64, and her more recent *Reading and the History of Race in the Renaissance* (Cambridge: Cambridge University Press, 2011) are partial exceptions. I will engage Spiller's arguments later in this introduction.

9. There are too many to name here, but on the prescientific formation of racial ideologies, see, for example, Kim Hall: "The easy association of race with modern science ignores the fact that language itself creates differences within social organization and that race was then (as it is now) a social construct that is fundamentally more about power and culture than biological difference." *Things of Darkness: Economies of Race and Gender in Early Modern England* (New York: Cornell University Press, 1995), 6. Also see Lara Bovilsky's more recent *Barbarous Play: Race on the English Renaissance Stage* (Minneapolis: University of Minnesota Press, 2008), 8–14; Ayanna Thompson, *Performing Race and Torture on the Early Modern Stage* (New York: Routledge, 2008), 3–6; and Ian Smith's *Race and Rhetoric in the Renaissance: Barbarian Errors* (New York: Palgrave, 2009), in which he provides a useful overview of scholarship that so forcibly wishes to deny the existence of "race" before the Enlightenment (11–12).

10. Dympna Callaghan, *Shakespeare Without Women: Representing Gender and Race on the Renaissance Stage* (New York: Routledge, 2000); Celia R. Daileader, *Racism, Misogyny, and the* Othello *Myth* (Cambridge: Cambridge University Press, 2005); Hall, *Things of Darkness*; Margo Hendricks and Patricia Parker, eds., *Women, 'Race,' and Writing in the Early Modern Period* (New York: Routledge, 1994); Sujata Iyengar, *Shades of Difference: Mythologies of Skin Color in Early Modern England* (Philadelphia: University of Pennsylvania Press, 2005); Arthur Little, *Shakespeare Jungle Fever: National-Imperial Re-Vision of Race, Rape and Sacrifice* (Stanford: Stanford University Press, 2000); Ania Loomba, *Gender, Race, Renaissance Drama* (Manchester: Manchester University Press, 1989) and *Shakespeare, Race, and Colonialism*; and Joyce Green MacDonald, *Women and Race in Early Modern Texts* (Cambridge: Cambridge University Press, 2002).

11. For an insightful discussion of interpretations of black skin in Western thought from the time of the ancient Hebrews through the nineteenth century, see David M. Goldenberg, *The Curse of Ham: Race and Slavery in Early Judaism, Christianity and Islam* (Princeton: Princeton University Press, 2003).

12. Mary Floyd-Wilson, *English Ethnicity and Race in Early Modern Drama* (Cambridge: Cambridge University Press, 2003); Jean Feerick, *Strangers in Blood: Relocating Race in the Renaissance* (Toronto: University of Toronto Press, 2010);

Ian Smith, *Race and Rhetoric in the Renaissance*; and Spiller, *Reading the History of Race*.

13. Smith, *Race and Rhetoric in the Renaissance*, 3. Also see MacDonald, *Women and Race in Early Modern Texts*, 44; she cautions critics not to attend solely to skin color.

14. Janet Adelman details the ambiguity of "Jew" in *Blood Relations*, and Emily C. Bartels details the ambiguity of "Moor" extensively in *Speaking of the Moor: from Alcatraz to Othello* (Philadelphia: University of Pennsylvania Press, 2009).

15. Also see James Shapiro, *Shakespeare and The Jews* (New York: Columbia University Press, 1996), in which he notes that inattention to theology has led to a flawed assumption that race and religion are distinct entities: "[race studies] ha[ve] been remarkably slow to acknowledge the extent to which theology shaped the way people thought about both racial and national differences in early modern times" (170).

16. Kwame Anthony Appiah, "Race," in *Critical Terms for Literary Study*, ed. Frank Lentricchia and Thomas McLaughlin, 2d ed. (Chicago: University of Chicago Press, 1995), 277–78. Equally influential in its assertion that "race" does not exist in the early modern period is Ivan Hannaford, *Race: The History of an Idea in the West* (Baltimore: Johns Hopkins University Press, 1996), esp. 147–84. In contrast, George M. Fredrickson provides a much more flexible definition of race in *Racism: A Short History* (Princeton: Princeton University Press, 2002): The concept of race exists whenever "one ethnic group or historical collectivity dominates, excludes, or seeks to eliminate another on the basis of differences that it believes are hereditary and unalterable" (170).

17. For example, see Hall, *Things of Darkness*, 3–4; MacDonald, *Women and Race in Early Modern Texts*, 23; Bovilsky, *Barbarous Play*, 10–11; Smith, *Race and Rhetoric in the Renaissance*, 10–12; and Lisa Lampert, "Race, Periodicity, and the (Neo-) Middle Ages," *MLQ* 65 (2004): 391–421.

18. Race as a biological category has been under scrutiny for some time; in 1999 the America Anthropological Association stated, "Racial beliefs constitute myths about diversity in the human species. . . . The myths fused behavior and physical features together in the public mind, impeding our comprehension of both biological variations and cultural behavior, implying that both are genetically determined" (quoted in Lundy Braun, "Race, Ethnicity and Health: Can Genetics Explain Disparities?" *Perspectives in Biology and Medicine* 45 [2002]: 162). Also see, for example, Daniel G. Blackburn, "Why Race Is Not a Biological Concept," in *Race and Racism in Theory and Practice*, ed. Berel Lang (Oxford: Rowman and Littlefield, 2000), 3–26; and Audrey Smedley and Brian D. Smedley, "Race as Biology Is Fiction, Racism as a Social Problem Is Real: Anthropological and Historical Perspectives on the Social Construction of Race," *American Psychologist* 60 (2005): 16–26.

19. On race as lineage, see Feerick's *Strangers in Blood*. Also see Spiller, who convincingly describes how older concepts of race as lineage merged with race determined by phenotypic difference in the early modern period ("From Imagination to Miscegenation," 50).

20. Colin Kidd, *The Forging of the Races: Race and Scripture in the Protestant Atlantic World, 1600–2000* (Cambridge: Cambridge University Press, 2006), 19.

21. In *The Forging of the Races*, Kidd examines early modern theological discussions of the peopling of the world through Noah and his three sons. Also see Kidd's *British Identities before Nationalism: Ethnicity and Nationhood in the Atlantic World, 1600–1800* (Cambridge: Cambridge University Press, 1999). Kidd, however, does not consult Protestant polemical texts in which particular doctrinal positions are articulated and which in turn define particular confessional communities. Apart from Kidd's work, see David N. Livingstone's *Adam's Ancestors: Race, Religion, and the Politics of Human Origin* (Baltimore: Johns Hopkins University Press, 2008), which examines early modern racial formation that emerges from exegesis of the story of Adam and his descendents.

22. See J. Kameron Carter, *Race: A Theological Account* (Oxford: Oxford University Press, 2008); and Willie James Jennings, *The Christian Imagination: Theology and the Origins of Race* (New Haven: Yale University Press, 2010).

23. Karen E. Spierling, *Infant Baptism in Reformation Geneva: The Shaping of Community, 1536–1564* (Aldershot, UK: Ashgate, 2005), 4.

24. Even what it meant for sacraments to signify rather than automatically confer grace was greatly contested. Zwingli insisted that sacraments are merely external signs and that they do no spiritual work in themselves, while Luther and Calvin maintained that sacraments inspire or in some way aid a believer's faith. For a clear and concise overview of differences between Protestant and Catholic sacraments, and differences among the sacramental theologies of Luther, Zwingli, and Calvin, see Euan Cameron, *The European Reformation*, 2d ed. (Oxford: Oxford University Press, 2012), 183–96.

25. See Cameron, *The European Reformation*, 187.

26. On English Protestant anxieties about the salvation of their infants, see David Cressy, *Birth, Marriage, and Death: Ritual, Religion, and the Life-Cycle in Tudor and Stuart England* (Oxford: Oxford University Press, 1997), 115–16.

27. John Bradford, *The Writings of John Bradford*, ed. Aubrey Townsend (Cambridge, UK: The University Press for The Parker Society, 1853), 123.

28. For an overview of these arguments, see Peter Marshall, "(Re)Defining the English Reformation," *Journal of British Studies* 48 (2009): 564–86; and the special issue of *Journal of Medieval and Early Modern Studies* 40, "English Reformations," eds. David Ayers and Nigel Smith (2010). Also see Eamon Duffy, *The Stripping of the Altars: Traditional Religion in England c. 1400–1580* (New

Haven: Yale University Press, 1992); and Christopher Haigh, *English Reformations: Religion, Politics and Society under the Tudors* (Oxford: Clarendon Press, 1993).

29. Ken Jackson and Arthur F. Marotti, "The Turn to Religion in Early Modern Studies," *Criticism* 46 (2004): 167–90.

30. Before Jackson and Marotti identified this "turn," Debora Kuller Shuger challenged the New Historicist conflation of politics and religion in *Habits of Thought in the English Renaissance: Religion, Politics, and the Dominant Culture* (Berkeley: University of California Press, 1990). On the relation between cultural studies and religious studies as academic disciplines, see Thomas Fitzgerald, *The Ideology of Religious Studies* (New York: Oxford University Press, 2000), 221–34.

31. Arthur F. Marotti, *Religious Ideology and Cultural Fantasy: Catholic and Anti-Catholic Discourses in Early Modern England* (South Bend, Ind.: University of Notre Dame Press, 2005). Murray notes the importance of infidel conversion in early modern literature, but she does not discuss it in her book (*The Poetics of Conversion*, 28).

32. Indeed, anxieties about conversion pervaded early modern England, as both the nation and individuals within it frequently converted from Catholicism to Protestantism and vice versa. On this culture of serial conversion, see Michael C. Questier, *Conversion, Politics and Religion in England, 1580–1625* (Cambridge: Cambridge University Press, 1996).

33. Ania Loomba, "Delicious traffick," in *Shakespeare and Race*, ed. Catherine M.S. Alexander and Stanley Wells (Cambridge: Cambridge University Press, 2000), 209.

34. Fitzgerald, *The Ideology of Religious Studies*, 222.

35. Julia Reinhard Lupton, "The Religious Turn (to Theory) in Shakespeare Studies," *Modern Language Notes* 44 (2006): 146–48. It is important to note that for Lupton, as the title of her essay suggests, the return to religion also affords the opportunity to return to theory.

36. Ibid., 146.

37. Ibid., 147.

38. Geraldine Heng, *Empire of Magic: Medieval Romance and the Politics of Cultural Fantasy* (New York: Columbia University Press, 2003), 71.

39. On the goals of Historical Formalism and its relation to New Historicism, see Stephen Cohen's cogent introduction to *Shakespeare and Historical Formalism* (New York: Palgrave, 2007), 1–27.

40. On formalist responses to the New Historicism and Cultural Studies, see Stephen Cohen, "Between Form and Culture: New Historicism and the Promise of a Historical Formalism," in *Renaissance Literature and Its Formal Engagements*, ed. Mark David Rasmussen (New York: Palgrave, 2002), 17–33. Cohen acknowledges, however, that New Historicism did not entirely reject formalism.

41. Cohen, "Introduction," 14.

42. Daniel Boyarin, *A Radical Jew: Paul and the Politics of Identity* (Berkeley: University of California Press, 1994), 7–8. There has been a renewed interest in Pauline universalism in early modern literary studies: see Lupton, *Citizen Saints*; Lisa Lampert, *Gender and Jewish Difference from Paul to Shakespeare* (Philadelphia: University of Pennsylvania Press, 2004); Gregory Kneidel, *Rethinking the Turn to Religion in Early Modern English Literature: The Poetics of All Believers* (New York: Palgrave, 2008); and Jane Hwang Degenhardt, *Islamic Conversion and Christian Resistance on the Early Modern Stage* (Edinburgh: University of Edinburgh Press, 2010).

43. On patristic and medieval readings of Jewish carnality and the inability to accept Christian truth, also see Lampert, "The Hermeneutics of Difference," in *Gender and Jewish Difference from Paul to Shakespeare*, 21–57.

44. Boyarin, *A Radical Jew*, 13. Also see Lambert: "Jews and Judaism not only come to signify a people but also become synonymous with a devalued hermeneutical practice" (*Gender and Jewish Difference*, 10).

45. Here, Erich Auerbach's definition of *figura* is also useful: "They point not only to the concrete future, but also to something that always has been and always will be; they point to something which is in need of interpretation, which will indeed be fulfilled in the concrete future, but which is at all times present." "*Figura*," trans. Ralph Manheim, in *Scenes from the Drama of European Literature: Six Essays* (New York: Meridian, 1959), 59.

46. See Judith H. Anderson and Joan Pong Linton's meditations on figure: "The figure is irreducibly substantive, material—itself a body or meaningfully comparable to a body." Introduction to *Go Figure: Energies, Forms, and Institutions in the Early Modern World* (New York: Fordham University Press, 2011), 1.

47. Sujata Iyengar has documented that this was a pervasive Protestant reading of the black woman in *Song of Solomon* (*Shades of Difference*, 44–79). On blackness and early modern standards of beauty, of course, see Hall's *Things of Darkness*.

48. Joannes Boemus, *The fardle of facions conteining the aunciente maners, customes, and lawes, of the peoples enhabiting the two partes of the earth, called Affrike and Asie* (London, 1555), sig. A6v.

49. See Mateo Salvidore, "The Ethiopian Age of Exploration: Prester John's Discover of Europe, 1306–1458," *Journal of World History* 21 (2010): 593–627.

50. Johnson may have drawn his white Prester John from Boemus: "[Prester John] is of the bloud of David, continued from one generation to another (as they are persuaded) by so many yeres of succession. And he is not as the most of the Ethiopians are, blacke, but white" (*The fardle of facions*, sig. C5v).

51. On romance's immense popularity, see Mary Ellen Lamb and Valarie Wayne, eds., *Staging Early Modern Romance: Prose Fiction, Dramatic Romance, and Shakespeare* (New York: Routledge, 2008); Steve Mentz, *Romance for Sale in Early*

Modern England: The Rise of Prose Fiction (Aldershot, UK: Ashgate, 2006); Lori Humphrey Newcomb, *Reading Popular Romance in Early Modern England* (New York: Columbia University Press, 2001); and Tiffany Werth, *The Fabulous Dark Cloister: Romance in England After the Reformation* (Baltimore: Johns Hopkins University Press, 2011). On its early modern detractors, see Werth. On the use of its motifs to imagine cross-cultural exchanges, see Barbara Fuchs, *Romance* (New York: Routledge, 2004) and *Mimesis and Empire: The New World, Islam, and European Identities* (Cambridge: Cambridge University Press, 2001); Joan Pong Linton, *The Romance of the New World: Gender and the Literary Formulations of English Colonialism* (Cambridge: Cambridge University Press, 1998), and Benedict Robinson, *Islam and Early Modern English Literature: The Politics of Romance from Spenser to Milton* (New York: Palgrave, 2007).

52. On the problem of definition, see Fuchs, *Romance,* 2; and Helen Cooper, *The English Romance in Time: Transforming Motifs from Geoffrey of Monmouth to the Death of Shakespeare* (Oxford: Oxford University Press, 2004), 7–15. Mentz argues that part of the reason romance has been so difficult to define, both in the early modern period and in our own, is because it lacks a classical exemplar, or, more precisely, that we have failed to recognize it (*Romance for Sale,* 73). The difference between a literary genre and a literary mode is vexed one, but see Paul Alpers, *What is Pastoral?* (Chicago: University of Chicago Press, 1996). He suggests, " 'Mode' is a suitable term for the literary category that includes a number of individual genres" (49). Along with pastoral, which is his main interest, he lists romance as one of several literary modes (46). Romance may be a literary mode, but I am most concerned with English responses to the genre of crusade romance, in which the infidel-conversion motif is prominently featured.

53. On the origins of "romance" as a term, see Nathaniel E. Griffin, "The Definition of Romance," *PMLA* 38 (1923): 50–70. Also see Dorothy Everett, "A Characterization of the English Medieval Romance," in *Essays on Middle English Literature,* ed. Patricia Kean (1929; repr., Oxford: Clarendon Press, 1955), 2–3. On romances as embodying aristocratic values, see Fredric Jameson, *The Political Unconscious: Narrative as a Socially Symbolic Act* (Ithaca: Cornell University Press, 1981), 103–50. On romance prose fiction and its appeal to popular tastes, see Mentz, *Romance for Sale,* and Newcomb, *Reading Popular Romance.*

54. Cooper, *The English Romance in Time,* 3.

55. Although this definition of romance may seem a bit tautological, genre theory often notes that genres emerge through principles of repetition. See, for example, Jacques Derrida, "The Law of Genre," trans. Avital Ronell, *Critical Inquiry* 7 (1980): 55–81; and Tzvetan Todorov, *Genres in Discourse,* trans. Catherine Porter (Cambridge: Cambridge University Press, 1990), 13–26.

56. See Fuchs, who suggests that romance can be understood not only as a genre but also as a "strategy" that can be employed to do specific kinds of work (*Romance,* 9).

57. On this debate, see Bernard Weinberg, *A History of Literary Criticism in the Italian Renaissance,* vol. 2 (Chicago: University of Chicago Press, 1963), esp. 960–90; and Daniel Javitch, *Proclaiming a Classing: The Canonization of Orlando Furioso* (Princeton: Princeton University Press, 1991), 21–47.

58. Philip Sidney speaks of "heroic poetry" as well throughout *The Defense of Poesy.*

59. Alistair Fowler, *Kinds of Literature: An Introduction to the Theory of Genres and Modes* (Cambridge: Harvard University Press, 1982), 42.

60. On the Renaissance application of this kind of Aristotelian mimesis, see Rosalie A. Colie, *The Resources of Kind: Genre-Theory in the Renaissance,* ed. Barbara K. Lewalski (Berkeley: University of California Press, 1973), 7–8.

61. Cooper, *The English Romance in Time,* 8. Cooper borrows the term "meme" from evolutionary theory to account for the appearance of recurrent motifs in romance: The meme comes to stand for "a unit within literature that proves so useful, so infectious, that it begins to take a life of its own . . . an idea that behaves like a gene in its ability to replicate faithfully and abundantly, but also on occasion to adapt, mutate, and therefore survive in different forms and cultures" (3).

62. My point is not to reaffirm the medieval-early modern period divide that, as James Simpson argues, is constructed by Protestant polemicists and our disciplinary conventions; see his *Reform and Cultural Revolutions* (Oxford: Oxford University Press, 2002), 7–9. Werth also notes that romance in particular bridges the medieval-early modern divide.

63. John Frow, *Genre* (New York: Routledge, 2006), 26.

64. Derrida, "The Law of Genre," 55.

65. Philip Sidney, "The Defense of Poetry," in *Sir Philip Sidney: Selected Poetry and Prose,* ed. Robert Kimbrough (Madison: University of Wisconsin Press, 1983), 155.

66. William Shakespeare, *Hamlet,* ed. Ann Thompson and Neil Taylor (London: Thomson Learning for The Arden Shakespeare, 1995), 2.2.333–5.

67. Giraldi Cinthio, *On Romances,* trans. Henry L. Snuggs (Lexington: University of Kentucky Press, 1968), 52.

68. Despite Cinthio's assertion, romance is not commonly understood as a didactic genre. Jeff Dolven, however, has shown that English romance authors were often interested in the types of instruction that this genre could offer. *Scenes of Instruction in Renaissance Romance* (Chicago: University of Chicago Press, 2007). Northrop Frye analyzes romance's tendency to distinguish good from evil: "Romance presents an idealized world: in romance heroes are brave, heroines beautiful, villains villainous, and the frustrations, ambiguities, and embarrassments of ordinary life are made little of." *Anatomy of Criticism: Four Essays* (Princeton: Princeton University Press, 1957), 151. In its very typology, for Frye, romance

attempts to make distinctions very clear through producing a world apparently devoid of ambiguity. My contrasting view is that in romance ambiguity (almost) always seems to clear itself up. Take, for instance, the paradoxical utterances of the Delphic oracle in *The Old Arcadia*; although they are at once the origin of the confusion and the plot, the romance narrative works through confusions to make all distinctions clear.

69. Jameson, *The Political Unconscious*, 118.

70. Ibid., 119.

71. Jameson begins *The Political Unconscious* with the call, "Always historicize!" (9).

72. We may find, however, a situation analogous to the one Jameson describes in the countless examples of the return-of-the-lost-child narrative. For examples of the reincorporation of previously unrecognized children, consider the return of Pastorella in Book 6 of *The Faerie Queene* and the return of children in Shakespeare's *Cymbeline* and *The Winter's Tale*.

73. Spiller, *Reading and the History of Race*, 42.

74. Spiller writes, "What we see in the literary record recodes what we see in the historical register: when conversion is introduced to save the romance narrative, race also enters in ways that threaten it and insist that identity is not subject to transformation." Ibid., 45.

75. Spiller also asserts, "Race emerged as a concept that was used to deny the theological and social possibility of conversion"; she sees an antagonism between race and theology. Ibid., 52. In Protestant England, however, race and theology often work together and not in opposition.

76. Northrop Frye, *The Secular Scripture: A Study of the Structure of Romance* (Cambridge, MA: Harvard University Press, 1976), 13 and 29–30. Harry Berger extends this concept of "kidnapped" romance in " 'Kidnapped Romance': Discourse in *The Faerie Queene*," in *Unfolded Tales: Essays on Renaissance Romance*, ed. George M. Logan and Gordon Teskey (Ithaca: Cornell University Press, 1989), 208–56.

77. This is an argument in Werth's *The Fabulous Dark Cloister*.

78. Whether *gestes* are romances or epics is a contested issue, but Sarah Kay argues that the line between the two is not a clear one in Old French literature. *The Chanson de Geste in the Age of Romance: Political Fictions* (Oxford: Clarendon, 1995), 2.

79. Both the French and the English translation are from *La Chanson de Roland*, trans. Gerard J. Brault (University Park: The Pennsylvania State University Press, 1984), ln. 3674.

80. See Sharon Kinoshita, *Medieval Boundaries: Rethinking Difference in Old French Literature* (Philadelphia: University of Pennsylvania Press, 2006); she discusses the importance of gender and the connection between Bramimond's conversion and the military victory (41–45).

81. *Song of Roland,* ln. 3672. On the efficacy of nonconsensual baptism see, for example, Thomas Aquinas, *The Summa Theologica of St. Thomas,* trans. Fathers of the English Dominican Province, vol. 17 (London: Burns, Oats and Washbourne LTD, 1923), 161; and Marina Caffiero, *Forced Baptism: Histories of Jews, Christians, and Converts in Papal Rome,* trans. Lydia G. Cochrane (Berkeley: University of California Press, 2012).

82. *Song of Roland,* ln. 3987. Although Brault translates the line as "She is a Christian out of sheer conviction," translating *"veire"* as "true" seems closer to the earlier conversions of the Jews and Muslims.

83. *Bevis of Hampton,* in *Four Romances of England: King Horn, Havelok the Dane, Bevis of Hampton, Athelston,* ed. Ronald B. Herzman, Graham Drake, and Eve Salisbury (Kalamazoo: Western Michigan University Medieval Publications, 1999), ln. 2583–84. The poem went through seven editions in the sixteenth century and four in the seventeenth.

84. Both *Orlando Furioso* and *Gerusalemme liberata* appeared in popular early modern English translations (Harington's *Orlando Furioso* in 1591 and Edward Fairfax's *Godfrey of Bulloinge, or The Recoverie of Jerusalem* in 1600), and both are alluded to or imitated by the authors I discuss. Two other editions of Harington's translation appeared after the 1591 edition, one in 1607 and another in 1634. Harington's is the most famous of the early modern English translations of the poem, but English readers and audiences also would have had access to the *Furioso* through a translation by Peter Beverley, who published a paraphrase of Canto 5 in 1571, and Robert Greene's stage adaptation, printed in 1594 and again in 1599. Fairfax's translation of *Gerusalemme liberata* went through another edition in 1624 and had a revival in late seventeenth century (it went through three editions in 1687). Prior to Fairfax, Richard Carew published the first five cantos of the poem in 1594.

Tasso's poem is certainly more epic than romance, but critics commonly acknowledge that it employs many romance conventions. See, for example, Andrew Fitcher, "Tasso's Epic of Deliverance," *PMLA* 93 (1978): 264–74; Kristen Olsen Murtaugh, "Erminia Delivered: Notes on Tasso and Romance," *Quaderni d'italianistica* 3 (1982): 12–25; Michael Sherberg, "Epic and Romance in Tasso's Rinaldo: The Conflict of Genre," *Stanford Italian Review* 9 (1990): 67–85; Richard Helgerson, "Tasso on Spenser: The Politics of Chivalric Romance," *The Yearbook of English Studies* 21(1991): 153–67; Jo Ann Cavallo, *The Romance Epics of Boiardo, Ariosto, and Tasso* (Toronto: University of Toronto Press, 2004), 186–228; and Marion A. Wells, *The Secret Wound: Love-Melancholy and Early Modern Romance* (Stanford: Stanford University Press, 2007), 137–78.

85. Ludovico Arisoto, *Orlando Furioso,* trans. Sir John Harington, ed. Robert McNulty (Oxford: Clarendon Press, 1972), 22.27.

86. On the erotics of conversion in medieval literature, see Heng, 195–97. On the complementary work of marriage and conversion, see Jacqueline de

Weever, *Sheba's Daughters: Whitening and Demonizing the Saracen Woman in Medieval French Epic* (New York: Garland, 1998); and Siobhan Bly Calkin, *Saracens and the Making of English Identity: The Auchinleck Manuscript* (New York: Routledge, 2005). Calkin notes that clerics play little to no role in these conversions (29).

87. For example, Daniel Vitkus, "Introduction," in *Three Turk Plays from Early Modern England* (New York: Columbia University Press, 2000), 1–53; Vitkus, *Turning Turk: English Theater and the Multicultural Mediterranean, 1570–1630* (New York: Palgrave, 2003); Jonathan Burton, *Traffic and Turning: Islam and English Drama, 1579–1624* (Newark: University of Delaware Press, 2005); and Degenhardt, *Islamic Conversion and Christian Resistance.*

88. Vitkus, Burton, and Degenhardt have been most interested in reading these interactions in terms of turning Turk, but on these interactions more generally see Nabil Matar's *Turks, Moors, and Englishmen in the Age of Discovery* (New York: Columbia University Press, 1999) and his *Britain and Barbary, 1589–1689* (Gainesville: University of Florida Press, 2005).

89. Mark Rose makes a connection between *Othello* and *Don Quixote*: "One might interpret Othello as a kind of tragic *Don Quixote*." "Othello's Occupation: Shakespeare and the Romance of Chivalry," *English Literary Renaissance* 15 (1985): 295. He issues the caveat that we should not accept this reading because Shakespeare does not parody romance in the way Cervantes does.

90. This is true in both English and Spanish contexts. See Daniel Bernardo Hershenzon, "Early Modern Spain and the Creation of the Mediterranean: Captivity, Commerce, and Knowledge" (Ph.D. diss., University of Michigan, 2011), 49–50; and Nabil Matar, "Introduction: England and Mediterranean Captivity, 1577–1704," in *Piracy, Slavery, and Redemption: Barbary Captivity Narratives from Early Modern England* (New York: Columbia University Press, 2001), 1–52. On captivity in the early modern world more generally, see Lisa Voigt, *Writing Captivity in the Early Modern Atlantic: Circulations of Knowledge in the Iberian and English Imperial Worlds* (Chapel Hill: University of North Carolina Press, 2009).

91. See María Antonia Garcés, *Cervantes in Algiers: A Captive's Tale* (Nashville, Tenn: Vanderbilt University Press, 2002). She sees captivity and trauma as recurrent themes in Cervantes' works and links them to the five years he spent in Algiers.

92. All citations for *Don Quixote* are from Miguel de Cervantes Saavedra, *The Adventures of Don Quixote*, trans. J. M. Cohen (New York: Penguin, 1950).

93. María Antonia Garcés, "Zoraida's Veil: 'The Other Scene' of The Captive's Tale," *Revista de Estudios Hispanicos* 23 (1989): 69.

94. Barbary and other Muslim locales often provided Europeans with opportunities to imagine new social—religious or national—identities. About the English, Burton writes, "Englishmen joined pirate crews raiding Atlantic

and Mediterranean shipping and formed their own, unofficial compacts with local authorities" (*Traffic and Turning*, 23). Also see Matar, *Islam in Britain*, 15. On anxieties about the religious identities of renegades, see Matar, "The Renegade in the Seventeenth-Century English Imagination," *SEL* 33 (1993): 489–505; and Fuchs, *Mimesis and Empire*, 139–63.

95. Miguel de Cervantes, *El Ingenioso Hildago Don Quijote de la Mancha*, ed. Salvador Farjardo and James A. Parr (Ashville, NC: Pegasus Press / University of North Carolina at Ashville, 1998), 336.

96. Deborah Root, "Speaking Christian: Orthodoxy and Difference in Sixteenth-Century Spain," *Representations* 23 (1988): 128. On Arabic being interpreted as a sign of crypto-Islamic faith, also see Consuelo Lopez-Marillos, "Language and Identity in Late Spanish Islam," *Hispanic Review* 63 (1995): 193–210. In 1567, Philip II made it illegal to speak Arabic in Granada. Nonetheless, Arabic was tolerated to varying degrees in different provinces, and some argued that it could be used to proselytize the Moors.

97. Ibid., 128–29.

98. Gracés suggests that this scene illustrates "the preoccupation with the borderline between the Christian and Muslim world," a borderline which Zoraida reveals as permeable (*Cervantes in Algiers*, 206). As Gracés notes, Zoraida's "double" status is further highlighted by her insistence that her name be changed to María, and by the Virgin Mary imagery that surrounds many of her descriptions (214–16). On Zoraida's relation to the Virgin Mary, also see Carroll B. Johnson, *Cervantes and the Material World* (Urbana: University of Illinois Press, 2000), 87–88.

99. William Childres, *Transnational Cervantes* (Toronto: University of Toronto Press, 2006), 178.

100. Ricote in part 2 may be another story, but in part 1 the narrative affirms that Zoraida is a Christian. See Judith A. Whitenack, "Don Quixote and the Romances of Chivalry Once Again: Converted *Paganos* and Enamoured *Magas*," *Cervantes: Bulletin of the Cervantes Society of America* 13 (1993): 71. Nevertheless, as Fuchs argues, "The Captive's Tale" and other Cervantean tales about renegades and Muslim to Christian conversion work within "the historical reality of early seventeenth-century Spain: Moriscos are not welcome, whatever their religion, and all New Christians are suspect" (*Passing for Spain,* 68). On the way in which race works in opposition to Catholic understandings of baptism, see Spiller, *Reading and the History of Race*, 48.

101. Romances were often considered to be "romanish" in Protestant England. See Werth, *The Fabulous Dark Cloister*, 19; and Cooper, *The English Romance in Time*, 38.

102. Frye, *The Secular Scripture*, 24.

103. On medieval English romance and proto-imperial, proto-national identities, see Heng, *Empire of Magic*, esp. 63–113.

104. For synopses, manuscript and printing histories, and overviews of these romances, see the introductions to the tales in *Three Middle English Charlemagne Romances,* ed. Alan Lupack (Kalamazoo, Mich.: Medieval Institute Publications, 1990). Shakespeareans may find the tale of *Otuel and Roland* of particular interest. Otuel (or Otinel) is a Saracen who, after a miraculous encounter that leads him to convert, fights for Charlemagne and eventually marries his daughter. On the possible relation of Othello to Otuel, see Cherrell Guilfoyle, "Othello, Otuel, and the English Charlemagne Romances," *Review of English Studies* 38 (1987): 50–55. Calkin discusses the recurrent presences of Saracens and religious conversion in the Auchinleck manuscript in *Saracens and the Making of English Identity.* She also notes that the presence of Saracens in texts illustrates that medieval English culture grappled with questions of how to incorporate difference (7). She does not note, however, that this is a feature of romance.

105. Citations are from *The King of Tars: Edited from the Auchinleck MS, Advocates' 19.2.1,* ed. Judith Perryman, Middle English Texts 12 (Heidelberg: C. Winter, 1980). Translations to modern English are mine.

106. Heng, *Empire of Magic,* 231.

107. See Lampert, "Race, Periodicity, and the (Neo-) Middle Ages," 406–10. Also see Heng, who notes that the poem "supposes *the normativity of whiteness*" (*Empire of Magic,* 231). Cord J. Whitaker, however, provides an alternative reading. Observing that the sultan's skin changes color before the conversion, he suggests that the transformation provides a metaphor of spiritual blackness inside the white Christian body: "Blackness and whiteness, of the internal and external varieties, can simultaneously cohere in a single being." "Black Metaphors in *The King of Tars,*" *JEGP: The Journal of English and Germanic Philology* 112 (2013): 169–93. Whitaker discusses various instances in medieval writings where black people are intended to be read metaphorically and describes the poem's later complication of the equation between whiteness and spiritual purity.

108. Bruce Holsinger, "The Color of Salvation: Desire, Death, and the Second Crusade in Bernard of Clairvaux's *Sermons on the Song of Songs,*" in *The Tongue of the Fathers: Gender and Ideology in Twelfth-Century Latin,* ed. David Townsend and Andrew Taylor (Philadelphia: University of Pennsylvania Press, 1998), 156–86. Holsinger provides an insightful discussion of the black female body in medieval literature as a metaphor for sinful nature. Also see Spiller, who notes that the poem "tells a story about the congruency of appearance and identity" (*Reading and the History of Race,* 45).

109. Calikin notes a literary tradition of monstrous births to interfaith couples. She suggests that these monstrous births affirm fundamental differences between Christians and heathens (*Saracens and the Making of English Identity,* 103–22).

110. Jane Gilbert, "Putting the Pulp into Fiction: The Lump-Child and its Parents in *The King of Tars*," in *Pulp Fictions of Medieval England,* ed. Nicola McDonald (Manchester: Manchester University Press, 2004), 105.

111. Spiller provides a compelling reading of this scene; she argues that once the lump is transformed into a beautiful white child, romance, a genre that is invested in genealogy and lineage, requires that the child's father become white (*Reading and the History of Race,* 44).

112. Lampert, "Race, Periodicity, and the (Neo-) Middle Ages," 409.

1. *"The Baptiz'd Race"*

1. The epigraphs are from Thomas Cranmer, *A Short Instruction into Christian Religion Being a Catechism Set Forth by Archbishop Cranmer,* ed. Edward Burton (Oxford: Oxford University Press, 1829), 182; James I, *Lepanto* (London, 1603), ln. 10–11.

2. For an overview of baptism as initiation, from the early church, into the Reformation, and into the present, see Maxwell E. Johnson, *The Rites of Christian Initiation: Their Evolution and Interpretation* (Collegeville, MN: Liturgical Press, 2007).

3. For a brief overview of Luther's, Zwingli's, and Calvin's baptismal theologies, see G. R. Evans, *Problems of Authority in the Reformation Debates* (Cambridge: Cambridge University Press, 1992), 143–51. For a more sustained discussion, see Hughes Oliphant Old's *The Shaping of the Reformed Baptismal Rite in the Sixteenth Century* (Grand Rapids, MI: William B. Eerdmans Publishing Co., 1992).

4. On differences among English baptismal theologies, see John Wheelan Riggs, *Baptism in the Reformed Tradition: A Historical and Practical Theology* (Louisville, KY: Westminster John Knox Press, 2002).

5. On race as genealogy and lineage, see Jonathan Burton and Ania Loomba, introduction to *Race in Early Modern England: A Documentary Companion* (New York: Palgrave Macmillan, 2007), 1–36.

6. In Book 4, chapter 15 of *Institutes of the Christian Religion,* which was widely read and translated in Reformation England, Calvin extensively discusses baptism in relation to circumcision; he uses notions of race—as lineage—to justify infant baptism, and asserts that children can be saved without being baptized. That said, these notions actually predate Calvin's influence in England. As Shannon McSheffrey shows, the Lollards had already questioned the necessity of baptism for salvation, positing instead that Christianity is passed from parents to children. See McSheffrey, *Gender and Heresy: Women and Men in Lollard Communities, 1420–1530* (Philadelphia: University of Pennsylvania Press, 1995), 85.

7. Maxwell E. Johnson notes that Calvin's theology of baptism conflicted with the Tertullian maxim (*Rites of Christian Initiation,* 333). He does not consider, however, the racial implications of this theological position.

8. Just as it is now impossible to talk about the "Reformation" since Christopher Haigh's *English Reformations: Religion, Politics and Society Under the Tudors* (Oxford: Oxford University Press, 1993), it is equally impossible to talk about the English Protestant baptismal theology because English Protestants took varying positions on the theology of Luther, Zwingli, Calvin, and others. Thus, attempting to illustrate a codified English understanding of baptism is an exercise in futility. Instead this chapter seeks only to show that the concept of race emerges with some consistency in order to clarify the English Church's doctrine concerning baptism.

9. Tyndale's influence on the English Reformation and on the Church of England's theology has been the cause of some controversy. See Patrick Collinson, "William Tyndale and the Course of the English Reformation," *Reformation* 1 (1996): 72–97 for a useful overview of the problems surrounding tracing Tyndale's influence. Also see Christopher Hill, "Tyndale and His Successors," *Reformation* 1 (1996): 98–112. Although I discuss Tyndale's baptismal theology throughout this chapter, I do not wish to make any overt claims that his theology influenced later theologians in the Church of England. That said, Tyndale's writings were continually published throughout the sixteenth century. Thus, looking at Tyndale is important for establishing that the various ideas about baptism discussed in this chapter were first announced in England by him.

10. Quotations are from William Tyndale, "*A briefe declaration of the Sacraments,*" in *Doctrinal Treatises and Introductions to Different Portions of the Holy Scriptures*, ed. Henry Walter (Cambridge, UK: The University Press for The Parker Society, 1848).

11. Protestant theologies vehemently disagreed among themselves about the efficacy of sacraments: whether they conferred spiritual grace, whether they were merely signs of grace given to those who have faith, or whether they are only miraculously efficacious for the believer. For concise discussions of differences among the sacramental theologies of prominent reformers such as Luther, Zwingli, and Calvin, see Carter Lindberg, *The European Reformations* (Oxford: Blackwell, 1996), 181–91; and Diarmaid MacCulloch's *The Reformation* (New York: Viking, 2004), 240–45.

12. *The boke of common praier, and administracion of the sacramentes, and other rites and ceremonies in the Churche of Englande* (London, 1552), sig. S2r–v.

13. Although the Black Rubric's baptismal service was clearly influenced by the Sarum Rite, unlike its medieval predecessor it incorporates biblical tales of God saving his people through water. The Sarum Rite baptismal service can be found in *Documents of the Baptismal Liturgy*, ed. E. C. Whitaker (1960), third edition revised and edited by Maxwell. E. Johnson (Bristle: The Bath Press for The Society for Promoting Christian Knowledge, 2003), 284–307.

14. Although Luther's impact on the English Reformation has been debated, there may be a Lutheran influence in the Church of England's baptismal liturgy that resides in the implied *fides aliena* that makes baptism effective. In *The Babylonian Captivity of the Church* (1520), Luther argues that the infant is regenerated by baptism because of the faith and prayers of the Church. I quote and discuss this passage later in the chapter. But for discussions of Luther's influence in Reformation England, see Basil Hall, "The Early Rise and Gradual Decline of Lutheranism in England (1520–1600)," in *Reform and Reformation: England and the Continent, c. 1500–c.1750*, ed. Derek Baker (Oxford: Basil Blackwell, 1979), 103–47; Alec Ryrie, "The Strange Death of Lutheran England," *Journal of Ecclesiastical History* 53 (2002): 64–92; and Carl R. Trueman, *Luther's Legacy: Salvation and English Reformers, 1525–1556* (Oxford: Clarendon Press, 1994).

15. In using the story of Noah to explicate baptism, the English service shows a clear Lutheran influence. Luther introduced the comparison between baptism and the flood in what is referred to as "The Flood Prayer" in his *Order of Baptism* (1523).

16. Thomas Aquinas provides a prominent example of a medieval scholastic understanding of the relation between baptism and circumcision. See *The "Summa Theologica of St. Thomas,"* vol. 17, trans. the Fathers of the English Dominican Province (London: Burns, Oats and Washbourne LTD, 1923), esp. 186–194. That said, many Protestant writers prove eager to discuss circumcision in order to illustrate that baptism, as they suggested was the case with circumcision, means nothing if it is not accompanied by faith and understanding.

17. On reformed baptism and typology, see Old, *Shaping of the Reformed Baptismal Rite*, 120–23. According to Old, "The whole idea behind any typological argument is that God works with human beings in an orderly, consistent pattern" (122).

18. Julia Reinhard Lupton, *Citizen Saints: Shakespeare and Political Theology* (Chicago: University of Chicago Press, 2005), 22. Christianity's conflicted relationship to its Jewish heritage is also an important concern for Janet Adelman in *Blood Relations: Christian and Jew in* The Merchant of Venice (Chicago: University of Chicago Press, 2008).

19. Achsah Guibbory, *Christian Identity, Jews, and Israel in the Seventeenth Century* (Oxford: Oxford University Press, 2010), 13. Guibbory does not discuss the circumcision/baptism analogy, however.

20. Although "Anabaptist" was used derisively to label those who rejected infant baptism and rebaptized adults, the term was often applied more generally to those who held what where considered radical Protestant beliefs. See Carrie Euler, "Anabaptism and Anti-Anabaptism in the Early English Reformation: Defining Protestant Heresy and Orthodoxy during the Reign of Edward VI," in *Heresy, Literature, and Politics in Early Modern English Culture,* eds. David Loewenstein and John Marshall (Cambridge: Cambridge University Press, 2006), 40. For a

more general overview of Protestant apologies for infant baptism, see Old, *Shaping of the Reformed Baptismal Rite*, 111–44.

21. On the English Church's theological positioning between Catholicism and Anabaptism, see Old, 111–44, and David Loewenstein and John Marshall, introduction to *Heresy, Literature, and Politics*, 1–10, esp. 6. Also see Euler, "Anabaptism and Anti-Anabaptism in the Early English Reformation."

22. Becon's catechism was written during the reign of Edward VI, but it was published in 1564 as part of *The Works of Thomas Becon*. The repeated publication of Becon's works in the sixteenth and seventeenth centuries illustrates that he was considered an important theologian of the Church of England. Quotations are from *The Catechism of Thomas Becon*, ed. John Ayer (Cambridge, UK: The University Press for the Parker Society, 1844).

23. Thomas Cranmer, "A confutation of unwritten verities" (1584), in *The Miscellaneous Letters and Writings of Thomas Cranmer*, ed. John Edmund Cox (Cambridge, UK: The University Press for The Parker Society, 1846), 60.

24. Alexander Nowell, *A Catechisme, or first Instruction and Learning of Christian Religion* (1570), trans. Thomas Norton (Cambridge, UK: The University Press for The Parker Society, 1853), 209.

25. Seeing baptism as the perfection of circumcision had been a Catholic belief as well. On the medieval Church's understanding of baptism as the perfection of the Jewish rite of circumcision, see Peter Cramer, *Baptism and Change in the Early Middle Ages, c. 200–c. 1150* (Cambridge: Cambridge University Press, 1993). Cramer notes that medieval theologians used the story of Cornelius's conversion by Peter, and Paul's assertion that gentiles do not need to be circumcised to become Christians, to argue that baptism is superior to circumcision (42).

26. Adelman, *Blood Relation*, and James Shapiro, *Shakespeare and the Jews* (New York: Columbia University Press), esp. 167–93.

27. Sharon Achinstein, "John Foxe and the Jews," *Renaissance Quarterly* 54 (2001): 89.

28. John Foxe, *A sermon preached at the christening of a certaine Iew at London by Iohn Foxe* (London, 1578), sig. A1v.

29. Adelman, *Blood Relations*, 116, note 25.

30. This doctrine proves to be wide-reaching; it is also seen in the baptismal theology of "radical" English Puritan sects and in colonial propaganda. The separatists Francis Johnson, for example, argued in *A brief treatise conteyning some grounds and reasons, against two errours of the Anabaptists* (Amsterdam, 1609) that children should be baptized "Because the children of beleevers are holy, and are Abrahams seed, and heirs by promise of the kingdome of heaven and eternal blessedness" (sig. A6r). In Johnson we see a complete substitution of Christian for Jew, such that "children of beleevers," of Christians, are now the descendents of Abraham. The pervasiveness of the English view of themselves as the new

chosen race may also be seen in its appearance outside theological discussions, especially in seventeenth-century English colonial writing. In *A Plain Pathway to Plantations* (1624), for example, Rev. Richard Eburne comments on his reading of English colonial writing: "I do thereby after a sort, as blessed Moses from Mount Nebo (Deuteronomy 34), view and behold with the eyes of my mind those goodly countries which there God doth offer to give unto us and our seed" (quoted in Paul Stevens, "'Leviticus Thinking' and the Rhetoric of Early Modern Colonialism," *Criticism* 34 [1993]: 451–52). Stevens discusses just how often English colonialists figured themselves as the Jews of the Old Testament.

31. The Swiss theologian Heinrich Bullinger, whose works were required reading for English clerics, argued for the baptism of infants not because they have faith but because God promised to be the god of Christian seed: "But though wilt say, the infants of Christians, which are to be baptized, believed not. I grant. Nor more did the infants of the Jews believe; which nevertheless were circumcised, and were in league with God, and made partakers of all good gifts" (Heinrich Bullinger, *The Decades of Henry Bullinger*, ed. Thomas Harding [Cambridge: the University Press for The Parker Society, 1849], 323). On Calvin's rejection of infant faith, see Riggs, *Baptism in the Reformed Tradition*, 68. After Becon's time, William Perkins, like Calvin and Bullinger, argued that infants do not have faith. Also like them, Perkins argued that the children of Christian parents were nevertheless included in the covenant of grace. See Perkins's "A golden chaine, or the description of theologie" (1592), in *The Work of William Perkins*, ed. Ian Breward (Appleford, UK: The Sutton Courtenay Press, 1970), 219–20. Perkins, a double predestinarian, also believed that infants could be reprobates (251).

32. Similarly, Muslim faith could be seen as a matter of race. See my discussion in chapter 4 of Meredith Hanmer's *The baptizing of a Turke*.

33. The position that the children of Christians ought to be baptized because they have faith and are the seed of the faithful was also articulated by John Whitgift, Archbishop of Canterbury during the last twenty years of Elizabeth's reign. Although his defense of pedobaptism against the Anabaptists is very similar to Becon's, Whitgift adds to the argument a better understanding of who Becon called the "household of faith," the parents of "the children of the faithful." In *The defense of the aunsvvere to the Admonition against the replie of T.C. By Iohn VVhitgift Doctor of Diuinitie* (1574), Whitgift responded to Thomas Cartwright's *Replye to an Answere of Dr Whitgifte* (1573), in which Cartwright critiqued Whitgift's earlier *A Second Admonition to the Parliament* (1573). In the discussion of infant baptism, we learn that the "household of faith" is more inclusive than we might have otherwise assumed. He argues that children should not be barred from baptism because of the impiety or erroneous beliefs of their parents:

> What if the parents be of evil behavior? what if it be the child of a drunkard, or of an harlot? what if the parents be papists? what if they be heretics? what if they err in some point or other in matters of faith? shall not their children be baptized? . . . May not a wicked father have a good son? may not a papist or heretic have a believing son? will you seclude for the parent's sake (being himself baptized) his seed from baptism? (135)

Putting aside the fact that drunkards, harlots, papists, and heretics all appear to be of the same faith in Whitgift's rhetoric, the category of the "faithful"—whose children are counted among the holy—is quite inclusive. In Whitgift baptism is conceived of as a rite belonging to the seed of the baptized; children have a right to be baptized if their parents were baptized, regardless of the beliefs or impiety of their parents. The work of baptism thus seems to operate beyond that of the spiritual state of parents who may indeed be out of God's grace because of heresy and sin. Although parents may be outside of God's favor, their children nevertheless are included in the covenant God established through baptism.

34. John Smyth, *The character of the beast* (Middelburg, 1609), sig. K2v.

35. Ibid., sig. I3v, my emphasis.

36. That this remained the common view well into the seventeenth century is illustrated in the work of the English Catholic John Brerely, *Sainct Austines Religion* (London, 1620): "It be now an ordinary opinion among Protestants that Children borne of faithful parents dying without baptisme may be saved" (71).

37. John Jewel, *The Works of John Jewel*, vol. 3, ed. John Ayre (Cambridge, UK: The University Press for The Parker Society), 366.

38. Ibid., 371.

39. Quoted by Jewel, *The Works of John Jewel*, 370.

40. John Calvin, *Institutes of the Christian Religion*, vol. 2., trans. Henry Beveridge (Grand Rapids, MI: Wm. B. Eerdmans Publishing Co., 1966), 531–32.

41. Ibid., 526–27.

42. Riggs, *Baptism in the Reformed Tradition*, 60.

43. Calvin, *Institutes,* 976.

44. Riggs discusses Calvin's defense of infant baptism in relation to his developing theory of predestination: "Calvin knew . . . that election into the visible covenant may not have meant ultimate predestination to salvation by God's decree, and by 1599, Calvin realized that he had to speak further about election into God's covenant because there were some who were born into the covenant who might not have received the second, secret election" (*Baptism in the Reformed Tradition*, 65). As far as I can tell, English theologians are never as explicit as Calvin is here, leaving room for the possibility that "seed of election" is a consequence of birth.

45. John Calvin, *Sermons of M. John Calvin vpon the Epistle of Sainct Paule to the Galatians* (London, 1574), sig. L7r–v.

46. Aquinas states that the third necessary sacrament is Orders, for the maintenance of the church and its sacraments.

47. Aquinas defended lay baptism and baptism by women for just this reason (129–31). Nevertheless, midwives were required to take an oath that they would correctly perform, among other things, the baptismal ritual. See Doreen Evendeen, *The Midwives of Seventeenth-Century London* (Cambridge: Cambridge University Press, 2000), 27–33. Also see David Cressy, *Birth, Marriage, and Death: Ritual, Religion and the Life-Cycle in Tudor and Stuart England* (Oxford: Oxford University Press, 1997), 63–70.

48. This residual anxiety may be seen in the fact that ministers who negligently allowed infants to die without baptism were often brought before church officials. Such cases are discussed by Marshall, "(Re)Defining the English Reformation," 204; Cressy, *Birth, Marriage, and Death*, 115–16; Judith Maltby, *Prayer Book and People in Elizabethan and Early Stuart England* (Cambridge: Cambridge University Press, 2000), 52–56; and Felicity Heal, *Reformation in Britain and Ireland* (Oxford: Oxford University Press, 2003), 452–53.

49. Despite Aquinas's critique of them, forced baptisms of Jews were performed well into the eighteenth century. See Marina Caffiero, *Forced Baptism: Histories of Jews, Christians, and Converts in Papal Rome*, trans. Lydia G. Cochrane (Berkeley: University of California Press, 2012).

50. In Aquinas, however, maybe Jewishness makes a difference. When the parents are Jewish, Aquinas argues that the desires of the parents have greater power—though still not so much that baptism has no effect. The difference Aquinas articulates may indeed point to a proto-racial thinking concerning Jews in particular that was already present in the medieval Church, a racialism that grows more pronounced in English Protestant discussions of baptism.

51. Martin Luther, "The Babylonian Captivity of the Church," trans. A. T. W. Steinhäuser, in *Luther's Works*, vol 36, ed. Abdel Ross Wentz (Philadelphia, PA: Fortress Press, 1955), 73.

52. William Hubbock, *An apologie of infants in a sermon* (London, 1594), sig. B5v.

53. Quoted in Cressy, *Birth, Marriage, and Death*, 115. Bancroft was Archbishop of Canterbury after Whitgift, from 1604–1610. Cressy also notes that later Laudian ministers under Charles I took the more Roman Catholic view that nonbaptized infants were damned (116).

54. Cressy, *Birth, Marriage, and Death*, 114.

55. John Hooper, *A Brief and Clear Confession of the Christian Faith*, in *Later Writings of Bishop Hooper: Together with His Letters and Other Pieces*, ed. Charles Nevinson (Cambridge, UK: The University Press for The Parker Society, 1852), 47.

56. Matthew Dimmock, *New Turkes: Dramatizing Islam and the Ottomans in Early Modern England* (Aldershot, UK: Ashgate), 68–70.

57. *The homilie against disobedience and wylfull rebellion* (London, 1570), sig. H3r.

58. Thomas More, *Responsio ad Lutherum,* in *The Complete Works of St. Thomas More,* ed. John M. Headley, vol. 5 (New Haven: Yale University Press, 1969), 221. Both the Latin and the English translation come from this edition.

59. More, *Responsio ad Lutherum,* 223.

60. See the 1570 preface to John Bale's *The Image of Both Churches.* Bale compares Catholics to Muslims, emphasizing that although Muslims believe incorrectly, they are still virtuous and pious. Also see Benedict S. Robinson's "Returning to Egypt: 'The Jew,' 'the Turk,' and the English Republic," in *Milton and the Jews,* ed. Douglas A. Brooks (Cambridge: Cambridge University Press, 2008), 178–99, in which he discusses the connections Protestants often made between Catholics, Jews, and Turks.

2. Ovidian Baptism in Book 2 of The Faerie Queene

1. There is a long tradition of reading this episode as questioning both the ability of baptism to erase original sin and to produce spiritual regeneration. A. C. Hamilton, looking to Spenser's letter to Raleigh, argued long ago that the nature of sin and spiritual regeneration through baptism is "the whole subject" of Book 2 ("A Theological Reading of *The Faerie Queene, Book II,*" *ELH* 25 [1958]: 155–162, esp. 155). In addition to Hamilton, see Alastair Fowler, "The Image of Mortality: 'The Faerie Queene,' II.i–ii," *The Huntington Library Quarterly* 24 (1961): 91–110; Carol V. Kaske, "The Bacchus Who Wouldn't Wash: *Faerie Queeen, Book II.i–ii,*" *Renaissance Quarterly* 29 (1976): 159-209; Kaske, *Spenser and Biblical Poetics* (Ithaca: Cornell University Press, 1999), chapter 4, 98–57; and Harold Weatherby, *Mirrors of Celestial Grace: Patristic Theology in Spenser's Allegory* (Toronto: University of Toronto Press, 1994), 172–79. Lewis H. Miller, Jr., however, reads Spenser's turn to Ovid as a rejection of the theological concerns that dominate Book I in "A Secular Reading of *The Faerie Queene, Book II,*" *English Literary History* 33 (1966):154–69.

2. The quotation is from Edmund Spenser, *The Faerie Queene,* ed. A. C. Hamilton (New York: Longman, 1977). All quotations of *The Faerie Queene* are from this edition.

3. Following Stephen Greenblatt's reading of the Bower of Bliss in *Renaissance Self-Fashioning,* locating Book 2 in the New World is now commonplace. See chapter 4 of Stephen Greenblatt's *Renaissance Self-fashioning: From More to Shakespeare* (Chicago: University of Chicago Press, 1980). In addition to Greenblatt, see Roland Greene's "A Primer of Spenser's Worldmaking: Alterity in the Bower of Bliss," in *Worldmaking Spenser: Explorations in the Early Modern Age,* eds. Patrick Cheney and Lauren Silberman (Lexington: University of Kentucky Press, 2000), 9–31; and David Read's *Temperate Conquests: Spenser and the Spanish New World* (Detroit: Wayne State University Press, 2000). As I will

show in this chapter, however, New World foreignness is not the only kind of
difference with which the poem engages. The poem also looks east through its
engagement with Ariosto's and Tasso's epic romances.

4. *The Faerie Queene* seems to operate through a poetics of absence on
numerous levels. See Susanne L. Wofford, "*The Faerie Queene,* Books I–III,"
in *The Cambridge Companion to Spenser,* ed. Andrew Hadfield (Cambridge:
Cambridge University Press, 2001), 107–12.

5. Armida's final words in the poem, "*Ecco l'ancilla tua: d'essa a tuo senno / —gli
disse—e le fia legge il cenno,*" are somewhat ambiguous, but they strongly suggest
conversion given the fact that her words are a response to Rinaldo's spoken
desire that "*al Cielo / ch'a la tua mente alcun de' raggi suoi / del paganesmo dissolvesse il
velo*" (Torqarto Tasso, *Gerusalemme liberata, Torquarto Tasso: Poesie* [Milan:
Riccardo Ricciadri Editore, 1964], 20.136 & 135). At the very least, Armida is
reconciled with Rinaldo.

6. Four times in Book 3, canto 3, Merlin explicitly lists Britomart and
Artegall's progeny as fighting "paynim" forces, and he tells Britomart that
Artegall in particular is ultimately to defeat the "forein Paynims, which invade
thy land" (3.3.27). These foreign forces are not explicitly denoted as Muslim
here, but "paynim" most often refers to a Saracen knight in romance. Spenser
shows that he draws from these associations in Book 2: Arthur, we learn, "hath
to Paynim knights wrought great distresse, / And thousand Sar'zins foully done
to dye" (2.8.18).

7. Unless otherwise noted, English translations of Ovid are from *Metamorphoses,*
trans. Charles Martin (New York: W. W. Norton & Company, 2004). The Latin
is from Ovid's *Metamorphosis,* ed. G.P. Goold, vol. 1 (London: Loeb Classical
Library, 1976).

8. Leonard Barkan, *The God's Made Flesh: Metamorphosis and the Pursuit of
Paganism* (New Haven: Yale University Press, 1990), 23.

9. Indeed, there are too many to name here. David Lee Miller, however,
notes this tradition in *The Poem's Two Bodies: The Poetics of the 1590 Faerie Queene*
(Princeton: Princeton University Press, 1988), 12, and there have been many
other readings of this type since Miller's study. Miller, however, nicely articulates
this mode of reading *The Faerie Queene*: "the poem, the world in the poem, and
the world that the poem is in share a common ontology that is itself allegorical.
It follows from this assumption that a certain formal reciprocity among poet,
protagonist and reader, or between the represented action and the act of
representation, must be a constant and integral dimension of the allegory, part of
its mirroring system" (13). For readings of this type that have particularly
influenced my reading, see, in addition to Miller, Susanne L. Wofford's readings
of *The Faerie Queene* in *The Choice of Achilles: The Ideology of Figure in Epic*
(Stanford: Stanford University Press, 1992), and, of course, Harry Berger's *The
Allegorical Temper: Vision and Reality in Book 2 of Spenser's* The Faerie Queene (New

Haven: Yale University Press, 1957). Also see Judith H. Anderson's more recent study, *Reading the Allegorical Intertext: Chaucer, Spenser, Shakespeare, Milton* (New York: Fordham University Press, 2008). On Spenser's treatment of the sacraments, see in particular *Reformation* 6 (2001/2002), which contains a set of essays by Margaret Christian, John N. King, James Schiavoni, H. L. Weatherby, Carol V. Kaske, Clinton Allen Brand, Kenneth Borris, Darryl Gless, and Anne Lake Prescott from a roundtable on Spenser and the sacraments at the 1998 Sixteenth Century Studies Conference.

10. John Jewel, *The Works of John Jewel, Bishop of Salisbury,* vol. 2, ed. John Ayre (Cambridge, UK: The University Press for the Parker Society, 1847), 593–94.

11. Maureen Quilligan, *The Language of Allegory: Defining the Genre* (Ithaca: Cornell University Press, 1979), 46. On allegory and *allegoresis,* also see Quilligan, *Milton's Spenser: The Poetics of Reading* (Ithaca: Cornell University Press, 1983), 24–26.

12. To be sure, and as it has been duly noted, theological concerns about the relation between signs and truth have close affinities with the structuralist and poststructuralist linguistic theories of Ferdinand de Saussure, Roland Barthes, and Jacques Derrida. For poststructuralist readings of Spenser's use of signs, see Jonathan Goldberg, *Endlesse Worke: Spenser and the Structures of Discourse* (Baltimore: Johns Hopkins University Press, 1981); and Åke Bergvall, "The Theology of the Sign: St. Augustine and Spenser's Legend of Holiness" *SEL: Studies in English Literature, 1500–1900* (1993): 21–42. But unlike these studies, I do not arrest Spenser's linguistic concerns from his purposeful engagement with theological matters.

13. Regina M. Schwartz, *Sacramental Poetics at the Dawn of Secularism: When God Left the World* (Stanford: Stanford University Press, 2008), 8.

14. Schwartz reads sacramental poetics as much more efficacious in calling forth things that are absent than I do, perhaps because Spenser does not figure into her conclusions, which are based in readings of Shakespeare, Donne, Herbert, and Milton. Additionally, Schwartz does not fully consider the theological nuances concerning the relationship between earthly signs and their respective spiritual graces.

15. Spenser, "A Letter of the Authors," 737.

16. On the etymology of the word, see Fletcher, *Allegory,* 2, note 1.

17. George Puttenham, *The Arte of English Poesy* (1591), eds. Gladys Doidge Willcock and Alice Walker (Cambridge: Cambridge University Press, 1936), 186.

18. See Wofford, *The Choice of Achilles,* 226–27. Also see James Nohrnberg, who argues that allegories work and indeed come into being through principles of differentiation and othering between "the figure and its significance" (*The Analogy of "The Faerie Queene"* [Princeton: Princeton University Press, 1992], ix and 101–2).

19. Angus Fletcher, *Allegory: The Theory of a Symbolic Mode* (Ithaca: Cornell University Press, 1964), 222. Fletcher also notes, "At the heart of any allegory will be found this conflict of authorities. One idea will be pitted against another, its opposite" (22). Here, Fletcher is discussing the way an author may use allegory to avoid censorship; the conflict is between the allegorist and his or her political opponents, even as a conflict is enacted in the very structure of the mode. On the contradictory nature of allegory, also see Anderson, *Reading the Allegorical Intertext*, 7.

20. Berger, *The Allegorical Temper*, 22.

21. Ibid., 145–46.

22. On the difference between the original and the reflections in the mirrors announced in Spenser's proems, see Wofford, *The Choice of Achilles,* 227. She goes on to note that Spenser's allegorical structure "tells (at least) two stories at once, and cannot reconcile or unite them" (235).

23. See Fletcher, who notes that allegory seeks to turn images "into something other (*allos*) than what the open and direct statement tells the reader" (*Allegory,* 2).

24. Michael Taussig, *Mimesis and Alterity: A Particular History of the Senses* (New York: Routledge, 1993), 52–53. Taussig extends James G. Frazer's theory of "contagious magic" in *The Golden Bough: A Study of Magic and Religion,* abridged, ed. Robert Frazier (1890, New York: Oxford University Press, 1995), 37–45. Fletcher makes a connection between contagious magic and allegory, suggesting that both work through metonymy (196), and that this is especially true in Christian allegory: "Contagion is the primary symbol of Christian allegory since that allegory is primarily concerned with sin and redemption" (*Allegory,* 199).

25. "Thirty-Nine Articles," in *Religion and Society in Early Modern England: A Source Book*, eds. David Cressy and Lori Anne Ferrell (New York: Routledge, 1996), 62.

26. Ibid., 66–67.

27. David Cressy, *Birth, Marriage, and Death: Ritual, Religion and the Life-Cycle in Tudor and Stuart England* (Oxford: Oxford University Press, 1997), 110 (his emphasis).

28. John Frith, *A myrroure or lokynge glasse wherin you may beholde the sacramente of baptisme described* (London, 1548), sig.B4v–C1r.

29. See Janet Adelman, *Blood Relations: Christian and Jew in* The Merchant of Venice (Chicago: University of Chicago Press, 2008), 79; and Joshua Trachtenberg, *The Devil and the Jews: The Medieval Conception of the Jew and its Relation to Modern Antisemitism* (New York: Harper & Row, 1966), 48–49. Trachtenberg notes, however, that it was also thought that the smell left after conversion because Christians were supposedly cleaner than Jews.

30. This distrust of the sincerity of conversions is very similar to the situation in Spain that prevailed at the time of the expulsion of *moriscos* in 1609,

very much against the wishes of some parts of the church hierarchy that saw them as Christians.

31. Patricia Crawford, *Blood, Bodies, and Families in Early Modern England* (Harlow, UK: Pearson/Longman, 2004), 114. Adelman also noted the importance of blood as determining race in *Blood Relations*.

32. Philip Sidney, "The Defense of Poetry," in *Sir Philip Sidney: Selected Poetry and Prose,* ed. Robert Kimbrough (Madison: University of Wisconsin Press, 1983), 109.

33. Michael C. Schoenfeldt, *Bodies and Selves in Early Modern England: Physiology and Inwardness in Spenser, Shakespeare, Herbert, and Milton* (Cambridge: Cambridge University Press, 1999), 40–41. Schoenfeldt provides a persuasive reading of the spiritual significance of bodily temperance.

34. Consequently, the blackness inherited by Ham's decedents is not unlike the blackness of the Ethiope that cannot be turned white.

35. See Benjamin Braude, "The Sons of Noah and the Construction of Ethnic and Geographical Identities in the Medieval and Early Modern Periods," *William and Mary Quarterly* 54 (1997): 103–42.

36. George Best, *A true discourse of the late voyages of discoverie, for finding of a passage to Cathaya by the Northwest, under the conduct of Martin Forbisher Generall: Divided into three Bookes* (London: The Argonaut Press, 1938), 34–35.

37. William Perkins, "A golden chaine, or the description of theologie" (1592), in *The Work of William Perkins,* ed. Ian Breward (Appleford, UK: The Sutton Courtenay Press, 1970), 192.

38. See Benedict Robinson, *Islam and Early Modern English Literature: The Politics of Romance from Spenser to Milton* (New York: Palgrave, 2007), in which he notes the Islamic status of the brothers and Spenser's engagement with Islamic otherness throughout *The Faerie Queene* (40).

39. Nabil Matar, *Turks, Moors, and Englishmen in the Age of Discovery* (New York: Columbia University Press, 1999), 13.

40. See Christopher Ivic, "Spenser and the Bounds of Race," *Genre* 32 (1999): 141–173; and Jean Feerick, "Spenser, Race, and Ireland," *English Literary Renaissance* 32 (2002): 85–117. Feerick compellingly argues that we can read the two brothers as Irish, especially since wrath and lust were also seen as Irish characteristics. Even so, I feel that their Saracen identity also needs to be considered.

41. See, for example, Gordon Teskey, *Allegory and Violence* (Ithaca: Cornell University Press, 1996), 175 and 187; Quilligan, *The Language of Allegory,* 46–51, and 166–72.

42. On the political uses of the polysemy inherent in allegory, see Kenneth Borris, *Allegory and Epic in English Renaissance Literature* (Cambridge: Cambridge University Press, 2000), 168–77; and Wofford, *Choice of Achilles,* 220.

43. Maurice Evans, "The Fall of Guyon," *ELH* 28 (1961): 216.

44. For example, see Kaske, "The Bacchus Who Wouldn't Wash," 208; Lauren Silberman, "*The Faerie Queene*, Book II and the Limitations of Temperance," *Modern Language Studies* 17 (1987): 12; and Wofford, *The Choice of Achilles*, 248–49.

45. The Palmer's assertion may be validated by the reemergence of a classical *topos* in the Renaissance that understood all waters as springing from a common source. See David Quint's *Origin and Originality in Renaissance Literature: Versions of the Source* (New Haven: Yale University Press, 1983), esp. 149–66, where Quint argues that this topos is central to Spenser's allegorical structuring of *The Faerie Queene*.

46. Accounts of magical waters often appeared in European travel narratives and in English lore. The origins and myths of English magical wells are catalogued in an old book, R. C. Hope's *The Legendary Lore of the Holy Wells of England* (London, 1893).

Additionally, as the water fails to change both Ruddymane's physical and spiritual state (his hands are still stained and inward infection remains), Spenser both questions the efficacy of baptismal waters and intervenes in a point of controversy between Anglicans and Puritans. In "A view of Popish abuses yet remaining in the English Church" (1572), we see a clear picture of how Puritans viewed the Church of England's sacrament. They believed that the ritual was still infused with Catholic superstitions: "The public baptism, that also is full of childish and superstitious toys. First in the prayer they say that God by the baptism of Jesus Christ did sanctify the flood Jordan, and all other waters, to the mystical washing away of sin, attributing that to the sign which is proper to the work of God in the blood of Christ, as though virtue were in water, to wash away sin" ("A View of Popish Abuses Yet Remaining in the English Church," in *Religion and Society in Early Modern England: A Source Book,* eds. David Cressy and Lori Anne Ferrell [New York: Routledge, 1996], 85). The notion that the Church of England, according to these Puritan writers, considers "all other waters" (meaning that not only the water of the river Jordan had these powers but the water in churches around the world has it as well—and not through baptism itself but through God's power in choosing to give the waters these powers at the time of Jesus' baptism) to have "mystical" powers comes surprisingly close to the words of Spenser's Palmer, that "In euery fountaine, and in euery lake" are "secrete vertues . . . infusd." And it may also call to mind the medieval practice of using water from magical wells in baptism. On this practice, see Keith Thomas, *Religion and the Decline of Magic* (New York: Charles Scribner's Sons, 1971), 48. "A view of Popish abuses" also suggests that despite the official theology of the "Thirty-Nine Articles," some Puritans felt that the English Church still believed in the power of sacramental water to wash away sin.

47. Ovid is careful to leave it unclear whether Daphne assents or not to Apollo's use of her; she bows her crown in assent, or *seems* to do so. Ovid makes

it clear that we can no longer know her consciousness and that all interpretations of her have now become projections onto her by Apollo or the reader.

48. See Cora Fox, who argues that Ovid provided a primary means for articulating female emotion in early Modern England in *Ovid and the Politics of Emotion in Elizabethan England* (New York: Palgrave, 2008).

49. See Barkan's reading of the Narcissus and Echo myth (*The Gods Made Flesh*, 51). Also see Wofford's reading of the Daphne and Apollo myth ("Epics and the Politics of the Origin Tale," in *Epic Traditions in the Contemporary World: The Poetics of Community,* eds. Margaret Beissinger, Jane Tylus and Susanne Wofford (Berkeley: University of California Press, 1999), 246.

50. Spenser is fond of punning on the word "dismay." When Florimell sees the Hyena—"That feeds of womens flesh, as others feede on gras" (3.7.22.9)— kill her horse, she sees what the Hyena would have done to her and "she was dismayd" (3.7.25.1). Her emotional response registers the threat against her virginity. Also, when the Blatant Beast seizes Serena in Book 6, Calidore and Calipine "Hastily starting up, like men dismayd, / Ran after fast to reskue the distressed mayde" (6.3.24). Also see Quilligan, *The Language of Allegory,* 25–85, where she notes the punning is a defining characteristic of allegory in general, Spenser's in particular.

51. Wofford, *The Choice of Achilles,* 301.

52. Kaske, *Spenser and Biblical Poetics,* 166.

53. For example, see N. I. Matar, "The Renegade in English Seventeenth-Century Imagination," *SEL: Studies in English Literature* 30 (1993): 489–505; Barbara Fuchs, *Mimesis and Alterity: The New World, Islam and European Identities* (Cambridge: Cambridge University Press, 2001), 154–63; and Dennis Britton, "Religious Conversion and Circumcision as Theater," in *Religion and Drama in Early Modern England*, eds. Jane Hwang Degenhardt and Elizabeth Williamson (Aldershot, UK: Ashgate, 2011), 71–86.

54. John Guillory, *Poetic Authority: Spenser, Milton and Literary History* (New York: Columbia University Press, 1983), 31.

55. Ibid., 32.

56. Kaske, "The Bacchus Who Wouldn't Wash," 208. Silberman is much more critical of the Palmer and describes him this way: "The Palmer is the simple-minded exegete who directs Guyon away from the stuff of human experience" ("*The Faerie Queene*, Book II and the Limitations of Temperance," 12). She argues that Spenser criticizes the Palmer's readings that attempt to privilege classical temperance's ability to provide solutions in a fallen world.

57. Teskey, *Allegory and Violence,* 156. On the longstanding debate and the romantic legacy, see Fletcher, *Allegory,* 13–18; Jeremy Tambling, *Allegory* (New York: Routledge, 2010), 81–84 and 109–77; and Teskey, *Allegory and Violence,* 149–56.

58. Tambling, *Allegory,* 178.

59. Wofford, "Epics and the Politics of Origin Tales," 247.

60. Anderson, *Reading the Allegorical Intertext*, 7.

61. In her study of Spenser's uses of the Hermaphroditus myth in Book III, Silberman argues that Spenser uses Ovid's myth to speak to the problems of knowledge and misreading—Hermphroditus allegorizes his sexual experience with Salmacis: "Ovid offers a myth of sexual identity in which the formal definition of manhood is set in paradoxical opposition to the active experience of it. Ovid's story presents a hermeneutical gap between a character's understanding of his own experience and what the narrator of that experience conveys to the reader" (Lauren Silberman, "The Hermaphrodite and the Metamorphosis of Spenserian Allegory," *English Literary Renaissance* 17 [1987]: 211. Silberman also argues that we see a shift in Spenserian allegory from Book I to Book III: In Book I, allegory reveals divine truth, while in Book III Spenser is concerned with human understanding and how to make meaning. In "*The Faerie Queene*, Book II and the Limits of Temperance," she argues that Book 2 marks the shift between the kinds of reading in Book 1 and Book 3.

62. Syrith Pugh, *Spenser and Ovid* (Aldershot, UK: Ashgate, 2005), 48–52 and 119–20.

63. See Chapter 5 of Daniel Javitch, *Proclaiming a Classic: The Canonization of Orlando Furioso* (Princeton: Princeton University Press), 65–71. The connection between the *Metamorphoses* and the *Furioso* became so entwined that, as Javitch goes on to note, Italians began to translate Ovid's poem in Octava Rima, the verse form of *Orlando Furioso*.

64. Book 10 provides a clear example of this, as the stories of Ganymede, Pygmalion, Myrrha, and Venus and Adonis, among others, are embedded within the story and song of Orpheus.

65. Especially in Spenser studies, Ovid is often set against Virgil. See, for example, Theresa M. Krier, *Gazing on Secret Sights: Spenser, Classical Imitation and the Decorums of Vision* (Ithaca: Cornell University Press, 1990), esp. 41–65; and Pugh's *Spenser and Ovid,* in which she argues that Spenser systematically uses Ovid to critique Virgilian epic. David Scott Wilson-Okamura, however, argues against this common reading in "Errors about Ovid and Romance," *Spenser Studies* 23 (2008): 215–34.

66. Ovid does this by unearthing the kinds of violence that such projects attempt to obscure. Wofford proposes in the context of discussing the *Metamorphoses* as a tale about origins, "One way to read these stories of origin, then, is to consider to what extent they are narratives about the naturalization of force or violence—to what extent they are stories in which a sudden, revolutionary, and instantaneous act of force is made to seem a natural event" ("Epics and the Politics of the Origin Tale," 244). Ovid continually reminds his readers of the violence and force behind "natural events."

67. See John Watkins, *The Specter of Dido: Spenser and Virgilian Epic* (New Haven: Yale University Press, 1995), 114.

68. Earlier criticism that was most concerned with the theology of baptism in Book II, which I cited earlier, was largely unconcerned with how such readings might affect how we understand the conclusion of Book II.

69. Arthur Golding, *The. xv. Bookes of P. Ouidius Naso, entyluted Metamorphoses, translated oute of Latin into English meeter, by Arthur Golding Gentleman, A work very pleasaunt and delectable* (London, 1567), in *Shakespeare's Ovid,* ed. W.H.D. Rouse (Carbondale: Southern Illinois University Press, 1961), 14.463.

70. Ibid., 14.468–72.

71. Guillory, *Poetic Authority,* 28.

72. Patricia Parker notes the threat that *carpe diem* lyric posses for Guyon in his encounters with both Acrasia and Phaedria in "The Progress of Phaedria's Bower: Spenser to Coleridge," *ELH* 40 (1973): 372–97; and in "Suspended Instruments: Lyric and Power in the Bower of Bliss," *Literary Fat Ladies: Rhetoric Gender, Property* (London: Methuen, 1987), 54–66, Parker connects the impulses of lyric to romance deferral. Also see Wendy Beth Hyman, "Seizing Flowers in Spenser's Bower and Garden," *English Literary Renaissance* 37 (2007): 193–214.

73. Maureen Quilligan, *Milton's Spenser: The Poetics of Reading* (Ithaca: Cornell University Press, 1983), 66.

74. Darryl J. Gless, *Interpretation and Theology in Spenser* (Cambridge: Cambridge University Press, 1994), 186.

75. See Wofford's explication of Grill: "Letting '*Grill* be *Grill*' rather than anything else . . . is a radically anti-allegorical step" (*The Choice of Achilles,* 305).

76. Watkins, *The Specter of Dido,* 137.

77. Ibid., 114.

78. On this episode seeking to establish Elizabeth's "proto-racial" identity, see Ivic, 150–55.

79. See Fox's discussion of Britomart's potentially dangerous Ovidian desire (*Ovid and the Politics of Emotion,* 76–77).

80. In terms of incest, Mary Douglas's now-classic reading of Leviticus shows that incest, like other biblical abominations, blurs clear categorical distinctions: "Holiness means keeping distinct categories of creation. It therefore involves correct definition, discrimination and order. Under this head all the rules of sexual morality exemplify holiness. Incest and adultery (Lev. XVII, 6–20) are against holiness" (*Purity and Danger: An Analysis of Concept of Pollution and Taboo* [New York: Routledge, 2002], 67). On Book 3's obsession with incest, see Kent R. Lenholf, "Incest and Empire in *The Faerie Queene*" *ELH* 73 (2006): 215–43; Miller, *The Poem's Two Bodies,* 278–81; Nohrnberg, *The Analogy of "The Faerie Queene,"* 436, and Maureen Quilligan, *Incest and Agency in Elizabethan England* (Philadelphia: University of Pennsylvania Press, 2005), chapter 5, 134–63.

81. That said, as Lenholf has convincingly shown, Book 3 does not completely reject incest. He argues that "the imperialist logic underpinning the epic is linked to an intense fear of miscegenation that, in turn, [it] privileges endogamous relations as a way of warding off foreign invasion and contamination. For Spenser, incest becomes a positive practice, one that ensures national and individual purity" ("Incest and Empire in *The Faerie Queene*," 216).

82. Fox, *Ovid and the Politics of Emotion*, 59.

83. Radigund is certainly a foreigner as an Amazon, but she may also be linked with an eastern identity. A.C. Hamilton notes in the Longman edition of *The Faerie Queene*, "The name may derive from the valorous Persian princess, Rhodogune, in Plutarch" (555, stanza 33, note 3).

3. Infidel Texts and Errant Sexuality: Translation, Reading, and Conversion in Harington's Orlando Furioso

1. William Tyndale, *The Pentateuch*, ed. F. F. Bruce (Carbondale: Southern Illinois University Press, 1967), 295. Also see Tiffany Jo Werth, who discusses Tyndale's conflicting treatment of allegory (*The Fabulous Dark Cloister: Romance in England after the Reformation* [Baltimore, MD: Johns Hopkins University Press, 2011], 55).

2. Stephen Greenblatt, *Renaissance Self-Fashioning from More to Shakespeare* (Chicago: University of Chicago Press, 1980), 102.

3. William Tyndale, *The exposition of the fyrste, seconde, and thyrde canonical epistles of S. Jhon* (London, 1538), sig. A4v.

4. On the Protestant rejection of medieval Catholic hermeneutics, see Ian Green, *Print and Protestantism in Early Modern England* (Oxford: Oxford University Press, 2000), 105. Green also notes that while Protestants rejected medieval hermeneutical practices, they did not reject typological readings that allowed the Old Testament to be understood as prefiguring the New Testament. Thus, what we actually see in the Reformation is a desire to distinguish "good" modes of figurative reading from "bad" ones.

5. "Thirty-Nine Articles," in *Religion and Society in Early Modern England: A Source Book*, eds. by David Cressy and Lori Anne Ferrell (New York: Routledge, 1996), 65.

6. Richard Helgerson, *Forms of Nationhood: The Elizabethan Writing of England* (Chicago: University of Chicago Press, 1992). This is an overarching argument of Helgerson's book, but especially relevant here is his discussion of Spenser and English versification in chapter 1, 21–62.

7. On the popularity of the poem in England, see Miranda Johnson-Haddad, "Englishing Ariosto: *Orlando Furioso* at the Court of Elizabeth I," *Comparative Literature Studies* 31 (1994): 323–50. To see how frequently Ariosto's name appears

on booksellers' lists and library inventories, see John L. Lievsay, *The Englishman's Italian Books 1500–1700* (Philadelphia: University of Pennsylvania Press, 1969).

8. There is a critical tradition of reading Harington's moralizing allegories as parody, but I follow T. G. A. Nelson's argument that the paratextual materials indeed produce a more earnest desire to instruct the reader; see his "Sir John Harington and the Renaissance Debate over Allegory," *Studies in Philology* 82 (1985): 359–79. At the very least, careful attention to the paratextual materials shows that Harington thoroughly engages with Protestant concerns about infidel texts.

9. Green, *Print and Protestantism*, 43

10. Su Fang Ng, "Translation, Interpretation, and Heresy: The Wycliffite Bible, Tyndale's Bible, and the Contested Origin," *Studies in Philology* 98 (2001): 315.

11. Green, *Print and Protestantism*, 101.

12. See Diarmaid MacCulloch's discussion of Cranmer's support for the Great Bible in chapter 7 of *Thomas Cranmer: A Life* (New Haven: Yale University Press, 1998), 237–96.

13. Citations are from *The First Authorized English Bible and the Cranmer Preface*, ed. Harold R. Willoughby (Chicago: University of Chicago Press, 1942), 39.

14. Katharine A. Craik, *Reading Sensations in Early Modern England* (New York: Palgrave, 2007), 21–34; and Elizabeth Spiller, *Reading and the History of Race in the Renaissance* (Cambridge: Cambridge University Press, 2011), esp. 23–32.

15. Spiller, *Reading and the History of Race*, 27. On the connection between reading and eating, also see Craik, *Reading Sensations*, 30.

16. Mary Floyd-Wilson, *English Ethnicity and Race in Early Modern Drama* (Cambridge: Cambridge University Press, 2003), 23 and 46–7. On early modern views of African sexuality, also see Ian Smith, "Barbarian Errors: Performing Race in Early Modern England," *Shakespeare Quarterly* 49 (1998): 179–80.

17. On uses of biblical marginalia to reduce heresy, see William W. E. Slights, "'Marginall Notes That Spoile the Text': Scriptural Annotation in the English Renaissance," *Huntington Library Quarterly* 55 (1992): 255–78. Slights also notes, however, that many Protestants were leery of glossing.

18. Green, *Print and Protestantism*, 75. Yet Slights also notes, "The story told in the margins of English Bibles produced between 1525 and 1611 appears from the foregoing to be one of restraint and consolidation of doctrinal positions" ("Marginall Notes That Spoile the Text," 268).

19. Illona N. Rashkow, "Hebrew Bible Translation and the Fear of Judaization," *The Sixteenth Century Journal* 21(1990): 223–24.

20. Ibid., 231.

21. Weith, *The Fabulous Dark Cloister*, 107–8

22. Slights, "'Marginall Notes'" 258.

23. All citations of *Orlando Furioso* will appear parenthetically within the text. Ludovico Arisoto, *Orlando Furioso,* trans. Sir John Harington (1591), ed. Robert McNulty (Oxford: Clarendon Press, 1972).

24. Werth, *The Fabulous Dark Cloister,* 5.

25. Roger Ascham, "The Schoolmaster," in *Roger Ascham: English Works,* ed. William Aldis Wright (Cambridge, UK: The University Press, 1904), 229.

26. Ibid., 230–31.

27. Ibid., 236

28. Quoted in Werth, *The Fabulous Dark Cloister,* 107.

29. Jane E. Everson, "Translating the Pope and the Apennines: Harington's Version of *Orlando Furioso,*" *Modern Language Review* 100 (2005): 647.

30. Ibid., 653.

31. Augustine, *Confessions,* trans. Henry Chadwick (Oxford: Oxford University Press, 1991), 152.

32. Ibid., 145.

33. I say "almost" because while Harington translates all the cantos of Ariosto's poem, he deletes and condenses quite a bit of the original material. On these deletions and condensations, see Townsend Rich, *Harington and Ariosto: A Study in Elizabethan Verse Translation* (New Haven: Yale University Press, 1940), 70–79; and Everson, "Translating the Pope and the Apennines."

34. See Rich, *Harington and Ariosto,* 23–24. Also see Jason Scott-Warren, *Sir John Harington and the Book as Gift* (Oxford: Oxford University Press, 2001). Scott-Warren suggests that if we take the apocryphal tale seriously, we can read the translation of Ariosto's entire poem as penitence for circulating the twenty-eighth canto, which he reads as an affront to the poetics of chastity and virginity that circulated in Elizabeth's court (25–26).

35. Colin Burrow, *Epic Romance: Homer to Spenser* (Oxford: Clarendon Press, 1993), 149. Also see Massimiliano Morini, *Tudor Translation in Theory and Practice* (Aldershot, UK: Ashgate, 2006). He suggests that the translation is much more serious than Ariosto's original poem (102–6).

36. On Harington's participation in the warfare between the attackers and defenders of poetry, see Rich, *Harington and Ariosto,* 36–50.

37. According to Morini, convincing readers that *Orlando Furioso* is a Virgilian epic, alongside making the poem acceptable to an English court readership, is a primary goal of Harington's translation ("Sir John Harington and the Poetics of Tudor Translation," in *Travels and Translation in the Sixteenth Century: Selected Papers from the Second International Conference of the Tudor Symposium,* ed. Mike Pincombe [Aldershot, UK: Ashgate, 2000], 121–36). Also see his *Tudor Translation in Theory and Practice,* 106–14. That said, various critics have argued that *Orlando Furioso* turns itself into epic by the end. See, for example, David Quint, "The Figure of Atlante: Ariosto and Boiardo's Poem,"

Modern Language Notes 94 (1979): 77–91; and Marion A. Wells, *The Secrete Wound: Love-Melancholy and Early Modern Romance* (Stanford: Stanford University Press, 2007), 96–136. Daniel Javitch, however, disagrees with these readings and argues that the poem is romance through and through. See his "Reconsidering the Last Part of *Orlando Furioso*: Romance to the Bitter End," *Modern Language Quarterly* 71 (2010): 385–405.

38. Werth, *The Fabulous Dark Cloister*, 97–98, 135–36; and Spiller, *Reading and the History of Race*, 27–30.

39. Judith Lee, "The English Ariosto: The Elizabethan Poet and the Marvelous," *Studies in Philology* 80 (1983): 289

40. This is an important foundation for Benedict. S. Robinson's exploration of what happens to romance in Reformation England, once the Reformation makes Christendom no longer possible; see his *Islam and Early Modern English Literature: The Politics of Romance from Spenser to Milton* (New York: Palgrave, 2007).

41. "recourse, v.1". OED Online. March 2012. Oxford University Press. http://www.oed.com/view/Entry/159920?rskey=UzreKu&result=3& isAdvanced=false (accessed May 23, 2012).

42. "The Form of Solemnization of Matrimony," in *The Book of Common Prayer 1599: The Elizabethan Prayer Book*, ed. John E. Booty (Charlottesville: The University of Virginia Press for The Folger Shakespeare Library, 2005), 290.

43. Fuchs, *Romance,* 69. Here Fuchs draws from Patricia Parker's study of romance deferral and dilation. For a reading similarly to Fuchs's, see David Quint's *Epic and Empire* (Princeton: Princeton University Press, 1993), 178–85.

44. *Oh gran bontá de' cavallieri antiqui!*
   Eran rivali, eran di fé diversi
   e si sentian degli aspri colpi iniqui
   per tutta la persona anco dolersi;
   e pur per selve oscure e calli obliqui
   insieme van senza sospetto aversi.
   Da quattro sponi il destrier punto arriva
   ove una strada in due si dipartiva. (1.22)

Ludovico Ariosto, *Orlando Furioso e Cinque Canti,* ed. Remo Ceserani and Sergio Zatti, vol. 1 (Torino: Unione Tipografico-Editrice Torinese, 1997).

45. Lee, "The English Ariosto," 283.

46. See Patricia Parker, *Inescapable Romance: Studies in the Poetics of a Mode* (Princeton, Princeton University Press, 1979), 10.

47. Albert Russell Ascoli, *Ariosto's Bitter Harmony: Crisis and Evasion in the Italian Renaissance* (Princeton: Princeton University Press, 1987).

4. Transformative and Restorative Romance: Re-"turning" Othello and Locating Christian Identity

1. See Elizabeth Williamson, *The Materiality of Religion in Early Modern English Drama* (Aldershot, UK: Ashgate, 2009) for a discussion of how various theatrical properties made religion present on the stage. For a discussion of how theatrical properties made Islam material and visible on the early modern stage, see Dennis Britton, "Muslim Conversion and Circumcision as Theater," in *Religion and Drama in Early Modern England,* eds. Jane Hwang Dengenhardt and Elizabeth Williamson (Aldershot, UK: Ashgate, 2011), 71–86.

2. Othello as outsider is such a critical commonplace that it is impossible to fully document here. See, however, Michael Neill, introduction to *Othello,* ed. Michael Neill (Oxford: Oxford University Press, 2006), 113–30. Neill gives a helpful overview of the criticism that discusses race in the play. See in particular, however, John Gillies, *Shakespeare and the Geography of Difference* (Cambridge: Cambridge University Press, 1994), 25. Gillies first asked us to consider the importance of Shakespeare's "poetic geography" in relation to the "construction of otherness" (3). Also see Daniel Vitkus, *Turning Turk: English Theater and the Multicultural Mediterranean* (New York: Palgrave, 2002). He reads Iago's comment that Othello is an "erring barbarian" (1.3.355–56) in light of Gillies's discussion (91).

3. Citations are from William Shakespeare, *Othello,* ed. E. A. J. Honigmann (Walton-on-Thames, Surrey: Thomas Nelson & Sons, LTD for the Arden Shakespeare, 1997). In contrast to readings that are most concerned with Othello's eastern or African origins, Jane Hwang Degenhardt notes that Othello's origins are ambiguous (*Islamic Conversion and Christian Resistance on the Early Modern Stage* [Edinburgh: Edinburgh University Press, 2010], 55).

4. Emily C. Bartels, *Speaking of the Moor: From* Alcazar *to* Othello (Philadelphia: University of Pennsylvania Press, 2009), 158. Apart from Bartels's study, work that has questioned the absoluteness of Othello's alterity has focused on his religious identity. See, for example, Degenhardt, *Islamic Conversion and Christian Resistance,* 49–72; Vitkus, *Turning Turk,* 77–106; and Julia Reinhard Lupton, *Citizen-Saints: Shakespeare and Political Theology* (Chicago: University of Chicago Press, 2005),105–23.

5. On *Othello* and anxieties about Ottoman expansion, see Matthew Dimmock, *New Turkes: Dramatizing Islam and the Ottomans in Early Modern England* (Aldershot, UK: Ashgate), 201–8; and Vitkus, *Turning Turk,* chapter 4, 77–106.

6. Critics have noticed the romance motifs and themes in the play for quite some time, but they have often mentioned them only in passing. Long ago, A. C. Bradley suggested that "Othello is, in one sense of the word, by far the most romantic of Shakespeare's heroes. . . . He does not belong to our world, and he seems to enter it from we know not whence—almost as if from wonderland." (*Shakespearean Tragedy: Lectures on* Hamlet, Othello, King Lear, *and* Macbeth [1904; repr. New York: St. Martin's Press, 1978], 187). Bradley's mysterious

wonderland, I suggest, should be identified as the world of Catholic romance. Nathaniel E. Griffin then noted that Othello's tales of "moving accidents" and acephali belong to the world of romance ("The Definition of Romance," *PMLA* 38 (1923): 55–56, note 3). Another classic discussion of romance in the play is G. Wilson Knight's, in which he linked Othello's jealousy to Leontes' in *The Winter's Tale*; see *The Crown of Life: Essays in Interpretation of Shakespeare's Final Plays* (1947; repr., New York: Methuen, 1958), 11. Other studies have discussed Shakespeare's indebtedness to romance in order to prove that Shakespeare read Italian and to uncover his source materials. See A. S. Cairncross, "Shakespeare and Ariosto: *Much Ado about Nothing, King Lear*, and *Othello*," *Renaissance Quarterly* 29 (1976): 178–82; Guilfoyle, "*Othello, Otuel*, and the English Charlemagne Romances," *Review of English Studies* 38 (1987): 50-55; and Roger Prior's "Shakespeare's Debt to Ariosto," *Notes and Queries* 48 (2001): 289–92. Othello's similarities to Otuel suggest that Shakespeare draws from more than one infidel-conversion narrative; in numerous Charlemagne romances, Otuel is a Moor who converts to Christianity and then marries Charlemagne's daughter. I focus on the infidel-conversion narrative as presented in *Orlando Furioso* because it is the one with which Shakespeare's play most explicitly engages.

The fullest treatments of *Othello's* indebtedness to romance to date are Mark Rose's "Othello's Occupation: Shakespeare and the Romance of Chivalry," *English Literary Renaissance* 15 (1985): 293-311; Michael L. Hays's discussion of Othello in *Shakespearean Tragedies as Chivalric Romance: Rethinking* Macbeth, Hamlet, Othello *and* King Lear (Cambridge: D.S. Brewer, 2003); and Benedict Robinson's discussion in *Islam and Early Modern English Literature: The Politics of Romance from Spenser to Milton* (New York: Palgrave, 2007). Rose reads the play as enacting a struggle between bourgeois interests, represented by the upstart Iago, and the aristocratic interests that are championed by Othello. Hays suggests that it is likely the case that critics have ignored romance in *Othello* because they have been more interested in exploring issues of gender and race (155–56). He is most interested in unearthing the traces of chivalric love in the play. It is certainly the case, however, that a study of romance in *Othello* need not preclude considerations of race or gender. Robinson's study is the only one that deals with the play's negotiation of racial and religious identities through romance. There are important similarities between Robinson's reading and my own: We both see the play's indebtedness to Ludovico Ariosto, and we both see Othello as using romance as a means to create his belonging in Venice. Robinson argues, however, that Shakespeare always converts romances of interracial desire into tragedy, thus revealing the failure of romance to represent such desire as anything but "against all rules of nature" (74). For Robinson, race remains that category of identity that makes Othello an outsider. I also depart from Robinson in seeing the play as engaging two competing types of romance.

7. See Bartels, *Speaking of the Moor*, chapter 4, 100–17.

8. In *Speaking of the Moor*, though she convincingly illustrates the various ways in which Moors belong in early modern Europe, Bartels does not fully consider Othello's Christian identity. Elsewhere she has disregarded Othello's Christian identity altogether: "The play does not make clear whether or not Othello is, like Africanus, a converted Moor; Othello obviously knows the rhetoric of Christianity, but he claims no allegiance to any religious faith" (*"Othello* and the Moor," in *Early Modern Drama: A Critical Companion*, eds. Garrett A. Sullivan, Patrick Gerard Cheney, and Andrew Hadfield [Oxford: Oxford University Press, 2006], 142). Bartels makes a similar statement in "Othello on Trial," in *Othello: New Case Books,* ed. Lena Cowen Orlin (New York: Palgrave, 2004), 157. Even so, Bartels has consistently (and importantly) questioned the tendency of *Othello* criticism to read Othello as only an outsider. See also her "Making More of the Moor: Aaron, Othello, and Renaissance Refashionings of Race," *Shakespeare Quarterly* 41 (1990): 433–54, where she reads Othello's belonging as originating from his similarity to Leo Africanus and other figures of the noble Moor.

9. I am not the first to notice this line. See Hays, *Shakespeare's Tragedies as Chivalric Romance*, 164; and Vitkus, who reads Othello as "a baptized moor turned Turk" (*Turning Turk*, 89–90). Jonathan Bate also reads Iago's desire to undo Othello's baptism as an example of the play's larger anxieties about "turning" in "Shakespeare's Island," in *Shakespeare and the Mediterranean*, eds. Susan Brook, Vicente Forés, and Thomas Clayton (Newark: University of Delaware Press, 2004), 289–307, esp. 293–94. But see Lupton in particular, who notes that Iago sets as his task to unconvert Othello (115), and Nabil Matar, who notes that Othello is a special case as a Christian Moor on the English stage (*Britain and Barbary, 1589-1689* [Gainesville: University Press of Florida Press, 2005], 30–31).

10. See Bartels, "Making More of the Moor," 448; and Hays, *Shakespeare's Tragedies as Chivalric Romance*, 157.

11. It should also be remembered that in addition to the *Furioso, Gerusalemme liberata* illustrates similar alternatives in the conversions of Clorinda and Armida.

12. In mentioning Othello's re-"turning," I am of course drawing from recent interest in anxieties about "turning Turk" and conversion in *Othello* in particular and drama staging European encounters with Islam in general. See, for example, Degenhardt, *Islamic Conversion and Christian Resistance*, Vitkus's *Turning Turk*, and Jonathan Burton's *Traffic and Turning: Islam and English Drama 1579-1624* (Newark: University of Delaware Press, 2005).

13. John Whitgift, *The defense of the aunswere to the Admonition against the replie of T. C. By Iohn VVhitgift Doctor of Diuinitie* (London, 1574), 134–35.

14. Merideth Hanmer, *The baptizing of a Turke, A sermon preached at the Hospitall of Saint Katherin* . . . (London, 1586), sig. 1v–2r. Hereafter, citations for Hanmer will appear parenthetically.

15. John Jewel, *A replie vnto M. Hardinges answeare*, in *The Works of John Jewel, Bishop of Salisbury*, ed. John Ayre (Cambridge, UK: The University Press for the Parker Society, 1847), 334–35.

16. Ephriam Pagitt, *Christianographie* . . . (London, 1635), sig. H1v.

17. Ibid., sig. B1v.

18. Ibid., sig. D3v.

19. In addition to Pagitt's text, English readings could have learn about African Christians in John Pory's translation of Leo Africanus's *A geographical historie of Africa* (London, 1600), in which Africanus notes that there are Christians in Egypt, Ethiopia, Angola, and the Congo (sig. Ll3r–v).

20. Gillies, *Shakespeare and the Geography of Difference*, 25; Valerie Traub, "Mapping the Global Body," in *Early Modern Visual Culture: Representation, Race, and Empire in Renaissance England*, eds. Peter Erickson and Clark Hulse (Philadelphia: University of Pennsylvania Press, 2000), 58.

21. That Mauritania was commonly understood to be the same location as Barbary can be seen in sources as diverse as Richard Eden's translation of Pietro Martire d'Anghiera's *The history of trauayle in the West and East Indies* (London, 1577), which would later be included in the first volume of Richard Hakluyt's *Principle Navigations* (London, 1599): "*Mauritania* (now called *Barbaria*) is diuided into two partes" sig. Yy1v; to E.K.'s description of "a merueilous highe mountaine in Mauritania, that now is Barbarie" in his gloss to May eclogue in Spenser's *Shepherd's Calender* (London, 1579), sig. F2r.

22. Degenhardt offers a different reading of Hanmer. Noting that Negroponte was once part of Christendom, she suggests, "Hanmer posits not the conversion of a Muslim to Christianity, but the long overdue *reconversion* of a subject whose native and natural religion was Christianity" (*Islam and Christian Resistance*, 61).

23. Chinano's life's story, at least as Hanmer recounts it, is quite remarkable. He was a merchant who was eventually captured by Spaniards—this is how he learned Spanish. He was eventually rescued by Sir Francis Drake and brought to England.

24. "The Ministration of Baptism to Be Used in Churches," in *Religion and Society in Early Modern England*, eds. David Cressy and Lori Anne Ferrell (New York: Routledge, 1996), 50.

25. Imtiaz Habib, *Black Lives in the English Archive, 1500–1677: Imprints of the Invisible* (Aldershot, UK: Ashgate, 2008), 92, 91 and 143.

26. Bernard Weinberg, *A History of Literary Criticism in the Italian Renaissance*, vol. 2 (Chicago: University of Chicago Press, 1961), 210. Here, Weinberg is

discussing Cinthio's "Prologues," which accompanied the 1583 collection of his tragedies. Also see Sarah Dewar-Watson, "Aristotle and Tragicomedy," in *Early Modern Tragedicomedy*, eds. Subha Mukherji and Raphael Lyne (Cambridge: D. S. Brewer, 2007), 15–27. She identifies similar ideas in Cinthio's *On the Composition of Comedies and Tragedies* (16).

27. Giraldi Cinthio, *On Romances*, trans. Henry L. Snuggs (Lexington: University of Kentucky Press, 1968), 72.

28. On the elements of romance in these plays, see P. R. Horne, *The Tragedies of Giambattista Cinthio Giraldi* (Oxford: Oxford University Press, 1962), 128–46.

29. Aristotle, *Poetics*, trans. James Hutton (New York: W. W. Norton & Company, 1982), 56.

30. The infamous debate over the *Furioso* between Cinthio and Tasso raised the question whether romance is really a genre or merely a degenerate form of epic. But such a debate would be avoided by English poets altogether through their use of more inclusive terminology. John Harington, for example, defends the *Furioso* as a "Heroical Poeme" by comparing it to the *Aeneid*; see "A Preface, or Rather, a Brief Apologie of Poetry and of the Author and Translator of this Poem," in *Orlando Furioso*, trans. John Harington, ed. Robert McNulty (Oxford: Clarendon Press, 1972), 9–12.

31. Both Steve Mentz and Sarah Dewar-Watson have demonstrated that early moderns often read the *Odyssey* as having characteristics akin to romance. See Mentz, *Romance for Sale in Early Modern England: The Rise of Prose Fiction* (Aldershot, UK: Ashgate, 2006), 73–74. Dewar-Watson notes that Cinthio in particular made connections between the *Odyssey* and romance ("Aristotle and Tragicomedy," 22–23).

32. For seminal discussions of the relation between romance and tragedy, see Knight, *The Crown of Life*, chapter 1, 9–31; E. M. W. Tillyard, *Shakespeare's Last Plays* (London: Chatto and Windus, 1951), 16–58; Howard Felperin, *Shakespearean Romance* (Princeton: Princeton University Press, 1972), 97–139; and Hallett Smith, *Shakespeare's Romances: A Study of Some Ways of the Imagination* (San Marino, CA: The Huntington Library, 1972), 55–69. For examples of the tradition of reading *Lear* and *Hamlet* in relation to romance, see Hays, *Shakespearean Tragedies as Chivalric Romance*.

33. Vitkus, *Turning Turk*, 78.

34. William Shakespeare, *Titus Andronicus*, in *The Norton Shakespeare*, ed. Stephen Greenblatt (New York: W.W. Norton & Co., 1997), 3.1.204.

35. George Peele, *The Battle of Alcazar*, ed. John Yoklavich, *The Dramatic Works of George Peele*, ed. Charles Tyler Prouty, vol. 2 (New Haven: Yale University Press, 1961), 1.5 and 1.13.

36. The ambiguity of the term "Moor" is now commonly noted, but see Michael Neill, " 'Mulattos,' 'Blacks,' and 'Indian Moors': *Othello* and Early Modern Constructions of Human Difference," *Shakespeare Quarterly* 49 (1998):

361–74; and Bartels, "Making More of the Moor." On the tradition of the tawny or "oriental" Othello, which was infamously suggested by Samuel Coleridge, see Michael Neill, "Unproper Beds: Race, Adultery, and the Hideous in *Othello*," *Shakespeare Quarterly* 40 (1989): 383–412; and Karen Newman, *Fashioning Femininity and English Renaissance Drama* (Chicago: University of Chicago Press, 1991), 71–93. On blackface and the presence of the white actor behind Othello, see Dympna Callaghan, *Shakespeare Without Women: Representing Gender and Race on the Renaissance Stage* (London: Routledge, 2000), 77–78; Ian Smith, "White Skin, Black Masks: Racial Cross-Dressing on the Early Modern Stage," *Renaissance Drama* 32 (2003): 33–67; and Virginia Mason Vaughan, *Performing Blackness on the English Stage, 1500–1800* (Cambridge: Cambridge University Press, 2005), 9–10.

37. See Richard Grinnell, "Witchcraft, Race, and the Rhetoric of Barbarism in *Othello* and *1 Henry IV*," *Upstart Crow* 24 (2004): 72–80. He argues that witchcraft is linked with racial alterity.

38. On romance in this speech, also see Robinson, *Islam and Early Modern English Literature*, 71; and Ian Smith, who notes that romance is part of Othello's larger task to use language as "proof of cultural belonging" (*Race and Rhetoric in the Renaissance: Barbarian Errors* [New York: Palgrave, 2009], 139–40).

39. Hays, *Shakespearean Tragedies as Chivalric Romance*, 159–61; 184–90. Greene's play deals solely with a love plot between Orlando and Angelica, who has become the daughter of Marsillus, Emperor of Africa. Angelica chooses to marry Orlando among suitors from Cuba and Mexico at the very beginning of the play. Orlando is tricked into believing that Angelica is in love with Medor, which drives him mad. He eventually recovers his wits, marries Angelica, and gains the throne of Africa in the end.

40. Hayes, *Shakespearean Tragedies as Chivalric Romance*, 160. See Robert Greene, *Orlando Furioso, A Textual Study of Robert Greene's* Orlando Furioso *with an Elizabethan Text,* ed. Tetsumaro Hayashi (Municie, IN: Ball State University, 1973), 1.1.119–125.

41. Tales of adventure and woe often lead to love. See Heather James, "Dido's Ear: Tragedy and the Politics of Response," *Shakespeare Quarterly* 52 (2001): 360–82, in which she argues that Desdemona's response to Othello's tale recalls Dido's response to Aeneas'.

42. See Lynda E. Boose, "'The Getting of a Lawful Race': Racial Discourse in Early Modern England, and the Unrepresentable Black Woman," in *Women, "Race," and Writing,* eds. Margo Hendricks and Patricia Parker (New York: Routledge, 1994), 38.

43. Critics have debated whether Desdemona's insistence that she sees beyond Othello's physical appearance implies a racial loathing of black skin. For example, see Michael D. Bristol, "Charivari and the Comedy of Abjection in *Othello*," *Renaissance Drama* 21 (1990): 11–12.

44. Patricia Parker, "Fantasies of 'Race' and 'Gender': Africa, *Othello* and Bringing to Light," in *Women, "Race," and Writing in the Early Modern Period*, eds. Margo Hendricks and Patricia Parker (New York: Routledge, 1994), 91.

45. Although he suggests that race is the main reason that Othello cannot fully belong, Robinson puts it quite nicely when he writes, "Romance gives Othello a place in Venice" (*Islam and Early Modern English Literature*, 72).

46. Ania Loomba, *Gender, Race, Renaissance Drama* (Manchester: University of Manchester Press, 1989), 50.

47. Callaghan, *Shakespeare without Women*, 78.

48. Habib, *Black Lives in the English Archive*, 268. For statistical analysis of the black presence in England at varying time periods and in varying locations, see the afterword, 261–72.

49. See Vaughan, who notes the language of dirt and soot in the play. She suggests that this language works metatheatrically to draw the audience's attention to the fact that Burbage's blackness, and maybe Othello's, can be washed off (*Performing Blackness*, 94). For a contrasting reading, see Degenhardt, who places the audience's perception of Othello's visible black body in a vexed relationship with his invisible Christian faith (*Islamic Conversion and Christian Resistance*, 49).

50. Michael Neill, "Changing Places in *Othello*," *Shakespeare Survey* 37 (1984): 118.

51. See Bartels, *Speaking of the Moor*, 158. On Venice as a cosmopolitan center, also see Lupton, *Citizen Saints*, 77; and Arthur Little, *Shakespeare Jungle Fever: National-Imperial Re-visions of Race, Rape and Sacrifice* (Stanford: Stanford University Press, 2000), 68–101.

52. Giraldi Cinthio, *Gli Hecatommithi* (Decade 3, Story 7), trans. Geoffrey Bullough, in *The Narrative and Dramatic Sources of Shakespeare*, 8 vol., ed. Geoffrey Bullough (London: Routledge and Kegan Paul, 1973), 7:242.

53. See Degenhardt, who notes that "Iago suggests an equation between Othello's conversion to Christian faith and his faith in Desdemona's love" (*Islamic Conversion and Christian Resistance*, 51).

54. Ludovico Ariosto, *Orlando Furioso*, trans. Sir John Harington, ed. Robert McNulty (Oxford: Clarendon Press, 1972), 22.27.1–8. Although I use the Italian spellings for character names throughout the chapter, citations of the poem are from this English translation.

55. Ibid., 41.48.6–8 to 41.49.1–8.

56. Ibid., 41.53.1–2.

57. Nabil Matar, *Britain and Barbary, 1589-1689* (Gainesville: University Press of Florida, 2005), 30.

58. Degenhardt, *Islamic Conversion and Christian Resistance*, 39.

59. See Martine van Elk, " 'This sympathizèd one day's error': Genre, Representation, and Subjectivity in *The Comedy of Errors*," *Shakespeare Quarterly*

60 (2009): 47–72. Van Elk also discusses the restoration of identity in romance, arguing that "romance locates a spiritual and physical essence at the core of identity, a core that is testable but ultimately inalienable" (48). Heather Dubrow too notes that romances move toward restoration, though she is most interested in the genre's fondness for restoring family relationships (*Shakespeare and Domestic Loss: Forms of Deprivation, Mourning and Recuperation* [Cambridge: Cambridge University Press, 1999], 101–3).

60. For a discussion of Shakespeare's indebtedness to Greek romance, see Stuart Gillespie, "Shakespeare and the Greek Romance: 'like an old tale still,'" in *Shakespeare and the Classics*, eds. Charles Martindale and A. B. Taylor (Cambridge: Cambridge University Press, 2004), 225–40.

61. Bate, "Shakespeare's Islands," 290.

62. Cinthio, *Gli Hecatommithi*, 7:243.

63. *The Riverside Shakespeare* glosses the line solely as "brunette" (*Othello, The Riverside Shakespeare*, ed. G. Blakemore Evans, 2nd ed. [Boston: Houghton Mifflin, 1997], 1261, note 131). The Arden edition, ed. E. A. J. Honigmann, 171, note 133; *The Norton Shakespeare*, ed. Stephen Greenblatt (New York: Norton, 1997), 2118, note 4; and Neill's edition for the *Oxford Shakespeare* (249, notes 132–33) offer that "black" may refer both to hair color and complexion. Also see Lara Bovilsky, *Barbarous Play: Race on the English Renaissance Stage* (Minneapolis: University of Minnesota Press, 2008), 37.

64. William Shakespeare, sonnet 127, in *The Norton Shakespeare*, lines 1 and 3.

65. Frances E. Dolan, *Dangerous Families: Representations of Domestic Crime in England, 1550–1700* (Ithaca: Cornell University Press, 1994), 114. On charivari in the play, also see Bristol, "Charivari and the Comedy of Abjection in *Othello*."

66. Cyprus itself "turned Turk" in 1571. In between the time Cinthio wrote his tale and the time Shakespeare rewrote it for the stage, Venice lost Cyprus to Turkey.

67. William Shakespeare, *The Merchant of Venice*, in *The Norton Shakespeare*, 2.3.18–20.

68. Here I disagree with Janet Adelman's reading that "though we might expect her to convert in order to marry, the rhetorical weight of this speech moves in the opposite direction, suggesting that she would marry in order to convert" (*Blood Relations*, 71). *Jessica's* conditional statement suggests that her becoming a Christian and a loving wife will happen simultaneously, and only after Lorenzo's promise is enacted. For a reading complementary to my own, see M. Lindsay Kaplan, "Jessica's Mother: Medieval Constructions of Jewish Race and Gender in *The Merchant of Venice*," *Shakespearean Quarterly* 58 (2007), 22–23.

69. See Vitkus, who notes that the phrase "to turn Turk" commonly held sexual connotations in Turk plays (*Turning Turk*, 88–89).

70. Rebecca Ann Bach, *Shakespeare and Renaissance Literature before Heterosexuality* (New York: Palgrave, 2007), 108. On the benefits and drawbacks

of reading *Othello* as domestic tragedy, see Lena Cowen Orlin, *Private Matters and Public Culture in Post-Reformation England* (Ithaca: Cornell University Press, 1994), 246–49.

71. "The Form of Solemnization of Matrimony," in *The Book of Common Prayer 1559: The Elizabethan Prayer Book*, ed. John E. Booty (Charlottesville: The University of Virginia Press for The Folger Shakespeare Library, 2005), 290.

72. Christine Peters, "Gender, Sacrament and Ritual: The Making and Meaning of Marriage in Late Medieval and Early Modern England," *Past and Present* 169 (2000): 63–96.

73. Robert N. Watson has noted that "the marriage between Othello and Desdemona represents the precious but unstable relationship between the sinner's soul and its Savior" ("*Othello* as Protestant Propaganda," in *Religion and Culture in Renaissance England,* eds. Claire McEachern and Debora Shuger [Cambridge: Cambridge University Press, 1997], 234.) I would not go as far as Watson does, however; he reads the play as a Protestant allegory with Desdemona figuring Christ and salvation.

74. The Italian quotation is from Ariosto, *Orlando Furioso*, ed. Lanfranco Caretti (Milan: Riccardo Ricciadi, 1954), 46.80.4. In the *Furioso*, the handkerchief has its own "travels' history" as it makes its way from Troy to Egypt. It remains in Egypt for several generations before it is eventually brought to Italy.

75. Roger Prior, "Shakespeare's Debt to Ariosto," *Notes and Queries* 48 (2001): 289. On the handkerchief's indebtedness to Ariosto, also see Robinson, *Islam and Early Modern English Literature*, 73–74.

76. Anthony Gerard Barthelemy, *Black Face, Maligned Race: The Representation of Blacks in English Drama from Shakespeare to Southern* (Baton Rouge: Louisiana State University Press, 1987), 72.

77. Burton, *Traffic and Turning*, 253.

78. Bate, "Shakespeare's Islands," 295.

79. On the equation between Islamic identity and circumcision, see Burton, *Traffic and Turning*, 99–100. There is a strong tradition of reading Othello's suicide as his killing of "the irrational and cruel Turk within" (Virginia Mason Vaughan, *Othello: A Contextual History* [Cambridge: Cambridge University Press, 1994], 34). For similar readings, see Lupton, *Citizen Saints*, 120; Vitkus, *Turning Turk*, 103–4; Hays, *Shakespearean Tragedies as Chivalric Romance*; and Kim Hall, "Race and Religion," in *Othello, the Moor of Venice: Texts and Context* (New York: Bedford/ St. Martins, 2007), 177–79. Matar, however, finds fault with these readings because they rely upon a historically inaccurate conflation of Turks and Moors. According to Matar, not only did the English see Morocco as a potential ally, but Morocco also continually sought to resist Ottoman imperialism in North Africa (*Britain and Barbary*, 31–32).

80. See G. W. F. Hegel, "Dramatic Motivation and Language," in *Hegel on Tragedy*, ed. Anne and Henry Paolucci (Westport: Greenwood Press, 1978), 169–82.

81. A. C. Bradley, "Hegel's Theory of Tragedy," in *Hegel on Tragedy*, 369.

82. See the introduction, in which I discuss Cinthio's argument that one of the goals of romance is to clarify distinctions between good and evil.

83. A. C. Bradley, *Shakespearean Tragedy: Lectures on* Hamlet, Othello, King Lear, Macbeth (1904: New York: Palgrave, 2007), 22.

84. For another reading of *Othello's* exploration of differing modes of racial discourse, see Mary Floyd-Wilson, who argues, "*Othello* stands at a crossroads in the history of ethnological ideas when emergent racial discourses clashed with still dominate classical and medieval geohumoralism" (*English Ethnicity and Race in Early Modern Drama* [Cambridge: Cambridge University Press], 2006). As I conclude my exploration of *Othello*, I borrow Floyd-Wilson's language of intersection.

5. Reproducing Christians: Salvation, Race, and Gender on the Early Modern English Stage

1. Boose asserts, "the black male–white woman union is, throughout this period and earlier, most frequently depicted as the ultimate romantic-transgressive model of erotic love." Lynda E. Boose. "'The Getting of a Lawful Race': Racial Discourse in Early Modern England and the Unrepresentable Black Woman," in *Women, 'Race', and Writing in the Early Modern Period*, eds. Margo Hendricks and Patricia Parker (London: Routledge, 1994), 41.

2. James Shapiro makes a similar claim in *Shakespeare and the Jews* (New York: Columbia University Press, 1996), 132.

3. Joyce Green MacDonald, *Women and Race in Early Modern Texts* (Cambridge: Cambridge University Press, 2003), 165.

4. On these plays' engagements with their romance sources, however, see for example Elizabeth Spiller, "From Imagination to Miscegenation: Race and Romance in Shakespeare's *The Merchant of Venice*," *Renaissance Drama* 29 (1998): 137-64; Michael Neill, "Material Flames: The Space of Mercantile Fantasy in John Fletcher's *The Island Princess*," *Renaissance Drama* 28 (1997): 9–13; and Carmen Nocentelli, "Spice Race: *The Island Princess* and the Politics of Transnational Appropriation," *PMLA* 125 (2010): 572–88.

5. On tragicomedy in particular, Valerie Forman argues that it "finds its narrative and structural basis in Christian redemption (the *felix culpa*)" (*Tragicomic Redemptions: Global Economics and the Early Modern English Stage* [Philadelphia: University of Pennsylvania Press, 2008], 7). Also see Michael Neill, "Turn and Counterturn: Merchanting, Apostasy, and Tragicomic Form in Massinger's *The Renegado*," in *Early Modern Tragicomedy*, eds. Subha Mukherji and Raphael Lyne

(Cambridge, UK: D. S. Brewer, 2007), 154–74; Neill observes that the tragicomic form provides a structure for *The Renegado*'s treatment of religious conversion, and he observes a relationship between these plays in their common interests in mercantilism, religious conversion, and the tragicomic form. On the affinities between romance and tragicomedy, see Forman, *Tragicomic Redemptions*, 7–9; Maurice Hunt, "Romance and Tragicomedy," in *A Companion to Renaissance Drama*, ed. Arthur Kinney (Oxford: Wiley-Blackwell, 2002): 384–98; Barbara Mowat, " 'What's in a Name?' Tragicomedy, Romance, or Late Comedy," in *A Companion to Shakespeare's Works*, vol. 4 *The Poems, Problem Comedies, Late Plays*, eds. Richard Dutton and Jean E. Howard (Oxford: Wiley-Blackwell, 2003), 12–49.

6. I thus see a connection between the plays' subject matters, racial "miscegenation," and tragicomedy as (according to Sir Philip Sidney) a "mongrel" form. I follow Jean Feerick's assertion that since "laws of literary kind are entangled with and around the laws governing human 'kinds,' we would be right in asking what is at stake when the boundaries of genres are redrawn, reconfigured, and rewritten, as they were when tragicomedy emerged as the unwanted 'mixed' offspring of dramatic form in the late sixteenth century" ("Tragicomic Transformations: Passion, Politics, and the 'Art to Turn' in Fletcher's *The Island Princess*," *Early Modern Literary Studies* 19 [2009] 3.1–24 URL: http://purl.oclc.org/emls/si-19/feerflet.html: para. 1.)

7. That early modern comedies either reproduce or criticize Protestant ideas about marriage is often an assumption rather than explicit argument. For more explicit discussions of comedy's engagement with Protestant theology, see, for example, Jean Howard, *The Stage and Social Struggle* (New York: Routledge, 1994), 93–128; Jennifer Panek, *Widows and Suitors in Early Modern Comedy* (Cambridge: Cambridge University Press, 2004); and Theodora A. Jankowski, *Pure Resistance: Queer Virginity in Early Modern English Drama* (Philadelphia: University of Pennsylvania Press, 2006), 113–35. I also believe that the comedic imperative to reproduce a race of Christians explains why, as Ania Loomba has observed, "Whereas converted men must remain single or be destroyed, [a woman's] religious turning is also a romantic turning to her Christian husband" (" 'Delicious traffick': Racial and Religious Difference on Early Modern Stages," in *Shakespeare and Race*, eds. by Catherine M.S. Alexander and Stanley Wells [Cambridge: Cambridge University Press, 2000], 213). I intend this examination of the religious conversions of Jessica, Quisara, and Donusa to provide another way of understanding early modern dramas that feature romantic relationships between European Christian men and non-European women. Although much persuasive scholarship has read these relationships as figuring proto-imperial and mercantile fantasies, and have read religious conversion as a trope of empire, I suggest that in a religious climate in which conversion comes under scrutiny, these plays can figure mercantile and imperial fantasy only to the extent that they

recuperate the infidel-conversion motif. Plays that stage interfaith and interracial relationships are in conversation with—though also for the sake of commerce and empire, perhaps—a Protestant theological system that established marriage and sexual reproduction as the primary means of propagating the baptized race. On the connection between interracial relationships and mercantile and imperial fantasy, in addition to work done by Daniel Vitkus, Jonathan Burton, Benedict Robinson, and Jane Hwang Degenhardt, see Kim F. Hall, "Guess Who's Coming to Dinner?: Colonization and Miscegenation in *The Merchant of Venice*," Renaissance Drama 23 (1992): 87–111; Jonathan Gil Harris, *Sick Economies: Drama, Mercantilism, and Shakespeare's England* (Philadelphia: University of Pennsylvania Press, 2003), 136–62; Michael Neill, "Material Flames: The Space of Mercantile Fantasy in John Fletcher's *The Island Princess*," Renaissance Drama 28 (1998): 99-131; Joan Pong Linton, *The Romance of the New World: Gender and the Literary Formations of English Colonialism* (Cambridge: Cambridge University Press), 1998; Andrea Remi Solomon, " 'A Wild Shambles of Strange Gods:' The Conversion of Quisara in Fletcher's *The Island Princess*," in *Christian Encounters with the Other*, ed. John C. Howely (New York: New York University Press, 1998), 17–32; Loomba, "Delicious traffick"; Loomba, "Break her will, and bruise no bone sir": Colonial and Sexual Mastery in Fletcher's *The Island Princess*," *Journal for Early Modern Cultural Studies* 2 (2002): 68–108; Shankar Raman, *Framing "India": The Colonial Imagination in Early Modern Culture* (Stanford: Stanford University Press, 2001), chapter 4, 155–88; Carmen Nocentelli, "The Erotics of Mercantile Imperialism: Cross-Cultural Requitedness in the Early Modern Period," *The Journal of Early Modern Cultural Studies* 8 (2008): 134–52; and Jean E. Feerick. "Tragicomic Transformations: Passion, Politics, and the 'Art to Turn' in Fletcher's The Island Princess," *Early Modern Literary Studies* 19 (2009), 1–24.

8. Adelman, *Blood Relations*, esp. 66–84; M. Lindsay Kaplan, "Jessica's Mother: Medieval Constructions of Jews, Race and Gender in *The Merchant of Venice*," Shakespeare Quarterly 58 (2007): 1–30; and Julia Reinhard Lupton, *Citizen Saints: Shakespeare and Political Theology* (Chicago: University of Chicago Press, 2005), in which she argues that the combination of marriage and conversion leads to Jessica's civic *"naturalization"* (85).

9. On the debate between mercy and the law in the play, see Barbara Lewalski, "Biblical Allusion and Allegory in *The Merchant of Venice*," Shakespeare Quarterly 13 (1962): 327–43.

10. This is not the only instance in which the connections between religion, biology, and sexual reproduction surface in *The Merchant of Venice*. In the play's first meditation on Jewish reproduction in act 1, scene 3, Shylock defends usury and tells Antonio to "Mark what Jacob did" (1.3.73). Shylock goes on to describe Jacob's contract with Lathan, that Jacob should have the "eanlings which were streaked and pied" (1.3.75). Elizabeth Spiller has argued that this moment in the play is but one example of early modern uses of Genesis to formulate ideas about

racial difference: "Shylock then uses this story of ewes and rams, in part, to tell a kinship narrative that distinguishes members of his family, from whom he does not demand interest, and those out outside his flock" ("From Imagination to Miscegenation," 140). According to Spiller, the story of breeding ewes and rams is also a story about Jewish lineage.

11. Shapiro, *Shakespeare and the Jews*, 120–21.

12. Lupton, *Citizen Saints*, 33. Also see Daniel Boyarin, who suggests that for the Jews of late antiquity, "circumcision became the most contested site of contention, precisely because of the way it concentrates in one moment representations of the significance of sexuality, genealogy, and ethnic specificity in bodily practice' (*Carnal Israel: Reading Sex in Talmudic Culture* [Berkeley: University of California Press, 1993], 7).

13. "seed, n.". *OED Online*. December 2011. Oxford University Press. http://www.oed.com/view/Entry/174754?rskey=DXEHU9&result=1 (accessed March 07, 2012).

14. Aristotle, *Generation of Animals*, trans. A. L. Peck (Cambridge: Harvard University Press, 1943), 111.

15. Ibid., 109.

16. Ibid., 155.

17. Kaplan, "Jessica's Mother."

18. Susan Snyder, *The Comic Matrix of Shakespeare's Tragedies: Romeo and Juliet, Hamlet, Othello and King Lear* (Princeton: Princeton University Press, 1979).

19. For a different reading of the reason that Jessica can be converted more easily than Shylock, see Lisa Lampert, *Gender and Jewish Identity from Paul to Shakespeare* (Philadelphia: University of Pennsylvania Press, 2004). She argues that Jessica's can more easily "pass" for Christian because, as a beautiful Jewess, her body does not bear the mark of non-Christian identity, namely circumcision (164). This logic would also apply to beautiful Muslim women.

Although I focus on unalterable Jewish masculinity, various scholars have illustrated that Jewish men were "feminized" in a variety of ways in the early modern period—they were said to menstruate and lactate. See, for example, Rachel Trubowitz, 'But Blood Whitened': Nursing Mothers and Others in Early Modern Britain," in *Maternal Measures: Figuring Caregiving in the Early Modern Period*, eds. Naomi J. Miller and Naomi Yavneh (Aldershot, UK: Ashgate, 2000), 88–96; and Matthew Biberman, *Masculinity, Anti-Semitism and Early Modern English Literature: From the Satanic to the Effeminate Jew* (Aldershot, UK: Ashgate, 2004). Also see Daniel Boyarin's *Unheroic Conduct: The Rise of Heterosexuality and the Invention of the Jewish Male* (Berkeley: University of California Press, 1997), in which he suggests that the trope of the feminine Jewish male goes back to at least thirteenth-century Europe (211).

20. On the Lopez incident, see David Katz, *The Jews in the History of England, 1485–1850* (Oxford: Clarendon Press, 1994), 49–106. Also see James O'Rourke,

"Racism and Homophobia in *The Merchant of Venice*," *ELH* 70 (2003): 375–97. He argues that the play contains a critique of the racism inherent in Lopez's conviction.

21. Northrop Frye, *Anatomy of Criticism: Four Essays* (Princeton: Princeton University Press, 1957), 170–71. Frye's assertion also allows us to recognize an important similarity between romance and comedy: The two often work in tandem. Frye also argued that romance is a mode of comedy (177). Also see Michael Ragussis's extension of Frye's argument, in which he provides another way of understanding Shylock's incompatibility with the comic form. Ragussis suggests that in English literature Jews must necessarily reside outside comedic resolution because the comedic form is structured to correspond with the Christian redemption plot (*Figures of Conversion: "The Jewish Question" & English National Identity* [Durham, NC: Duke University Press, 1995], 77).

22. Lewalski, "Biblical Allusion and Allegory in *The Merchant of Venice*."

23. Susanne Penuel, "Castrating the Creditor in *The Merchant of Venice*," *SEL: Studies in English Literature 1500–1900* 44 (2004): 256. Also see Adelman, *Blood Relations,* esp. 38–65.

24. See Lupton, *Citizen Saints*, 86; Shapiro, *Shakespeare and the Jews*, 132–46; and Lewalski, "Biblical Allusion and Allegory in *The Merchant of Venice*," 342.

25. Here we might also consider the distinction between Abigail and Barabas in *The Jew of Malta*. On the relation between Jessica's and Abigail's conversions, see Shapiro, *Shakespeare and the Jews*, 157.

26. Best, *A true discourse*, 33–4. We might contrast this account with the description of "the coniunction betweene the men of Europe and the Negro women [which] are bred a generation of browne or tawnie people" in John Pory's preface to Leo Africanus's *Geographical Historie of Africa* (London, 1600), sig. e3r. It seems that the blackness of the African woman can be tempered by the European male's seed, but the whiteness of European woman has no effect on the African male's seed.

27. Janet Adelman, *Blood Relations: Christian and Jew in* The Merchant of Venice (Chicago: University of Chicago Press, 2008), 68.

28. Kaplan acknowledges this fact, but she nevertheless reads the play solely in relation to Aristotle's theory.

29. John Calvin, *A commentarie vpon S. Paules Epistles to the Corinthians* (London, 1577), sig. K8r.

30. *Geneva Bible,* sig. W3v.

31. See my discussion of Jewel's debate with Harding in chapter 1.

32. See Mary Lindemann, *Medicine and Society in Early Modern Europe* (Cambridge: Cambridge University Press, 1999), 66–91.

33. Ibid., 13–14.

34. Thomas Laqueur, *Making Sex: Body and Gender from Greeks to Freud* (Cambridge: Harvard University Press, 1999), 62. For an early modern example, see Helkiah Crooke's *Mikrokosmographia* (London, 1615): "Wherefore say they, if

a Woman may become man and her parts of generation which did before lay hid within may come foorth and hang as mens do, then do women differ from men onley in the seite or position of their parts of generation" (sig. Y3r).

35. Crooke, *Mikrokosomgraphia*, sig.T6v-V1r, It is important to note, however, that Crooke later rejects the Galenic model. Nonetheless, woman's perfection is based in her reproductive function.

36. Patricia Crawford, *Women and Religion in England, 1500–1720* (New York: Routledge, 1996), 7. Religion not only influenced the medical understandings of the female body, but medical understands were also used to make religious arguments. See Sara Mendelson and Patricia Crawford, *Women in Early Modern England, 1550–1720* (Oxford: Clarendon Press, 1998), 18.

37. Crooke, *Mikrokosomgraphia*, sig. Z5v.

38. "The Form of Solemnization of Matrimony," in *The Book of Common Prayer 1559: The Elizabethan Prayer Book*, ed. John E. Booty (Charlottesville: The University of Virginia Press for The Folger Shakespeare Library, 2005), 290.

39. Thomas Vicary, *The Englishemans treasure* (London, 1587), sig. H2r.

40. Julie Crawford, *Marvelous Protestantism: Monstrous Births in Post-Reformation England* (Baltimore, MD: Johns Hopkins University Press, 2005), 15.

41. Dorothy Leigh, *The mothers blessing: or, The godly counsell of a gentle-woman* (London, 1616), sig. B1v–B3r.

42. See Naomi J. Miller, " 'Hens should be served first': Prioritizing Maternal Production in Early Modern Pamphlet Debate," in *Debating Gender in Early Modern England, 1500–1700*, eds. Cristina Malcomson and Mihoko Susuki (New York: Palgrave, 2002), 171; on salvation coming though women, 173.

43. On this understanding in the seventeenth-century, see Patricia Crawford, "The Construction and Experience of Maternity in Seventeenth-Century England," in *Women as Mothers in Pre-Industrial England*, ed. Valerie Fildes (New York: Routledge, 1990), 6–7

44. Even so, Miller points out that male authors usually discuss childbirth in exclusively medical terms. She suggests that this allowed men to divorce its importance from female sexuality ("Hens should be served first," 170).

45. Thomas Raynalde, *The byrth of mankynde* (London, 1540), sig. D3v.

46. Trubowitz, "But Blood Whitened," 83–84.

47. On fears about breast milk and racial contamination, also see Jean Feerick, *Strangers in Blood: Relocating Race in the Renaissance* (Toronto: University of Toronto Press, 2010), 55–77.

48. On Jessica's ambiguous postconversion identity and her less-than-harmonious incorporation at the end of the play, see Lampert, *Gender and Jewish Difference*, 143–44 and 164–66.

49. For an extended discussion of anxieties about miscegenation in the play, see Spiller, "From Imagination to Miscegenation."

50. Michael Neill discusses evidence that *The Renegado* is an explicit response to Fletcher's *The Island Princess* ("Turn and Counterturn," 159–60).

51. Citations are from John Fletcher, *The Island Princess*, in *The Dramatic Works in the Beaumont and Fletcher Canon*, vol. 5, ed. Fredson Bowers (Cambridge: Cambridge University Press, 1966).

52. Claire Jowitt, "*The Island Princess* and Race," in *Early Modern English Drama: A Critical Companion,* eds. Garrett A. Sullivan, Jr., Patrick Cheney, and Andrew Hadfield (Oxford: Oxford University Press, 2006), 293.

53. See Forman, *Tragicomic Redemptions*, 113–145. Although Forman reads the play's interest in economic redemption in relation to Quisara's conversion, she takes the play's treatment of that conversion for granted. She does note in her discussion of *The Renegado,* however, that redemption in tragicomedy addresses "religious anxiety, which is real in and of itself" (181).

54. Ibid., 121.

55. Feerick, "Tragicomic Transformation," para. 3.

56. The Malaccan's, referred to as Moors in the play, represent a strange confluence of paganism and Islam. In this confluence, however, they are similar to romance Saracens who swear by Mohammed and Termagaunt.

57. This was an idea that was commonly expressed on the stage. Along with the examples already cited, we might also consider one of the reasons that Ward initially refuses to turn Turk in *A Christian Turned Turk*: Ward states that turning Turk is to "abjure / [His] name—and the belief [his] ancestors / Left to [his] being!" (Robert Daborne, *A Christian Turned Turk,* in *Three Turk Plays from Early Modern England,* ed. Daniel J. Vitkus [New York: Columbia University Press, 2000], 7.74–6).

58. See "breed, v.". *OED Online*. December 2011. Oxford University Press. http://www.oed.com/view/Entry/23020?rskey=Rs41No&result=2& isAdvanced=false (accessed March 12, 2012). Also see the *OED's* definition of "breed" as a noun: "1. generation, birth; parentage, extraction; natal or racial origin. of breed: of breeding age" ("breed, n." OED Online. December 2011. Oxford University Press. http://www.oed.com/view/Entry/23019 [accessed March 12, 2012]).

59. Neill, "'Material Flames,'" 119. Also see Solomon, "A Wild Shambles of Strange Gods," 27.

60. Quoted in Brad S. Gregory, *Salvation at Stake: Christian Martyrdom in Early Modern Europe* (Cambridge: Harvard University Press, 1999), 162.

61. I thus read this scene differently than Ania Loomba does in "Break her will." She reads this scene in relation to discourses of colonial and sexual mastery, and sees Armusia as wooing Quisara in such a way that the erotic becomes indistinguishable from the religious. I, however, do not see this as a scene of wooing—in which an individual attempts to inspire or elevate the romantic feelings in another—because Quisara's feelings toward Armusia

remain the same. Moreover, I see the play as disintegrating the romantic ties for the sake of religion.

62. I thus disagree with Jowitt's reading that Quisara's religious faith is ambiguous at the end ("*The Island Princess* and Race," 292). Not only does the discourse of martyrdom help verify her faith—she has nothing to gain, not even Armusia, in her death—but the redemption of the mercantile plot requires the audience's faith in her conversion.

63. Constancy is indeed a male characteristic in the play, which creates striking similarities between the king of Tidore and Armusia. Before Armusia is tortured for his blaspheme, the king endures torture while in prison. Both men remain resolute in their convictions, even as they face of torture.

64. In his edition of *The Renegado*, Michael Neill notes numerous similarities between the two plays, especially in the climactic conversions of the infidel women ("Introduction," in *The Renegado*, ed. Michael Neill [London: Methuen for The Arden Shakespeare, 2010], 9–10). Citations of *The Renegado* are from this edition.

65. See chapter 3 of Jane Hwang Degenhardt's *Islamic Conversion and Christian Resistance on the Early Modern Stage* (Edinburgh: University of Edinburgh Press, 2010), in which she argues *The Renegado* produces forms of religious embodiment that resist the threat of turning Turk (121–51).

66. Benedict Robinson, *Islam and Early Modern English Literature: The Politics of Romance from Spenser to Milton* (New York: Palgrave, 2007), 140.

67. For examples of reading moments like these as proof of Massinger's crypto-Catholic faith, see Frederick Boas, *An Introduction to Stuart Drama* (Oxford: Oxford University Press, 1946), 308; Alfred Cruickshank, *Philip Massinger* (New York: Frederic A. Stokes, 1920), 2; Thomas Dunn, *Philip Massinger: The Man and the Playwright* (London: Thomas Nelson, 1957), 191.

68. See my discussion of Jewel and *allegoresis* in chapter 2.

69. Degenhardt, *Islamic Conversion and Christian Resistance*, 149.

70. Jonathan Burton, *Traffic and Turning: Islam and English Drama, 1579–1624* (Newark: University of Delaware Press, 2005), 155.

71. See Robinson, *Islam and Early Modern English Literature*, 130–36; Degenhardt, 138–41; and Neill, "Turn and Counterturn," 162–67.

72. James Arminius, "Seventy-nine Private Disputation," in *The Works of James Arminius*, vol. 2, trans. James Nichols (Grand Rapids, MI: Baker Book House, 1986), 440.

73. See Susannah Brietz Monta, *Martyrdom and Literature in Early Modern England* (Cambridge: Cambridge University Press, 2005): "Protestant and Catholic authors shared the conviction, rooted in biblical precepts, that suffering identifies the true Christian" (117). On the exalted place of martyrdom in the English Protestant imagination, also see John R. Knott, *Discourses of Martyrdom in English Literature, 1563–1694* (Cambridge: Cambridge University Press, 1993).

Additionally, the connection between martyrdom and salvation was not only shared between Catholics and Anglicans. Anabaptists also connected baptism and martyrdom. See Gregory's discussion of the Anabaptist concept of "baptism in blood" (211).

74. See Everett Ferguson, *Baptism in the Early Church: History, Theology, and Liturgy in the First Five Centuries* (Grand Rapids, MI: WM. B. Eerdmans Publishing Co.), 417–19.

75. Robert Southwell, *An epistle of comfort* (London, 1587), sig. S4r.

76. Nicholas Ridley, "Letter XXXII. (Coverdale)," in *The Works of Nicholas Ridley, D.D.*, ed. Henry Christmas (Cambridge, UK: The University Press for The Parker Society, 1841), 397.

77. For example, see Ellen Macek, "The Emergence of a Feminine Spirituality in the Book of Martyrs," *Sixteenth Century Journal* 19 (1988): 62–80.

78. Loomba, "Delicious traffick," 215–16.

79. Mary Janell Metzger suggests that Jessica's "incorporation into Christian society is essential to defining her father's alien status" ("'Now by My Hood, a Gentle an No Jew': Jessica, *The Merchant of Venice*, and the Discourse of Early Modern English Identity," *PMLA* 113 [1998]: 59).

80. Loomba, "Delicious traffick," 215.

81. Degenhardt, *Islamic Conversion and Christian Resistance*, 138–39.

6. Afterword: A Political Afterlife of a Theology of Race and Conversion

1. Thomas Newton, *A notable historie of the Saracens* (London, 1575), sig. A2v.

2. Michael Dimock, "Belief that Obama is Muslim is Durable, Bipartisan—but Most Likely to Sway Democratic Votes," *Pew Research Center Publications*, http://pewresearch.org/pubs/898/belief-that-obama-is-muslim-is-bipartisan -but-most-likely-to-sway-democrats (Accessed April 2, 2012).

Bibliography

Primary

A proclamation giuen by the discreet lords and states, against the slanders laid vpon the euangelicall and reformed religion, by the Arminians and separatists: containing all the points, accusations, declarations and confessions, taken out of the last prouinciall synode holden at Arnhem, the 15 day of September last past. 1618. Together with the seuerall examinations and confessions (at Vtrecht and the Hage) of one Leydenberg, pentioner of Leyden, and Taurinus; with their sodaine and fearefull ends. London, 1618.

"A View of Popish Abuses Yet Remaining in the English Church." In *Religion and Society in Early Modern England: A Source Book*, ed. by David Cressy and Lori Anne Ferrell, 82–90. New York: Routledge, 1996.

Africanus, Leo. *A Geographical Historie of Africa.* London, 1600.

Ariosto, Ludovico. *Orlando Furioso.* Trans. by John Harington. Ed. by Robert McNulty. Oxford: Clarendon Press, 1972.

———. *Orlando Furioso e Cinque Canti.* 2 vols. Ed. by Remo Ceserani and Sergio Zatti. Torino: Unione Tipografico-Editrice Torinese, 1997.

Aristotle. *Generation of Animals.* Trans. by A. L. Peck. Cambridge: Harvard University Press, 1943.

———. *Poetics.* Trans. by James Hutton. New York: Norton, 1982.

Aquinas, Thomas. *The "Summa Theological of St. Thomas."* Vol. 17, trans. by The Fathers of the English Dominican Province. London: Burns, Oats and Washbourne Ltd., 1923.

Arminius, James. "Seventy-nine Private Disputation." In *The Works of James Arminius.* Vol. 2, trans. by James Nichols, 318–469. Grand Rapids, MI: Baker Book House. 1986.

Ascham, Roger. *The Schoolmaster.* In *English Works of Roger Ascam,* ed. by William Aldis Wright, 171–302. Cambridge, UK: The University Press, 1904.

Augustine. *Confessions.* Trans. by Henry Chadwick. Oxford: Oxford University Press, 1991.

Bale, John. *The image of bothe churches after the moste wonderfull and heauenly Reuela-cion of Sainct Iohn the Euangelist, contayning a very frutefull exposicion or paraphrase vpon the same. Wherin it is conferred with the other scripturs, and most auctorised his-toryes. Compyled by Iohn Bale an exile also in this life for the faythfull testimonye of Iesu.* London, 1570.

Becon, Thomas. *The Catechism of Thomas Becon.* Ed. by John Ayer. Cambridge, UK: The University Press for the Parker Society, 1844.

Best, George. *A true discourse of the late voyages of discoverie, for finding of a passage to Cathaya by the Northwest, under the conduct of Martin Forbisher Generall: Divided into three Bookes.* London: The Argonaut Press, 1938.

Bevis of Hampton. In *Four Romances of England: King Horn, Havelock the Dane, Bevis of Hampton, Athelston,* ed. by Ronald B. Herzman, Grahm Drake, and Eve Salsbury, 187–340. Kalamazoo: Western Michigan University Medieval Pub-lications, 1999.

Boemus, Joannes. *The fardle of facions conteining the aunciente maners, customes, and lawes, of the peoples enhabiting the two partes of the earth, called Affrike and Asie.* London, 1555.

Bradford, John. *The Writings of John Bradford.* Ed. by Aubrey Townsend. Cam-bridge, UK: The University Press for The Parker Society, 1853.

Brerely, John. *Sainct Austines Religion.* London, 1620.

Bullinger, Heinrich. *The Decades of Henry Bullinger.* Ed. by Thomas Harding. Cambridge, UK: The University Press for The Parker Society, 1849.

Calvin, John. *Institutes of the Christian Religion,* 2 vols. Trans. by Henry Beveridge. Grand Rapids, MI: WM. B. Eerdmans Publishing Co., 1966.

———. *Sermons of M. John Calvin vpon the Epistle of Sainct Paule to the Galatians.* London, 1574.

———. *A commentarie vpon S. Paules Epistles to the Corinthians.* London, 1577.

Cervantes, Miguel de. *The Adventures of Don Quixote.* Trans. by J. M. Cohen. New York: Penguin, 1951.

———. *El Ingenioso Hildago Don Quijote de la Manch.* Ed. by Salvador Farjardo and James A. Parr. Ashville: Pegasus Press/University of North Carolina at Ashville, 1998.

Chintio, Giraldi. *Gli Hecatommithi* (Decade 3, Story 7). Trans. by Geoffrey Bullough. In *The Narrative and Dramatic Sources of Shakespeare,* vol. 8, ed. by Geoffrey Bullough. London: Routledge and Kegan Paul, 1973.

———. *On Romances.* Trans. by Henry L. Snuggs. Lexington: University of Kentucky Press, 1968.

Cranmer, Thomas. *A Short Instruction into Christian Religion being a Catechism set forth by Archbishop Cranmer.* Ed. by Edward Burton. Oxford: Oxford Univer-sity Press, 1829.

———. *The Miscellaneous Letters and Writings of Thomas Cranmer.* Ed. by John Ed-mund Cox. Cambridge, UK: The University Press for The Parker Society, 1846.

Crashaw, Richard. *Steps to the Temple.* London, 1646.

Crooke, Helkiah. *Mikrokosmographia. A description of the body of man. Together vvith the controversies and figures thereto belonging. Collected and Trans. out of all the best authors of anatomy, especially out of Gasper Bauhinus, and Andreas Laurentius. By Helkiah Crooke Doctor in Physicke, phisitian to His Maiesty, and His Hignesse [sic] professor in anatomy and chirurgery. Published by the Kings Maiesties especiall direction and warrant, according to the first integrity, as it was originally written by the avthor.* London, 1615.

Daborne, Robert. *A Christian Turned Turk.* In *Three Turk Plays from Early Modern England,* ed. by Daniel J. Vitkus, 146–239. New York: Columbia University Press, 2000.

Documents of the Baptismal Liturgy. Ed. by E. C. Whitaker (1960). 3d edition, ed. by Maxwell. E. Johnson. Bristle: The Bath Press for Society for Promoting Christian Knowledge, 2003.

Fletcher, John. *The Island Princess.* In *The Dramatic Works in the Beaumont and Fletcher Canon.* Vol. 5, ed. by Fredson Bowers, 539–670. Cambridge: Cambridge University Press, 1966.

Foxe, John. *A sermon preached at the christening of a certaine Iew at London by Iohn Foxe.* London, 1578.

Frith, John. *A myrroure or lokynge glasse wherin you may beholde the sacramente of baptisme described.* London, 1548.

Geneva Bible. Geneva, 1560.

Greene, Robert. *Orlando Furioso.* Ed. by Robert B. McKerrow. Oxford: Malone Society Reprints, 1907.

Hanmer, Merideth. *The baptizing of a Turke. A sermon preached at the Hospitall of Saint Katherin, adioyning vnto her Maiesties Towre the 2. of October 1586. at the baptizing of one Chinano a Turke, borne at Nigropontus: by Meredith Hanmer, D. of Diuinitie.* London, 1586.

Harding, Thomas. *A confutation of a booke intituled An apologie of the Church of England.* London, 1565.

Hooper, John. *Later Writings of Bishop Hooper: together with his letters and other pieces.* Ed. by Charles Nevinson. Cambridge, UK: The University Press for The Parker Society, 1852.

Hubbock, William. *An apologie of infants in a sermon, prouing, by the reuealed will of God, that children preuented by death of their baptisme, by Gods election, may be saued.* London, 1594.

James I. *His Maiesties Lepanto, or heroicall song being part of his poeticall exercises at vacant houres.* London, 1603.

Jewel, John. *The Works of John Jewel, Bishop of Salisbury.* Ed. by John Ayre. Cambridge, UK: The University Press for the Parker Society, 1847.

Johnson, Francis. *A brief treatise conteyning some grounds and reasons, against two errours of the Anabaptists.* Amsterdam, 1609.

Johnson, Robert. *Tom a Lincoln*. Oxford: Oxford University Press for The Malone Society, 1992.

La Chanson de Roland. Trans. by Gerard J. Brault. University Park: The Pennsylvania State University Press, 1984.

Leigh, Dorothy. *The mothers blessing: or, The godly counsell of a gentlewoman, not long since deceased, left behind her for her children. Containing many good exhortations and good admonitions profitable for all parents, to leaue as a legacy to their children. By Mrs. Dorothy Leigh.* London, 1616.

Luther, Martin. "The Babylonian Captivity of the Church." Trans. by A. T. W. Steinhäuser. In *Luther's Works*, vol. 36, ed. by Abdel Ross Wentz, 2-126. Philadelphia, PA: Fortress Press, 1955), 73.

Massinger, Philip. *The Renegado*. Ed. by Michael Neill. London: Methuen for The Arden Shakespeare, 2010.

More, Thomas. *Responsio ad Lutherum*. In *The Complete Works of St. Thomas More*, vol. 5, ed. by John M. Headley. New Haven: Yale University Press, 1969.

Newton, Thomas. *A notable historie of the Saracens Briefly and faithfully descrybing the originall beginning, continuaunce and successe aswell of the Saracens, as also of Turkes, Souldans, Mamalukes, Assassines, Tartarians and Sophians.* London, 1575.

Nowell, Alexander. *A Catechisme, or first Instruction and Learning of Christian Religion*. Trans. by Thomas Norton. Cambridge, UK: The University Press for The Parker Society, 1853.

Ovid. *Metamorphoses*. Ed. by G. P. Goold. 2 vols. London: Loeb Classical Library, 1976.

———. *The. xv. Bookes of P. Ouidius Naso, entyluted Metamorphoses, Trans. oute of Latin into English meeter, by Arthur Golding Gentleman, A work very pleasaunt and delectable.* In *Shakespeare's Ovid*, trans. by Arthur Golding. Ed. by W.H.D. Rouse. Carbondale: Southern Illinois University Press, 1961.

———. *Metamorphoses*. Trans. by Charles Martin. New York: W. W. Norton & Company, 2004.

Pagitt, Ephraim. *Christianographie, or The description of the multitude and sundry sorts of Christians in the world not subiect to the Pope. With their vnitie, and how they agree with us in the principall points of difference betweene us and the Church of Rome.* London, 1635.

Perkins, William. *The Work of William Perkins*. Ed. by Ian Breward. Appleford, UK: The Sutton Courtenay Press, 1970.

Prynne, William. *The Church of Englands old antithesis to new Arminianisme. Where in 7. anti-Arminian orthodox tenents, are euidently proued; their 7. opposite Arminian (once popish and Pelagian) errors are manifestly disproued, to be the ancient, established, and vndoubted doctrine of the Church of England; by the concurrent testimony of the seuerall records and writers of our Church, from the beginning of her reformation, to this present. By William Prynne Gent. Hospitij Lincolniensis.* London, 1629.

Puttenham, George. *The Arte of English Poesy*. Ed. by Gladys Doidge Willcock and Alice Walker. Cambridge: Cambridge University Press, 1936.

Raynalde, Thomas. *The byrth of mankynde, newly Trans. out of Laten into Englysshe. In the which is entreated of all suche thynges the which chaunce to women in theyr labor, and all suche infyrmitees whiche happen vnto the infantes after they be delyuered. And also at the latter ende or in the thyrde or last boke is entreated of the conception of mankynde, and howe manye wayes it may be letted or furtheryd, with diuers other fruytefull thynges, as doth appere in the table before the booke*. London, 1540.

Ridley, Nicholas. *The Works of Nicolas Ridley, D.D.* Ed. by Henry Christmas. Cambridge, UK; The University Press for The Parker Society, 1841.

Rous, Francis. *The truth of three things, viz, the doctrine of predestination, free-will, and certainty of saluation. As it is maintayned by the Church of England, Wherein the grounds of Arminianisme is discouered, and confuted*. London, 1630.

Shakespeare, William. *Antony and Cleopatra*. Ed. by Michael Neill. Oxford: Oxford University Press, 1994.

———. *Hamlet*. Ed. by Ann Thompson and Neil Taylor. London: Thomson Learning for The Arden Shakespeare, 1995.

———. *Othello*. Ed. by E. A. J. Honigamann. Walton-on-Thames, Surrey, UK: Thomas Nelson & Sons, LTD for The Arden Shakespeare, 1997.

———. *Othello*. Ed. by Michael Neil. Oxford: Clarendon Press, 2006.

———. *Titus Andronicus*. Ed. by Jonathan Bate. New York: Routledge for The Arden Shakespeare, 1995.

———. *The Merchant of Venice*. Ed. by John Drakakis. London: Methuen for The Arden Shakespeare, 2010.

———. *The Norton Shakespeare*. Ed. by Stephen Greenblatt. New York: Norton, 1997.

———. *The Riverside Shakespeare*. 2d edition, ed. by G. Blakemore Evans. New York: Houghton Mifflin Company, 1997.

Sidney, Philip. *The Defense of Poesy*. In *Sir Philip Sidney: Selected Poetry and Prose*. 2d edition, ed. by Robert Kimbrough, 99-158. Madison: University of Wisconsin Press, 1983.

Smyth, John. *The character of the beast: or The false constitution of the church. Discovered in certayne passages betwixt Mr. R. Clifton & Iohn Smyth, concerning true Christian baptisme of new creatures, or new borne babes in Christ: &nd false baptisme of infants borne after the flesh. Referred to two propositions. 1. That infants are not to bee baptized. 2. That antichristians converted are to bee admitted into the true church by baptisme*. Middelburg, 1609.

Southwell, Robert. *An epistle of comfort, to the reuerend priestes, & to the honorable, worshipful, & other of the laye sort restrayned in durance for the Catholicke fayth*. London, 1588.

Spenser, Edmund. *The Faerie Queene*. Ed. by A. C. Hamilton. New York: Longman, 1977.

The boke of common praier, and administracion of the sacramentes, and other rites and cer-emonies in the Churche of Englande. London, 1552.

The First Authorized English Bible and the Cranmer Preface. Ed. by Harold R. Wil-loughby. Chicago: University of Chicago Press, 1942.

"The Form of Solemnization of Matrimony." In *The Book of Common Prayer 1559: The Elizabethan Prayer Book*, ed. John E. Booty, 290–9. Charlottes-ville: The University of Virginia Press for The Folger Shakespeare Library, 2005.

The homilie against disobedience and wylfull rebellion. London, 1570.

The King of Tars: Ed. from the Auchinleck MS, Advocates' 19.2.1. Ed. by Judith Per-ryman. *Middle English Texts* 12. Heidelberg: C. Winter, 1980.

"The Ministration of Baptism to be used in Churches." In *Religion and Society in Early Modern England*, ed. by David Cressey and Lori Anne Ferrell, 48–51. New York: Routledge, 1996.

"The Sarum Rite." In *Documents of the Baptismal Liturgy.* Ed. by E. C. Whitaker (1960). 3d edition, ed. by Maxwell. E. Johnson, 284–307. Bristle: The Bath Press for The Society for Promoting Christian Knowledge, 2003.

"Thirty-Nine Articles." In *Religion and Society in Early Modern England: A Source Book*, ed. by David Cressy and Lori Anne Ferrell, 59–70. New York: Rout-ledge, 1996.

Three Middle English Charlemagne Romances. Ed. by Alan Lupack. Kalamazoo: Me-dieval Institute Publications, 1990.

Torqarto, Tasso. *Gerusalemme liberata, Torquarto Tasso: Poesie.* Milan: Riccardo Ricciadri Editore, 1964.

———. *Discourses on the Heroic Poem.* Trans. by Mariella Cavalchini and Irene Samuel. Oxford: Clarendon Press, 1973.

Tyndale, William. *The exposition of the fyrste, seconde, and thyrde canonical epistles of S. Jhon.* London, 1538.

———. *Doctrinal Treatises and Introductions to Different Portions of the Holy Scriptures.* Ed. by Henry Walter. Cambridge, UK: The University Press for The Parker Society, 1848.

———. *The Pentateuch.* Ed. by F. F. Bruce. Carbondale: Southern Illinois Uni-versity Press, 1967.

Vicary, Thomas. *The Englishemans treasure: with the true anatomie of mans bodie: compiled by that excellent chirurgion maister Thomas Vicary Esquier, Sergeant Chirurgion to King Henry the 8. To King Edward the 6. To Queene Mary. And to our soueraigne lady Queene Elizabeth. And also chiefe chirurgion to S. Barthol-mewes Hospitall. Whereunto are annexed many secretes appertayning to chirurgerie, with diuers excellent approued remedies for all diseases the which are in man or woman, with emplasters of speciall cure, with other potions and drinkes approued in phisicke. Also the rare treasure of the English bathes: written by William Turner, doctor in phisicke. Gathered and set forth for the benefite of his friendes and countreymen in England by William Bremer practitioner in physicke and chirurgerie.* London, 1587.

Whitgift, John. *The defense of the aunswere to the Admonition against the replie of T. C. By Iohn VVhitgift Doctor of Diuinitie.* London, 1574.

Whitney, Geffrey. *A choice of emblemes, and other deuises, for the moste parte gathered out of sundrie writers, Englished and moralized. And diuers newly deuised, by Geffrey Whitney. A worke adorned with varietie of matter, both pleasant and profitable: wherein those that please, maye finde to fit their fancies: bicause herein, by the office of the eie, and the eare, the minde maye reape dooble delighte throughe holsome precepts, shadowed with pleasant deuises: both fit for the vertuous, to their incoraging: and for the wicked, for their admonishing and amendment.* Leiden, 1586.

Secondary

Achinstein, Sharon. "John Fox and the Jews." *Renaissance Quarterly* 54 (2001): 86–120.

Adelman, Janet. "Iago's Alter Ego: Race as Projection in *Othello*." *Shakespeare Quarterly* 48 (1997): 125–44.

———. *Blood Relations: Christian and Jew in* The Merchant of Venice. Chicago: University of Chicago Press, 2008.

Alpers, Paul. *What Is Pastoral?* Chicago: University of Chicago Press, 1996.

Anderson, Judith H. *Reading the Allegorical Interetext: Chaucer, Spenser, Shakespeare, Milton.* New York: Fordham University Press, 2008.

Anderson, Judith, and Joan Pong Linton. Introduction to *Go Figure: Energies, Forms, and Institutions in the Early Modern World*, ed. by Judith Anderson and Joan Pong Linton, 1–18. New York: Fordham University Press, 2011.

Appiah, Kwame Anthony. "Race." In *Critical Terms for Literary Studies,* ed. by Frank Lentricchia and Thomas McLaughlin, 277–78. Chicago: University of Chicago Press, 1995.

Ascoli, Albert Russell. *Ariosto's Bitter Harmony: Crisis and Evasion in the Italian Renaissance.* Princeton: Princeton University Press, 1987.

Auerbach, Erich. "Figura." In *Scenes from the Drama of European Literature: Six Essays*, trans. by Ralph Manheim, 11–71. New York: Meridian, 1959.

Ayers, David, and Nigel Smith, eds. "English Reformations," special issue of *Journal of Medieval and Early Modern Studies* 40 (2010).

Bach, Rebecca Ann. *Shakespeare and Renaissance Literature before Heterosexuality.* New York: Palgrave, 2007.

Barkan, Leonard. *The Gods Made Flesh: Metamorphosis and the Pursuit of Paganism.* New Haven: Yale University Press, 1986.

Bartels, Emily C. "Making more of the Moor. Aaron, Othello, and Renaissance Refashionings of Race." *Shakespeare Quarterly* 41 (1990): 433–54.

———. "Othello on Trial." In *New Casebooks: Othello*, ed. by Lena Cowin Orlin, 148–70. New York: Palgrave, 2004.

———. "*Othello* and the Moor." In *Early Modern Drama: A Critical Companion*, ed. by Garret A. Sullivan Jr. and Patrick Cheney, 140–51. Oxford: Oxford University Press, 2006.

———. *Speaking of the Moor: From* Alcatraz *to* Othello. Philadelphia: University of Pennsylvania Press, 2009.

Barthelemy, Anthony Gerard. *Black Face, Maligned Race: The Representation of Blacks in English Drama from Shakespeare to Southerne*. Baton Rouge: Louisiana State University Press, 1987.

Bate, Jonathan. "Shakespeare's Islands." In *Shakespeare and the Mediterranean*, ed. by Susan Brook, Vicente Forés and Thomas Clayton, 289–307. Newark: University of Delaware Press, 2004.

Berger, Harry. *The Allegorical Temper: Vision and Reality in Book II of* The Faerie Queene. New Haven: Yale University Press, 1957

———. "'Kidnapped Romance': Discourse in *The Faerie Queene*." In *Unfolding Tales: Essays on Renaissance Romance*, ed. by George M. Logan and Gordon Teskey, 208–56. Ithaca: Cornell University Press, 1989.

Bergvall, Åke. "The Theology of the Sign: St. Augustine and Spenser's Legend of Holiness" *SEL: Studies in English Literature, 1500–1900* 33 (1993): 21–42.

Biberman, Matthew. *Masculinity, Anti-Semitism and Early Modern English Literature: From the Satanic to the Effeminate Jew*. Aldershot, UK: Ashgate, 2004.

Blackburn, Daniel G. "Why Race Is not a Biological Concept." In *Race and Racism in Theory and Practice*, ed. by Berel Lange, 3–26. Oxford: Rowman and Littlefield, 2000.

Boose, Lynda E. "The Getting of a Lawful Race: Racial Discourse in Early Modern England and the Unrepresentable Black Woman." In *Women, 'Race,' and Writing*, ed. by Margo Hendricks and Patricia Parker, 35–54. New York: Routledge, 1994.

Borris, Kenneth. *Allegory and Epic in English Renaissance Literature: Heroic Form in Sidney, Spenser, and Milton*. Cambridge: Cambridge University Press, 2000.

Bovilsky, Lara. *Barbarous Play: Race on the English Renaissance Stage*. Minneapolis: University of Minnesota Press, 2008.

Boyarin, Daniel. *Carnal Israel: Reading Sex in Talmudic Culture*. Berkeley: University of California Press, 1993.

———. *A Radical Jew: Paul and the Politics of Identity*. Berkeley: University of California Press, 1994.

———. *Unheroic Conduct: The Rise of Heterosexuality and the Invention of the Jewish Male*. Berkeley: University of California Press, 1997.

Bradley, A. C. "Hegel's Theory of Tragedy." In *Hegel on Tragedy*, ed. by Anne Paolucci and Henry Paolucci, 367–88. Westport, CT: Greenwood Press, 1978.

————. *Shakespearean Tragedy: Lectures on* Hamlet, Othello, King Lear, *and* Macbeth. New York: Palgrave, 2007.

Braude, Benjamine. "The Sons of Noah and the Construction of Ethnic and Geographical Identities in the Medieval and Early Modern Periods." *William and Mary Quarterly* 54 (1997): 103–42.

Braun, Lundy. "Race, Ethnicity and Health: Can Genetics Explain Disparities?" *Perspectives in Biology and Medicine* 45 (2002): 159–74.

Bristol, Michael D. "Charivari and the Comedy of Abjection in *Othello*." *Renaissance Drama* 21 (1990): 3–21.

Britton, Dennis. "Religious Conversion and Circumcision as Theater." In *Religion and Drama in Early Modern England*, ed. by Jane Hwang Degenhardt and Elizabeth Williamson, 71–86. Aldershot, UK: Ashgate, 2011.

Burrow, Colin. *Epic Romance: Homer to Spenser*. Oxford: Clarendon Press, 1993.

Burton, Jonathan. *Traffic and Turning: Islam and English Drama, 1579–1624*. Newark: University of Delaware Press, 2005.

Caffiero, Marina. *Forced Baptism: Histories of Jews, Christians, and Converts in Papal Rome*. Trans. by Lydia G. Cochrane. Berkeley: University of California Press, 2012.

Cairncross, A. S. "Shakespeare and Ariosto: *Much Ado About Nothing, King Lear,* and *Othello*." *Renaissance Quarterly* 29 (1976): 178–82.

Calkin, Shiobhan Bly. *Saracens and the Making of English Identity: The Auchinleck Manuscript*. New York: Routledge, 2005.

Callaghan, Dympna. *Shakespeare Without Women: Representing Gender and Race on the Renaissance Stage*. New York: Routledge, 2000.

Cameron, Euan. *The European Reformation*. 2d edition. Oxford: Oxford University Press, 2012.

Carter, J. Kameron. *Race: A Theological Account*. Oxford: Oxford University Press.

Cavallo, Jo Ann. *The Romance Epics of Bioardo, Ariosto, and Tasso*. Toronto: University of Toronto Press, 2004.

Childres, William. *Transnational Cervantes*. Toronto: University of Toronto Press, 2006.

Cohen, Stephen. "Between Form and Culture: New Historicism and Cultural Studies." In *Renaissance Literature and Its Formal Engagements*, ed. by Mark David Ramussen, 17–33. New York: Palgrave, 2002.

————. Introduction to *Shakespeare and Historical Formalism*. Ed. by Stephen Cohen, 1–27. New York: Palgrave, 2007.

Colie, Rosalie A. *The Resources of Kind: Genre-Theory in the Renaissance*. Berkeley: University of California Press, 1973.

Collinson, Patrick. "William Tyndale and the Course of the English Reformation." *Reformation* 1 (1996): 72–97.

Cooper, Helen. *The English Romance in Time: Transforming Motifs from Geoffrey of Monmouth to the Death of Shakespeare*. Oxford: Oxford University Press, 2005.

Craik, Katherine A. *Reading Sensations in Early Modern England.* New York: Palgrave, 2007.

Cramer, Peter. *Baptism and Change in the Early Middle Ages, c. 200–c. 1150.* Cambridge: Cambridge University Press, 1993.

Crawford, Julie. *Marvelous Protestantism: Monstrous Births in Post-Reformation England.* Baltimore: Johns Hopkins University Press, 2005.

Crawford, Patricia. "The Construction and Experience of Maternity in Seventeenth-Century England." In *Women as Mothers in Pre-Industrial England,* ed. by Valerie Fildes, 3–38. New York: Routledge, 1990.

———. *Women and Religion in England, 1500–1720.* New York: Routledge, 1996.

———. *Blood, Bodies, and Families in Early Modern England.* Harlow, UK: Pearson / Longman, 2004.

Cressy, David. *Birth, Marriage, and Death: Ritual, Religion and the Life-Cycle in Tudor and Stuart England.* Oxford: Oxford University Press, 1997.

Daileader, Celia R. *Racism, Misogyny, and the* Othello *Myth.* Cambridge: Cambridge University Press, 2005.

de Weever, Jacqueline. *Sheba's Daughters: Whitening and Demonizing the Saracen Woman in Medieval French Epic.* New York: Garland, 1998.

Degenhardt, Jane Hwang. *Islamic Conversion and Christian Resistance on the Early Modern Stage.* Edinburgh: University of Edinburgh Press, 2010.

Dolven, Jeff. *Scenes of Instruction in Renaissance Romance.* Chicago: University of Chicago Press, 2007.

Derrida, Jacques. "The Law of Genre." *Critical Inquiry* 7 (1980): 55–81.

Dewar-Watson, Sarah. "Aristotle and Tragicomedy." In *Early Modern Tragicomedy,* ed. by Subha Mukherji and Raphael Lyne, 15–27. Cambridge: D. S. Brewer, 2007.

Dimmock, Matthew. *New Turkes: Dramatizing Islam and the Ottomans in Early Modern England.* Aldershot, UK: Ashgate.

Dimock, Michael. "Belief that Obama Is Muslim Is Durable, Bipartisan—but Most Likely to Sway Democratic Votes," *Pew Research Center Publications.* http://pewresearch.org/pubs/898/belief-that-obama-is-muslim-is-bipartisan-but-most-likely-to-sway-democrats (Accessed April 2, 2012).

Dolan, Frances E. *Dangerous Families: Representations of Domestic Crime in England, 1550–1700.* Ithaca: Cornell University Press, 1994.

Douglas, Mary. *Purity and Danger: An Analysis of Concept of Pollution and Taboo.* New York: Routledge, 2002.

Dubrow, Heather. *Shakespeare and Domestic Loss: Forms of Deprivation, Mourning, and Recuperation.* New York: Cambridge University Press, 1999.

Duffy, Eamon. *The Stripping of the Altars: Traditional Religion in England, 1400–1580.* New Haven: Yale University Press, 1992.

Elk, Martine van. "'This sympathizèd one day's error': Genre, Representation, and Subjectivity in *The Comedy of Errors.*" *Shakespeare Quarterly* 60 (2009): 47–72.

Euler, Carrie. "Anabaptism and Anti-Anabaptism in the Early English Reformation: Defining Protestant Heresy and Orthodoxy during the Reign of Edward VI." In *Heresy, Literature, and Politics in Early Modern English Culture,* ed. by David Loewenstein and John Marshall, 40–58. Cambridge: Cambridge University Press, 2006.

Evans, G. R. *Problems of Authority in the Reformation Debates.* Cambridge: Cambridge University Press, 1992.

Evans, Maurice. "The Fall of Guyon." *ELH* 28 (1961): 215–24.

Everett, Dorothy. "A Characterization of the English Medieval Romance," 1929. In *Essays on Middle English Literature,* ed. by Patricia Kean, 1–22. Oxford: Clarendon Press, 1955.

Evendeen, Doreen. *The Midwives of Seventeenth-Century London.* Cambridge: Cambridge University Press, 2000.

Everson, Jane E. "Translating the Pope and the Apennines: Harington's Version of *Orlando Furioso.*" *Modern Language Review* 100 (2005): 645–58.

Feerick, Jean. "Spenser, Race, and Ireland." *English Literary Renaissance* 32 (2002): 85–117.

———. "Tragicomic Transformations: Passion, Politics, and the 'Art to Turn' in Fletcher's *The Island Princess.*" *Early Modern Literary Studies* 19 (2009) 3.1–24. http://purl.oclc.org/emls/si-19/feerflet.html.

———. *Strangers of Blood: Relocating Race in the Renaissance.* Toronto: University of Toronto Press, 2010.

Felperin, Howard. *Shakespearean Romance.* Princeton: Princeton University Press, 1972.

Ferguson, Everett. *Baptism in the Early Church: History, Theology, and Liturgy in the First Five Centuries.* Grand Rapids, MI: Wm. B. Eerdmans Publishing Co., 2009.

Fitcher, Andrew. "Tasso's Epic of Deliverance." *PMLA* 93 (1978): 264–74.

Fitzgerald, Thomas. *The Ideology of Religious Studies.* New York: Oxford University Press, 2000.

Fletcher, Angus. *Allegory: The Theory of a Symbolic Mode.* Ithaca: Cornell University Press, 1964.

Fredrickson, George M. *Racism: A Short History.* Princeton: Princeton University Press, 2002.

Floyd-Wilson, Mary. *English Ethnicity and Race in Early Modern Drama.* Cambridge: Cambridge University Press, 2003.

Forman, Valerie. *Tragicomic Redemptions: Global Economics and the Early Modern English Stage.* Philadelphia: University of Pennsylvania Press, 2008.

Fowler, Alistair. "The Image of Mortality: 'The Faerie Queene,' II.i–ii." *The Huntington Library Quarterly* 24 (1961): 91–110.

———. *Kinds of Literature: An Introduction to the Theory of Genres and Modes.* Cambridge, MA: Harvard University Press, 1982.

Fox, Cora. *Ovid and the Politics of Emotion in Elizabethan England.* New York: Palgrave, 2008.

Frazer, James G. *The Golden Bough: A Study of Magic and Religion.* 1890. Abridged edition, ed. by Robert Frazier. New York: Oxford University Press, 1995.

Fredrickson, George M. *Racism: A Short History.* Princeton: Princeton University Press, 2002.

Frow, John. *Genre.* New York: Routledge, 2006.

Frye, Northrop. *Anatomy of Criticism: Four Essays.* Princeton: Princeton University Press, 1957.

———. *Secular Scriptures: A Study of the Structure of Romance.* Cambridge, MA: Harvard University Press, 1976.

Fuchs, Barbara. *Mimesis and Empire: The New World, Islam and European Identities.* Cambridge: Cambridge University Press, 2001.

———. *Passing for Spain: Cervantes and the Fictions of Identity.* Urbana: University of Illinois Press, 2003.

———. *Romance.* New York: Routledge, 2004.

Garcés, María Antonia. "Zoraida's Veil: 'The Other Scene' of The Captive's Tale." *Revista de Estudios Hispanicos* 23 (1989): 65–98.

———. *Cervantes in Algiers: A Captive's Tale.* Nashville: Vanderbilt University Press, 2002

Gilbert, Jane. "Putting the Pulp into Fiction: The Lump-Child and its Parents in *The King of Tars.*" In *Pulp Fictions of Medieval England*, ed. by Nicola McDonald, 102–23. Manchester: Manchester University Press, 2004.

Gillespie, Stuart. "Shakespeare and the Greek Romance: 'like an old tale still.'" In *Shakespeare and the Classics*, ed. by Charles Martindale and A. B. Taylor, 225–40. Cambridge: Cambridge Univ. Press, 2004.

Gillies, John. *Shakespeare and the Geography of Difference.* New York: Cambridge University Press, 1994.

Gless, Darryl J. *Interpretation and Theology in Spenser.* Cambridge: Cambridge University Press, 1994.

Goldenberg, David M. *The Curse of Ham: Race and Slavery in Early Judaism, Christianity and Islam.* Princeton: Princeton University Press, 2003.

Goldberg, Jonathan. *Endlesse Worke: Spenser and the Structures of Discourse.* Baltimore: Johns Hopkins University Press, 1981.

Green, Ian. *Print and Protestantism in Early Modern England.* Oxford: Oxford University Press, 2000.

Greenblatt, Stephen. *Renaissance Self-Fashioning: From More to Shakespeare.* Chicago: University of Chicago Press, 1980.

Greene, Roland. "A Primer of Spenser's Worldmaking: Alterity in the Bower of Bliss." In *Worldmaking Spenser: Explorations in the Early Modern Age*, ed. by Patrick Cheney and Lauren Silverman, 9–31. Lexington: University of Kentucky Press, 2000.

Gregory, Brad S. *Salvation at Stake: Christian Martyrdom in Early Modern Europe*. Cambridge, MA: Harvard University Press, 1999.

Griffin, Nathaniel E. "The Definition of Romance." *PMLA* 38 (1923): 50–70.

Grinnell, Richard. "Witchcraft, Race, and the Rhetoric of Barbarism in *Othello* and *1 Henry IV*." *Upstart Crow* 24 (2004): 72–80.

Guibbory, Achsah. *Christian Identity, Jews, and Israel in the Seventeenth Century*. Oxford: Oxford University Press, 2010.

Guilfoyle, Cherrell. "Othello, Otuel, and the English Charlemagne Romances." *Review of English Studies* 38 (1987): 50–55

Guillory, John. *Poetic Authority: Spenser, Milton and Literary History*. New York: Columbia University Press, 1983.

Habib, Imtiaz. *Black Lives in the English Archive, 1500–1677: Imprints of the Invisible*. Aldershot, UK: Ashgate, 2008.

Haigh, Christopher. *English Reformations: Religion, Politics and Society Under the Tudors*. Oxford: Oxford University Press, 1993.

Hall, Basil. "The Early Rise and Gradual Decline of Lutheranism in England (1520–1600)." In *Reform and Reformation: England and the Continent, c. 1500–c.1750*, ed. by Derek Baker, 103–47. Oxford: Basil Blackwell, 1979.

Hall, Kim. "Guess Who's Coming to Dinner?: Colonization and Miscegenation in *The Merchant of Venice*." *Renaissance Drama* 23 (1992): 87–111.

———. *Things of Darkness: Economies of Race and Gender in Early Modern England*. New York: Cornell University Press, 1995.

———. "Race and Religion." *Othello: Texts and Contexts*, ed. by Kim Hall, 171–85. New York: Bedford/St. Martin's, 2007.

Hamilton, A. C. "A Theological Reading of *The Faerie Queene*, Book II." *ELH* 25 (1958): 155–162

Hannaford, Ivan. *Race: The History of an Idea in the West*. Baltimore: Johns Hopkins University Press, 1996.

Harris, Jonathan Gil. *Sick Economies: Drama, Mercantilism, and Shakespeare's England*. Philadelphia: University of Pennsylvania Press, 2003.

Hays, Michael L. *Shakespeare's Tragedies as Chivalric Romance: Rethinking* Macbeth, Hamlet, Othello *and* King Lear. Cambridge, UK: D. S. Brewer, 2003.

Heal, Felicity. *Reformation in Britain and Ireland*. Oxford: Oxford University Press, 2003.

Hegel, G. W. F. *Hegel on Tragedy*. Ed. by Anne and Henry Paolucci. Westport, CT: Greenwood Press, 1978.

Helegerson, Richard. "Tasso on Spenser: The Politics of Chivalric Romance." *The Yearbook on English Studies* 21 (1991): 153–67.

———. *Forms of Nationhood: The Elizabethan Writing of England*. Chicago: University of Chicago Press, 1992.

Hendricks, Margo, and Patricia Parker, eds. *Women, "Race," and Writing in the Early Modern Period*. New York: Routledge, 1994.

Heng, Geraldine. *Empire of Magic: Medieval Race and the Politics of Cultural Fantasy*. New York: Columbia University Press, 2003.

Hershenzon, Daniel Bernardo. *Early Modern Spain and the Creation of the Mediterranean: Captivity, Commerce, and Knowledge*. Ph.D. diss., University of Michigan, 2011.

Hill, Christopher. "Tyndale and His Successors." *Reformation* 1 (1996): 98–112.

Holsinger. Bruce. "The Color of Salvation: Desire, Death, and the Second Crusade in Bernard of Clairvaux's *Sermons on the Song of Songs*." In *The Tongue of the Fathers: Gender and Ideology in Twelfth-Century Latin*, ed. by David Townsend and Andrew Taylor, 156–86. Philadelphia: University of Pennsylvania Press, 1998.

Hope, R. C. *The Legendary Lore of the Holy Wells of England*. London, 1893.

Horne, P. R. *The Tragedies of Giambattista Cinthio Giraldi*. Oxford: Oxford University Press, 1962.

Howard, Jean. *The Stage and Social Struggle in Early Modern England*. New York: Routledge, 1994.

Hunt, Maurice. "Romance and Tragicomedy." In *A Companion to Renaissance Drama*, ed. by Arthur Kinney, 384–98. Oxford: Wiley-Blackwell, 2002.

Hyman, Wendy Beth. "Seizing Flowers in Spenser's Bower and Garden." *English Literary Renaissance* 37 (2007): 193–214.

Ivic, Christopher. "Spenser and the Bounds of Race." *Genre* 32 (1999): 141–173.

Iyengar, Sujata. *Shades of Difference: Mythologies of Skin Color in Early Modern England*. Philadelphia: University of Pennsylvania Press, 2005.

Jackson, Ken, and Arthur F. Marotti. "The Turn to Religion in Early Modern Studies." *Criticism* 46 (2004): 167–90.

James, Heather. "Dido's Ear: Tragedy and the Politics of Response." *Shakespeare Quarterly* 52 (2001): 360–82.

Jameson, Fredric. *The Political Unconscious: Narrative as a Socially Symbolic Act*. Ithaca: Cornell University Press, 1981.

Jankowski, Theodora A. *Pure Resistance: Queer Virginity in Early Modern English Drama*. Philadelphia: University of Pennsylvania Press, 2006.

Javitch, Daniel. *Proclaiming a Classic: The Canonization of Orlando Furioso*. Princeton: Princeton University Press, 1991.

———. "Reconsidering the Last Part of *Orlando Furioso*: Romance to the Bitter End." *Modern Language Quarterly* 71 (2010): 385–405.

Jennings, Willie James. *The Christian Imagination: Theology and the Origins of Race*. New Haven: Yale University Press, 2011.

Johnson, Carroll B. *Cervantes and the Material World*. Urbana: University of Illinois Press, 2000.

Johnson, Maxwell E. *The Rites of Christian Initiation: Their Evolution and Interpretation*. Collegeville, MN: Liturgical Press, 2007.

Johnson-Haddad, Miranda. "Englishing Ariosto: *Orlando Furioso* at the Court of Elizabeth I." *Comparative Literature Studies* 31 (1994): 323–50.

Jowitt, Claire. "*The Island Princess* and Race." In *Early Modern English Drama: A Critical Companion,* ed. by Garrett A. Sullivan, Jr., Patrick Cheney, and Andrew Hadfield. Oxford: Oxford University Press, 2006.

Kaplan, M. Lindsay. "Jessica's Mother: Medieval Constructions of Jewish Race and Gender in *The Merchant of Venice*." *Shakespeare Quarterly* 58 (2007): 1–30.

Kaske, Carol V. "The Bacchus Who Wouldn't Wash: *Faerie Queeen,* Book II.i–ii." *Renaissance Quarterly* 29 (1976): 159–209.

———. *Spenser and Biblical Poetics*. Ithaca: Cornell University Press, 1999

Katz, David. *The Jews in the History of England, 1485–1850*. Oxford: Clarendon Press, 1994.

Kay, Sarah. *The Chanson de Geste in the Age of Romance: Political Fictions*. Oxford: Clarendon Press, 1995.

Kidd, Colin. *British Identities Before Nationalism: Ethnicity and Nationhood in the Atlantic World, 1600–1800*. Cambridge: Cambridge University Press, 1999.

———. *The Forging of the Races: Race and Scripture in the Protestant Atlantic World, 1600–2000*. Cambridge: Cambridge University Press, 2006.

Kinoshita, Sharon. *Medieval Boundaries: Rethinking Difference in Old French Literature*. Philadelphia: University of Pennsylvania Press, 2006.

Kneidel, Gregory. *Rethinking the Turn to Religion in Early Modern English Literature: The Poetics of All Believers*. New York: Palgrave, 2008.

Knight, G. Wilson. *The Crown of Life: Essays in Interpretation of Shakespeare's Final Plays*. 1965. New York: Methuen, 1985.

Knott, John R. *Discourses of Martyrdom in English Literature, 1563–1694*. Cambridge: Cambridge University Press, 1993.

Korhone, Anu. "Washing the Ethiope White: Conceptualizing Black Skin in Renaissance England." In *Black Africans in Renaissance Europe*, ed. by T. F. Earle and K. J. P. Lowe, 94–112. Cambridge: Cambridge University Press, 2005.

Krier, Theresa M. *Gazing on Secret Sights: Spenser and the Decorums of Vision*. Ithaca: Cornell University Press, 1990.

Lamb, Mary Ellen, and Valarie Wayne, eds. *Staging Early Modern Romance: Prose Fiction, Dramatic Romance, and Shakespeare*. New York: Routledge, 2008.

Lampert, Lisa. "Race, Periodicity, and the (Neo-) Middle Ages." *Modern Language Quarterly* (2004): 391–421.

———. *Gender and Jewish Difference from Paul to Shakespeare*. Philadelphia: University of Pennsylvania Press, 2004.

Laqueur, Thomas. *Making Sex: Body and Gender from the Greeks to Freud*. Cambridge: Harvard University Press, 1999.

Lee, Judith. "The English Ariosto: The Elizabethan Poet and the Marvelous." *Studies in Philology* 80 (1983): 277–99.

Lenholf, Kent R. "Incest and Empire in *The Faerie Queene*." *ELH* 73 (2006): 215–43.

Lewalski, Barbara. "Biblical Allusion and Allegory in *The Merchant of Venice*." *Shakespeare Quarterly* 13 (1962): 327–43.

Lievsay, John L. *The Englishman's Italian Books, 1500–1700*. Philadelphia: University of Pennsylvania Press, 1969.

Little, Arthur. *Shakespeare Jungle Fever: National-Imperial Re-Visions of Race, Rape and Sacrifice*. Stanford: Stanford University Press, 2000.

Lindmann, Mary. *Medicine and Society in Early Modern Europe*. Cambridge: Cambridge University Press, 1999.

Linton, Joan Pong. *The Romance of the New World: Gender and Literary Formations of English Colonialism*. Cambridge: Cambridge University Press, 1998.

Livingston, David N. *Adam's Ancestors: Race, Religion, and the Politics of Human Origin*. Baltimore: Johns Hopkins University Press, 2008.

Loewenstein, David, and John Marshall. Introduction to *Heresy, Literature, and Politics in Early Modern English Culture,* ed. by David Loewenstein and John Marshall, 1–10. Cambridge: Cambridge University Press, 2006.

Loomba, Ania. *Gender, Race, Renaissance Drama*. Manchester: University of Manchester Press, 1989.

———. "'Break her will, and bruise no bone sir': Colonial and Sexual Mastery in Fletcher's *The Island Princess*." *Journal for Early Modern Cultural Studies* 2 (2002): 68–108

———. "'Delicious traffick': Racial and Religious Difference on Early Modern Stages." In *Shakespeare and Race*, ed. by Catherine M.S. Alexander and Stanley Wells, 203–24. Cambridge: Cambridge University Press, 2000.

———. *Shakespeare, Race, and Colonialism*. Oxford: Oxford University Press, 2002.

Loomba, Ania, and Jonathan Burton. "Aesop, *Fables*." In *Race in Early Modern Europe: A Documentary Companion*, ed. by Ania Loomba and Jonathan Burton, 39–40. New York: Palgrave, 2007.

Lupton, Julia Reinhard. *Citizen-Saints: Shakespeare and Political Theology*. Chicago: University of Chicago Press, 2005.

———. "The Religious Turn (to Theory) in Shakespeare Studies." *Modern Language Notes* 44 (2006): 146–8.

MacCulloch, Diarmaid. *Thomas Cranmer: A Life*. New Haven: Yale University Press, 1998.

MacDonald, Joyce Green. *Women and Race in Early Modern Texts.* Cambridge: Cambridge University Press, 2003.

Macek, Ellen. "The Emergence of a Feminine Spirituality in the Book of Martyrs." *Sixteenth Century Journal* 19 (1988): 62–80.

Maltby, Judith. *Prayer Book and People in Elizabethan and Early Stuart England.* Cambridge: Cambridge University Press, 2000.

Marotti, Arthur F. *Religious Ideology and Cultural Fantasy: Catholic and Anti-Catholic in Early Modern England.* South Bend, IN: University of Notre Dame Press, 2005.

Marshal, Peter. "(Re)Defining the English Reformation." *Journal of British Studies* 48 (2009): 564–86.

Matar, Nabil. *Islam in Britain, 1558–1685.* Cambridge: Cambridge University Press, 1998.

———. *Turks, Moors, and Englishmen in the Age of Discovery.* New York: Columbia University Press, 1999.

———. "English Accounts of Captivity in North Africa and the Middle East: 1577–1625." *Renaissance Quarterly* 54 (2001): 53–72.

———. Introduction to *Piracy, Slavery and Redemption: Barbary Captivity Narratives in Early Modern England*, ed. by Daniel Vitkus, 1–52. New York: Columbia University Press, 2001.

———. *Britain and Barbary, 1589–1689.* Gainesville: University Press of Florida, 2005.

McSheffrey, Shannon. *Gender and Heresy: Women and Men in Lollard Communities, 1420–1530.* Philadelphia: University of Pennsylvania Press, 1995.

Mentz, Steve. *Romance for Sale in Early Modern England: The Rise of Prose Fiction.* Aldershot, UK: Ashgate, 2006.

Metzger, Mary Janell. "'No by My Hood, a Gentle and No Jew': Jessica, *The Merchant of Venice*, and the Discourse of Early Modern English Identity." *PMLA* 113 (1998): 52–63.

Miller, David Lee. *The Poem's Two Bodies: The Poetics of the 1590 Faerie Queene.* Princeton: Princeton University Press, 1988.

Miller, Lewis H. "A Secular Reading of *The Faerie Queene*, Book II." *ELH* 33 (1966): 154–169.

Miller, Naomi J. "'Hens should be served first': Prioritizing Maternal Production in Early Modern Pamphlet Debate." In *Debating Gender in Early Modern England, 1500–1700*, ed. by Cristina Malcomson and Mihoko Susuki, 161–84. New York: Palgrave, 2002.

Monta, Susannah Brietz. *Martyrdom and Literature in Early Modern England.* Cambridge: Cambridge University Press, 2005.

Morini, Massimiliano. "Sir John Harington and the Poetics of Tudor Translation." In *Travels and Translation in the Sixteenth Century: Selected Papers from the Second International Conference of the Tudor Symposium*, ed. by Mike Pincombe, 121–36. Aldershot, UK: Ashgate, 2000.

————. *Tudor Translation in Theory and Practice*. Aldershot, UK: Ashgate, 2006.

Mowat, Barbara. "'What's in a Name?' Tragicomedy, Romance, or Late Comedy." In *A Companion to Shakespeare's Works*, vol. 4: *The Poems, Problem Comedies, Late Plays*, ed. by Richard Dutton and Jean E. Howard, 12–49. Oxford: Wiley-Blackwell, 2003.

Murray, Molly. *The Poetics of Conversion in Early Modern English Literature*. Cambridge: Cambridge University Press, 2009.

Neill, Michael. "Unproper Beds: Race, Adultery, and the Hideous in *Othello*." *Shakespeare Quarterly* 40 (1989): 383–412.

————. "Material Flames: The Space of Mercantile Fantasy in John Fletcher's *The Island Princess*." *Renaissance Drama* 28 (1997): 99–131.

————. "'Mulattos,' 'Blacks,' and 'Indian Moors': *Othello* and Early Modern Constructions of Human Difference." *Shakespeare Quarterly* 49 (1998): 361–74.

————. "Turn and Counterturn: Merchanting, Apostasy and Tragicomic Form in Massinger's *The Renegado*." In *Early Modern Tragicomedy*, ed. by Subha Mukherji and Raphael Lyne, 154–74. Cambridge, UK: D. S. Brewer, 2007.

Nelson, T. G. A. "Sir John Harington and the Renaissance Debate over Allegory." *Studies in Philology* 82 (1985): 359–79.

Newcomb, Lori Humphrey. *Reading Popular Romance in Early Modern England*. New York: Columbia University Press, 2002.

Newman, Karen. *Fashioning Femininity and English Renaissance Drama*. Chicago: University of Chicago Press, 1991.

Ng, Su Fang. "Translation, Interpretation, and Heresy: The Wycliffite Bible, Tyndale's Bible, and the Contested Origin." *Studies in Philology* 98 (2001): 315–38.

Nocentelli, Carmen. "The Erotics of Mercantile Imperialism: Cross-Cultural Requitedness in the Early Modern Period." *The Journal of Early Modern Cultural Studies* 8 (2008): 134–52.

————. "Spice Race: *The Island Princess* and the Politics of Transnational Appropriation." *PMLA* 125 (2010): 572–88.

Nohrnberg, James. *The Analogy of "The Faerie Queene."* Princeton: Princeton University Press, 1992.

Old, Hughes Oliphant. *The Shaping of the Reformed Baptismal Right in the Sixteenth Century*. Grand Rapids, MI: Wm. B. Eerdmans Publishing Co., 1992.

Olsen, Kristen. "Erminia Delivered: Notes on Tasso and Romance." *Quaderni d'italianistica* 3 (1982): 12–25.

Orlin, Lena Cowen. *Private Matters and Public Culture in Post-Reformation England*. Ithaca: Cornell University Press, 1994.

O'Rourke, James. "Racism and Homophobia in *The Merchant of Venice*." *ELH* 70 (2003): 375–97.

Panek, Jennifer. *Widows and Suitors in Early Modern Comedy.* Cambridge: Cambridge University Press, 2004.

Parker, Patricia. "The Progress of Phaedria's Bower: Spenser to Coleridge." *ELH* 40 (1973): 372–97.

———. *Inescapable Romance: Studies in the Poetics of a Mode.* Princeton: Princeton University Press, 1979.

———."Suspended Instruments: Lyric and Power in the Bower of Bliss." In *Literary Fat Ladies: Rhetoric Gender, Property,* ed. by Patricia Parker, 54–66. London: Methuen, 1987.

———. "Fantasies of 'Race' and 'Gender': Africa, *Othello* and Bringing to Light." In *Women, "Race," and Writing in the Early Modern Period,* ed. by Margo Hendricks and Patricia Parker, 84–117. New York: Routledge, 1994.

Penuel, Susanne. "Castrating the Creditor in *The Merchant of Venice*," *SEL: Studies in English Literature 1500–1900* 44 (2004): 255–75.

Peters, Christine. "Gender, Sacrament and Ritual: The Making and Meaning of Marriage in Late Medieval and Early Modern England." *Past and Present* 169 (2000): 63–96.

Prager, Carolyn. " 'If I be Devil': English Renaissance Responses to the Proverbial and Ecumenical Ethiopian." *Journal of Medieval and Renaissance Studies* 17 (1987): 257–79.

Prior, Roger. "Shakespeare's Debt to Ariosto." *Notes and Queries* 48 (2001): 289–92.

Pugh, Syrith. *Spenser and Ovid.* Aldershot, UK: Ashgate, 2005.

Questier, Michael C. *Conversion, Politics, and Religion in England, 1580–1625.* Cambridge: Cambridge University Press, 1996.

Quilligan, Maureen. *The Language of Allegory: Defining the Genre.* Ithaca: Cornell University Press, 1979.

———. *Milton's Spenser: The Poetics of Reading.* Ithaca: Cornell University Press, 1983.

———. *Incest and Agency in Elizabethan England.* Philadelphia: University Of Pennsylvania Press, 2005.

Quint, David. The Figure of Atlante: Ariosto and Boiardo's Poem." *Modern Language Notes* 94 (1979): 77–91.

———. *Origin and Originality in Renaissance Literature: Versions of the Source.* New Haven: Yale University Press, 1983.

———. *Epic and Empire: Politics and Generic Form from Virgil to Milton.* Princeton: Princeton University Press, 1993

Ragussis, Michael. *Figures of Conversion: "The Jewish Question" & English National Identity.* Durham, NC: Duke University Press, 1995.

Raman, Shankar. *Framing "India": The Colonial Imaginary in Early Modern Culture.* Stanford: Stanford University Press, 2002.

Rashkow, Illona N. "Hebrew Bible Translation and the Fear of Judaization." *The Sixteenth Century Journal* 21(1990): 237–33.

Reed, David. *Temperate Conquests: Spenser and the Spanish New World.* Detroit: Wayne State University Press, 2000.

Rich, Townsend. *Harington and Ariosto: A Study in Elizabethan Verse Translation.* New Haven: Yale University Press, 1940.

Riggs, John Wheelan. *Baptism in the Reformed Tradition: A Historical and Practical Theology.* Louisville, KY: Westminster John Knox Press, 2002.

Robinson, Benedict S. *Islam and Early Modern English Literature: The Politics of Romance from Spenser to Milton.* New York: Palgrave, 2007.

———."Returning to Egypt: 'The Jew,' 'the Turk,' and the English Republic.' In *Milton and the Jews,* ed. by Douglas A. Brooks, 178–99. Cambridge: Cambridge University Press, 2008.

Root, Deborah. "Speaking Christian: Orthodoxy and Difference in Sixteenth-Century Spain." *Representations* 23 (1988): 118–34.

Rose, Mark. "Othello's Occupation: Shakespeare and the Romance of Chivalry." *English Literary Renaissance* 15 (1985): 293–311

Ryrie, Alec. "The Strange Death of Lutheran England." *Journal of Ecclesiastical History* 53 (2002): 64–92.

Salvidore, Mateo. "The Ethiopian Age of Exploration: Prester John's Discovery of Europe, 1306–1458." *Journal of World History* 21 (2010): 593–627.

Schoenfeldt, Michael C. *Bodies and Selves in Early Modern England: Physiology and Inwardness in Spenser, Shakespeare, Herbert, and Milton.* Cambridge: Cambridge University Press, 1999.

Schwartz, Regina. M. *Sacramental Poetics at the Dawn of Secularism: When God Left the World.* Stanford: Stanford University Press, 2008.

Scott-Warren, Jason. *Sir John Harington and the Book as Gift.* Oxford: Oxford University Press, 2001.

Simpson, James. *Reform and Cultural Revolution.* Oxford: Oxford University Press, 2002.

Shapiro, James. *Shakespeare and the Jews.* New York: Columbia University Press, 1996.

Sherberg, Michael. "Epic and Romance in Tasso's Rinaldo: The Conflict of Genre." *Stanford Italian Review* 9 (1990): 67–85.

Shuger, Debora Kuller. *Habits of Thought in the English Renaissance: Religion, Politics, and the Dominant Culture.* Berkeley: University of California Press, 1990.

Silberman, Lauren. "The Hermaphrodite and the Metamorphosis of Spenserian Allegory." *English Literary Renaissance* 17 (1987): 208–23.

———. "*The Faerie Queene,* Book II and the Limits of Temperance." *Modern Language Studies* 17 (1987): 9–22.

Slights, William W. E. "'Marginall Notes That Spoile the Text': Scriptural Annotation in the English Renaissance." *Huntington Library Quarterly* 55 (1992): 255–78.

Smedley, Audrey, and Brian D. Smedley. "Race as Biology Is Fiction, Racism as a Social Problem Is Real: Anthropological and Historical Perspectives on the Social Construction of Race." *American Psychologist* 60 (2005): 16–26.

Smith, Hallett. *Shakespeare's Romances: A Study of Some Ways of the Imagination.* San Marino, CA: The Huntington Library, 1972.

Smith, Ian. "Barbarian Errors: Performing Race in Early Modern England." *Shakespeare Quarterly* 49 (1998): 168–86.

———. "White Skin, Black Masks: Racial Cross-Dressing on the Early Modern Stage." *Renaissance Drama* 32 (2003): 33–67.

———. *Race and Rhetoric in the Renaissance: Barbarian Errors.* New York: Palgrave, 2009.

Snyder, Susan. *The Comic Matrix of Shakespeare's Tragedies: Romeo and Juliet, Hamlet, Othello and King Lear.* Princeton: Princeton University Press, 1979.

Solomon, Andrea Remi. "'A Wild Shambles of Strange Gods:' The Conversion of Quisara in Fletcher's *The Island Princess.*" In *Christian Encounters with the Other,* ed. by John C. Howely, 17–32. New York: New York University Press, 1998.

Spierling, Karen E. *Infant Baptism in Reformation Geneva: The Shaping of Community, 1536–1564.* Aldershot, UK: Ashgate, 2005.

Spiller, Elizabeth A. "From Imagination to Miscegenation: Race and Romance in Shakespeare's *The Merchant of Venice.*" *Renaissance Drama* 29 (1998): 137–64.

———. *Reading and the History of Race in the Renaissance.* Cambridge: Cambridge University Press, 2011.

Stevens, Paul. "'Leviticus Thinking' and the Rhetoric of Early Modern Colonialism." *Criticism* 34 (1993): 441–61.

Tambling, Jeremy. *Allegory.* New York: Routledge, 2010.

Taussig, Michael. *Mimesis and Alterity: A Particular History of the Senses.* New York: Routledge, 1993.

Teskey, Gordon. *Allegory and Violence.* Ithaca: Cornell University Press, 1996.

Thomas, Keith. *Religion and the Decline of Magic.* New York: Charles Scribner's Sons, 1971.

Thompson, Ayanna. *Performing Race and Torture on the Early Modern Stage.* New York: Routledge, 2008.

Tillyard, E. M. W. *Shakespeare's Last Plays.* London: Chatto and Windus, 1951.

Todorov, Tzvetan. *Genres in Discourse.* Trans. by Catherine Porter. Cambridge: Cambridge University Press, 1990.

Trachtenberg, Joshua. *The Devil and the Jews: The Medieval Conception of the Jew and its Relation to Modern Antisemitism.* New York: Harper & Row, 1966.

Traub, Valerie. "Mapping the Global Body." In *Early Modern Visual Culture: Representation, Race and Empire in Early Modern England*, ed. by Peter Erickson and Clark Hulse. 44–97. Philadelphia: University of Pennsylvania Press, 2000.

Trubowitz, Rachel. "'But Blood Whitened': Nursing Mothers and Others in Early Modern Britain." In *Maternal Measures: Figuring Caregiving in the Early Modern Period*, ed. by Naomi J. Miller and Naomi Yavneh, 88–96. Aldershot, UK: Ashgate, 2000.

Trueman, Carl R. *Luther's Legacy: Salvation and English Reformers, 1525–1556*. Oxford: Clarendon Press, 1994.

Vaughan, Virginia Mason. *Othello: A Contextual History*. Cambridge: Cambridge University Press, 1991.

———. *Performing Blackness on English Stages, 1500–1800*. New York: Cambridge University Press, 2005.

Vitkus, Daniel. Introduction to *Three Turk Plays from Early Modern England*, ed. by Daniel Vitkus, 1–53. New York: Columbia University Press, 2000.

———. *Turning Turk: English Theater and the Multicultural Mediterranean, 1570–1630*. New York: Palgrave, 2003.

Voigt, Lisa. *Writing Captivity in the Early Modern Atlantic: Circulations of Knowledge in the Iberian and English Imperial Worlds*. Chapel Hill: University of North Carolina Press, 2009.

Watkins, John. *The Specter of Dido: Spenser and Virgilian Epic*. New Haven: Yale University Press, 1995.

Watson, Robert N. "*Othello* as Protestant Propaganda." In *Religion and Culture in Renaissance England*, ed. by Claire McEachern and Debora Shuger, 235–57. Cambridge: Cambridge University Press, 1997.

Weatherby, Harold. *Mirrors of Celestial Grace: Patristic Theology in Spenser's Allegory*. Toronto: University of Toronto Press, 1994.

Weinberg, Bernard. *A History of Literary Criticism in the Italian Renaissance*. 2 vols. Chicago: University of Chicago Press, 1963.

Wells, Marion A. *The Secrete Wound: Love-Melancholy and Early Modern Romance*. Stanford: Stanford University Press, 2007.

Werth, Tiffany Jo. *The Fabulous Dark Cloister: Romance in England after the Reformation*. Baltimore, MD: Johns Hopkins University Press, 2011.

Whitaker, Cord. "Black Metaphors in *The King of Tars*." *Journal of English and Germanic Philology* 112 (2013): 169–93.

Whitenack, Judith A. "Don Quixote and the Romances of Chivalry Once Again: Converted *Paganos* and Enamoured *Magas*." *Cervantes: Bulletin of the Cervantes Society of America* 13 (1993): 69–91.

Williamson, Elizabeth. *The Materiality of Religion in Early Modern English Drama*. Aldershot, UK: Ashgate, 2009.

Wilson-Okamura, David Scott. "Errors about Ovid and Romance." *Spenser Studies* 23 (2008): 215–34.

Wofford, Susanne Lindgren. *The Choice of Achilles: The Ideology of the Figure in the Epic.* Stanford: Stanford University Press, 1992.

———. "Epics and the Politics of the Origin Tale: Virgil, Ovid, Spenser, and Native American Aetiology." In *Epic Traditions in the Contemporary World: The Poetics of Community,* ed. by Margaret Beissinger, Jane Tylus and Susanne Wofford, 239–69. Berkeley: University of California Press, 1999.

———. "*The Faerie Queene,* Books I–III." In *The Cambridge Companion to Spenser,* ed. by Andrew Hadfield, 103–23. Cambridge: Cambridge University Press, 2001.

Index

Achinstein, Sharon, 42
Acts and Monuments (Foxe), 42
Adelman, Janet, 6, 43, 145, 149, 150
"Aethiopem lavare" (Whitney), 1–3, 4
allegoresis, 63, 166
allegory: Christian allegorizing of
 non-Christian racialized bodies,
 14–16; compared to symbolism, 79;
 in *The Faerie Queene*, 64–66, 72–73;
 Harington's allegorical reading of
 Orlando Furioso, 101–8; in *The
 Merchant of Venice*, 149–50; Protestant
 ambivalence about, 91; relationship
 to sacramental theology, 62–66
Anabaptist baptismal theology, 40–41,
 43, 45
anagnorisis, 124–25
Anderson, Judith H., 80
Answer to Sir Thomas More's Dialogue
 (Tyndale), 56, 57
Apologia Ecclesiae Anglicanae (Jewel), 46–47
Apologie of infants, An (Hubbock), 52
Appiah, Kwame Anthony, 7
Aquinas, Thomas, 49, 51
Aristotle, 124, 147–48
Arminianism, 168–69
Arminius, Jacob, 168–69
Arte of English Poesy, The (Puttenham), 64
Ascham, Roger, 100
Augustine, 63, 102

Babylonian Captivity of the Church, The
 (Luther), 51
Bancroft, Richard, 52

baptism/baptismal theology (Church
 of England): baptismal service in
 A baptizing of a Turke, 121–23;
 circumcision/baptism analogy,
 14, 39–45, 49–50, 54; correct
 interpretation of Scripture and, 91;
 infidel conversion and, 68–69,
 114–23; linked to marriage and
 martyrdom in *The Renegado*, 164–69;
 linked to race and original sin in
 The Faerie Queene, 66–73; linked
 to romance in *Orlando Furioso* and
 Othello, 130–33; magical nature
 of water, 74, 202n46; martyrdom
 exceeding baptism in Christian
 thought, 169–71; original sin and,
 67–69; Ovidian metamorphosis in
 The Faerie Queene and, 61–62, 73–81;
 pedobaptism and concept of English
 election, 40–48; poetically figured
 through Ethiopians/blackness, 1–4;
 racialized understanding of salvation
 and, 8–11, 35–37, 42–53; reformed
 sacramental theology and, 37–39;
 romance's infidel-conversion motif
 and, 4–5; Turk/infidel as figure of
 alterity, 53–58. *See also* Anabaptist
 baptismal theology; Catholic
 baptismal theology
Baptizing of a Turke, A (Hanmer),
 116–18, 121–23
Barkan, Leonard, 62
Bartels, Emily C., 112, 174
Barthelemy, Anthony Gerard, 138

Bate, Jonathan, 134

Battle of Alcazar, The (Peele), 126

Becon, Thomas: circumcision/baptism
analogy, 40–42; on martyrdom, 170;
on race/lineage, baptism, and faith,
43–44, 52; on Turks and Turk/infidel
baptism without salvation, 54, 115

Berger, Harry, 64–65

Best, George, 70–71, 150

Bevis of Hampton, 23

Bible: paratexts and correct
interpretation of Scripture, 91, 94,
97–98; Protestant emphasis on
reading and translation, 92, 93–98

black skin and blackness: baptism
poetically figured through, 1–4;
George Best on, 70–71; Christian
allegorization of, 14–16; in early
modern London, 129; in *The King of
Tars*, 28–31; medieval morality plays
and, 138. *See also* race and racial
identity

Blood Relations (Adelman), 6

Bovilsky, Lara, 135

Bower of Bliss (*The Faerie Queene*),
81–87

Boyarin, Daniel, 13–14

Bradford, John, 10, 161

Bradley, A. C., 140, 141

breastfeeding, 155

*Brief and Clear Confession of the Christian
Faith, A* (Hooper), 53

Briefe declaration of the sacraments, A
(Tyndale), 37, 39, 114–15

Burrow, Colin, 103

Burton, Jonathan, 138

Byrth of mankynde, The (Raynalde),
154–55

Callaghan, Dympna, 128

Calvin, John, 35, 46, 47–48, 151

"Captive's Tale, The" (Cervantes),
24–27

Carter, J. Kameron, 8

Cartwright, Thomas, 115–16

Catechisme, A (Nowell), 41–42

Catholic baptismal theology, 46–47, 49,
51, 69

Cervantes, Miguel de, 24. *See also*
"Captive's Tale, The"

Chanson de Roland, La, 22–23

chansons de gestes, 22

Character of the beast, The (Smyth), 45

Charlemagne romances, 22

Childers, William, 27

Christianographie (Pagitt), 118–20

Christian Turned Turk, A, 155–56

Chrysostom, St. John, 95, 96

Cinthio, Giraldi, 17, 19, 124

circumcision: analogized to baptism, 14,
39–45, 49–50, 54; as linking sexual
and religious identity, 147

Cohen, Stephen, 13

comedy, 142–44, 149, 162. *See also*
tragicomedy

*Commonwealth and Government of Venice,
The* (Lewkenor), 129

concupiscence: Bible reading as means
to curb, 95–97; original sin and,
67–68, 69–70. *See also* sexuality and
sexual errancy

Confessions (Augustine), 102

Confutation of a booke, A (Harding), 46–47

conversion: Bible reading and
translation linked to, 93–98;
Harington's translation of *Orlando
Furioso* as, 92–93, 98–108; infidel
conversion and baptism, 68–69,
114–23; in *The Island Princess*, 156–62;
rejected in *The Faerie Queene*, 66–73;
in *The Renegado*, 162–69; restorative
romance in *Othello* as, 133–41;
theology of race and, 11–12, 173–76.
See also infidel-conversion motif;
salvation

Cooper, Helen, 16–19

Craik, Katharine A., 96

Cranmer, Thomas, 35–36, 41, 94–97

Crashaw, Richard, 1, 3, 4

Crawford, Julie, 153

Crawford, Patricia, 69, 152

Cressy, David, 52–53, 68

Crooke, Helkiah, 152–53, 154

*Defence of the Apologie of the Churche of
Englande, A* (Jewel), 63

Defense to the Answer to the Admonition, The (Whitgift), 115–16
Degenhardt, Jane Hwang, 133
Dimmock, Matthew, 55
Dolan, Frances E., 135
Don Quixote (Cervantes). *See* "Captive's Tale, The"
Dreams from My Father (Obama), 175

early modern England: appearance of Ethiopians in literary works, 15–16; definitions and role of romance in, 16–21; racial discourse in, 141; understandings of human reproduction in, 143, 146–48, 152–55
early modern English stage: interplay of race, gender, and infidel-conversion motif, 142–44, 155–56, 171–72; portrayal of Moors, 125–26, 128–29, 133
early modern literary studies, 5–8, 11–13
English Bibles, 94–95
Englishemans treasure, The (Vicary), 153
epic, 17, 81, 86
Epistle of comfort, An (Southwell), 170
Ethiopian Church, 118
Ethiopians: appearance in early modern English literary works, 15–16; baptism poetically figured through, 1–4; racialized sexuality and, 96–97
Evans, Maurice, 74
Everson, Jane E., 101
Exposition of the fyrste, seconde, and thyrde canonical epistles of S. Jhon, The (Tyndale), 91

Faerie Queene, The (Spenser): allegorical and sacramental poetics of, 62–66, 72–73; baptism, race, and original sin in, 66–73, 86–87; Bower of Bliss and rejection of romantic transformation in, 81–87; infidel-conversion motif rejected in, 61, 73; Ovidian baptism, originary identity, and figurative unity in, 61–62, 73–81; poetics of absence and traces in, 59–62, 64–66; race conjoined with religion in, 72–73, 86–90

fatherhood. *See* paternity
Feerick, Jean, 158
Fletcher, Angus, 64
Fletcher, John. *See Island Princess, The*
Floyd-Wilson, Mary, 96
Form and Solemnization of Matrimony, The, 137, 153
Fowler, Alastair, 17
Fox, Cora, 88
Foxe, John, 42
Frith, John, 68–69
Frow, John, 18
Frye, Northrop, 21, 28, 149
Fuchs, Barbara, 109

Galenic theory of reproduction, 152–55
Garcés, María Antonia, 25
gender: interplay with race and infidel-conversion motif, 142–44, 155–56, 171–72; salvation and maternity in *The Merchant of Venice*, 150–56; salvation and paternity in *The Merchant of Venice*, 145–50
Generation of Animals (Aristotle), 147–48
Genesis covenant, 147
Geneva Bible, 97–98, 151
genres and genre classification, 17–19. *See also* comedy; epic; romance; tragicomedy
Gerusalemme liberata (Tasso), 23
Gilbert, Jane, 31
Gillies, John, 120
Gless, Darryl J., 85
Golding, Arthur, 82–83
Great Bible, 94–95
Green, Ian, 93, 94, 98
Greenblatt, Stephen, 91
Greene, Robert, 127
Guibbory, Achsah, 40
Guillory, John, 78, 83

Habib, Imtiaz, 123, 129
Hanmer, Meredith, 116–18, 121–23
Harding, Thomas, 46–47
Harington, Sir John, 101, 102–3. *See also Orlando Furioso* (Harington translation)
Hays, Michael L., 127

Hecatommithi (Cinthio), 129–30, 134
Hegel, G. W. F., 140
Helgerson, Richard, 92
Heng, Geraldine, 12, 30
"heroic poetry," 17
Hippocratic/Galenic theory of
    reproduction, 152–55
historical formalism, 13
History of Italy (Thomas), 129
Hooper, John, 53
Hubbock, William, 52
human reproduction: early modern
    understandings of, 143, 146–48,
    152–55; linked to spiritual
    reproduction, 151–56

infant baptism. *See* pedobaptism
infection, language of, 69–71
infidel-conversion motif: history of,
    21–31; interplay with race and
    gender, 142–44, 155–56, 171–72; as
    key romance motif, 4–5, 21; in
    Othello, 173–74; recuperation of in
    The Island Princess, 156–62, 170–72;
    recuperation of in *The Renegado*,
    164–69, 170–72; rejected in *The
    Faerie Queene*, 61, 73; repurposed in
    Orlando Furioso, 93, 102
infidels: baptism and conversion of,
    68–69, 114–23; as figures of alterity
    in English baptismal theology, 53–58.
    See also Ethiopians; Jews and Judaism;
    Moors; Turks
Institutes of Christian Religion (Calvin), 47
Island Princess, The (Fletcher): function
    of martyrdom in, 160–62, 170–72;
    interplay of race, gender, and
    infidel-conversion motif, 142–44;
    recuperation of infidel-conversion
    motif, 156–62, 170–72; turning-Turk
    motif in, 158–59

Jackson, Ken, 11
James VI and I, 35–36
Jameson, Fredric, 19–20
Javitch, Daniel, 80
Jennings, Willie James, 8
Jewel, John, 46–47, 62–63, 118

Jews and Judaism: Christianity's
    relationship to, 149–50; circumcision/
    baptism analogy, 14, 39–45, 49–50, 54;
    Protestant anxieties over Hebrew
    Bible, 98; as racial category, 42–43;
    salvation and paternity in *The
    Merchant of Venice*, 145–50; theological
    arguments over baptism and
    conversion of, 68–69, 115–16
Johnson, Richard, 15–16
Jowitt, Claire, 157
"judaization," 98

Kaplan, M. Lindsay, 145, 148
Kaske, Carole V., 77, 79
Kidd, Colin, 8
King of Tars, The, 28–31
Kirkpatrick, Thomas, 12

Lampert, Lisa, 31
Laqueur, Thomas, 152
Lee, Judith, 105, 110
Leigh, Dorothy, 154
Lewkenor, Lewes, 129
Lindmann, Mary, 152
Loomba, Ania, 11–12, 171, 172
Lupton, Julia Reinhard, 12, 39, 145, 147
Luther, Martin, 35, 51, 56, 93

MacDonald, Joyce Green, 143
Making Sex (Laqueur), 152
Marotti, Arthur F., 11
marriage, 137, 151–55
martyrdom: as exceeding power of
    baptism in Christian thought,
    169–71; in *The Island Princess*, 144,
    160–62, 170–71; in *The Renegado*,
    144, 162–68, 170–71
Massinger, Philip. See *Renegado, The*
Matar, Nabil, 72, 133
maternity and salvation, 150–56
Merchant of Venice, The (Shakespeare):
    interplay of race, gender, and
    infidel-conversion motif in, 142–44,
    155–56, 171–72; love as motivation
    for conversion in, 136; salvation and
    maternity in, 150–56; salvation and
    paternity in, 145–50

Metamorphoses (Ovid), 61–62. *See also* Ovidian metamorphosis
metamorphosis. *See* Ovidian metamorphosis
Mikrokosmographia (Crooke), 152–53
mimesis, 65
misogynist discourse, 135, 136–37
Moors: conversion narratives involving, 24–27; early modern racial characterizations, 72; Hanmer's genealogical origins of, 121–22; portrayal on early modern English stage, 125–26, 128–29, 133; theological arguments over baptism and conversion of, 115–16. See also *Othello* (Shakespeare)
More, Thomas, 56
motherhood. *See* maternity and salvation
Mother's Blessing, The (Leigh), 154
motifs, 16–17. *See also* infidel-conversion motif; turning-Turk motif
Murray, Molly, 11
Myrroure or lokynge glasse, A (Frith), 68–69

Neill, Michael, 129, 160
"New Catechisme, A" (Becon), 41–42, 43–44, 52, 54, 115, 170
Newton, Thomas, 173
Ng, Su Fang, 94
Notable historie of the Saracens, A (Newton), 173
Nowell, Alexander, 41–42
Nymph's well episode (*The Faerie Queene*): baptismal theology linked to race and original sin in, 66–73; Ovidian baptism, originary identity, and figurative unity in, 61–62, 73–81

Obama, Barack Hussein, 174–75
On Romances (Cinthio), 19, 124
"On the Baptized Aethiope" (Crashaw), 1, 3, 4
Origen, 169–70
original sin: English baptismal theology and, 67–69; linked to race and baptism in *The Faerie Queene*, 66–73
originary identities: restoration of in Shakespearean romance, 114, 133–34;

Spenser's concern with in *The Faerie Queene*, 73–81
Orlando Furioso (Ariosto): controversy over genre of, 17; conversion, baptism, and romance in, 23, 130–33; interracial affection in, 109–10; as source material for *Othello*, 113–14, 137–38
Orlando Furioso (Greene's play), 127
Orlando Furioso (Harington translation): converted and allegorized into a Protestant poem, 92–93, 98–108; race and racial identity in, 93, 104–11
Othello (Shakespeare): ambiguity of Othello's racial identity and otherness in, 112–13, 125–30; conversion and transformative romance in, 126–33; infidel-conversion motif in, 173–74; other romance motifs and themes in, 210–11n6; reversion and restorative romance in, 133–41; romance, tragedy, and *anagnorisis* in, 113–14, 123–26, 140–41
Ovidian metamorphosis (in *The Faerie Queene*): linked to concern with racial and religious purity, 87–90; refiguring of Circe and rejection of romantic transformation, 81–87; relationship to baptism, originary identity, and figurative unity, 61–62, 73–81

Pagitt, Ephraim, 118–20
Parker, Patricia, 110
paternity: Obama's religious identity and, 175; salvation and, 145–50
Paul, Saint, 14, 39
Pauline universalism, 14
pedobaptism, 40–48
Peele, George, 126
Penuel, Suzanne, 149
Perkins, William, 71
"poetic geography," 120
Poetics (Aristotle), 124
Print and Protestantism in Early Modern England (Green), 93
Pugh, Syrith, 80
Puttenham, George, 64

Quilligan, Maureen, 63, 84

race and racial identity: ambiguity of in
Othello, 112–13, 125–30; black skin
and blackness in *The King of Tars*,
28–31; breastfeeding linked to, 155;
Christian allegorizing of racialized
non-Christian bodies, 14–16;
conjoined with religion in *The Faerie
Queene*, 72–73, 86–90; explored
within early modern literary studies,
5–8; figures of alterity in English
baptismal theology, 53–58; in
Harington's *Orlando Furioso*, 93,
104–11; interplay with gender and
infidel-conversion motif in English
tragicomedy, 142–44, 155–56, 171–72;
language of infection and, 70–71;
linked to original sin and baptism in
The Faerie Queene, 66–73, 86–87;
linked to religion and geography,
114–23; racial discourse in *Othello*,
113, 128, 134–35, 141; racialization of
sexuality, 96–97; racialized
understandings of salvation and
baptism, 8–11, 35–37, 42–53; salvation
and paternity in *The Merchant of
Venice*, 145–50; theology of race and
conversion, 11–12, 173–76
Rashkow, Ilona N., 98
Raynalde, Thomas, 154–55
reading and translation: of Bible linked
to conversion, 92, 93–98, 102;
Harington's translation of *Orlando
Furioso*, 92–93, 98–108; Protestant
anxieties surrounding, 91–93;
relationship to sexuality, 95–97,
101–2, 104–5
religious identity: conjoined with race
in *The Faerie Queene*, 72–73, 86–90;
explored within early modern
literary studies, 6–8, 11–13; in
Harington's *Orlando Furioso*, 93,
104–11; linked to race and geography,
114–23; linked to race in *The Kings of
Tars*, 28–31; Obama's paternity and,
175; oscillations of in *Othello*, 133–41;
racialized understandings of, 8–11,
35–37, 42–53; salvation and maternity
in *The Merchant of Venice*, 150–56;

salvation and paternity in *The
Merchant of Venice*, 145–50
Renegado, The (Massinger): baptism,
marriage, and martyrdom in, 162–68,
170–71; interplay of race, gender, and
infidel-conversion motif in, 142–44;
recuperation of infidel-conversion
motif in, 156–57, 164–69, 170–72;
turning-Turk motif in, 158–59
Replye to an Answere of Dr Whitgifte
(Cartwright), 115–16
reproduction. *See* human reproduction
Responsio and Lutherum (More), 56
restorative romance, 133–41
Ridley, Thomas, 170
Riggs, John Wheelan, 47
Robinson, Benedict S., 71, 165
romance: affinities between Ovid and,
80–81; connections to tragedy and
anagnorisis in *Othello*, 113–14, 123–26,
140–41; definitions and genre
classifications of, 16–21; Harington's
Orlando Furioso as turning away from,
101, 104–5; infidel-conversion motif
in, 4–5, 21 (*see also* infidel-conversion
motif); linked to sexuality and
hybrid identity, 100, 104–5; rejection
of in *The Faerie Queene*, 81–87;
restorative romance in *Othello*,
133–41; transformative romance in
Othello, 126–33; turning-Turk motif
in, 23–24, 155–56, 158–59
romance *anagnorisis*, 125
romance motifs, 16–17. *See also* infidel-
conversion motif; turning-Turk motif
Root, Deborah, 26

sacramental theology: linked to allegory,
62–66; marriage as sacrament, 137;
reformed baptism arising from, 37–39
salvation: maternity and, 150–56;
nonbaptized Turks/infidels and,
53–58; paternity and, 145–50;
racialized understandings of baptism
and, 8–11, 35–37, 42–53
Schoenfeldt, Michael C., 70
Schoolmaster, The (Ascham), 100
Schwartz, Regina M., 63–64

sexuality and sexual errancy: effects of reading on, 95–97, 100, 101–2; Harington's *Orlando Furioso* and, 102–5

sexual reproduction. *See* human reproduction

Shakespeare, William, 18. *See also Merchant of Venice, The*; *Othello*

Shapiro, James, 147

Slights, William W. E., 99

Smith, Ian, 6

Smyth, John, 45

Southwell, Robert, 170

Spenser, Edmund, 64. *See also Faerie Queene, The*

Spierling, Karen E., 9

Spiller, Elizabeth, 20, 96

Summa Theologica (Aquinas), 49, 51

symbolism, 79

Tambling, Jeremy, 79

Tasso, Torquato, 17, 23, 86

Taussig, Michael, 65

Teskey, Gordon, 79

"Thirty-Nine Articles, The," 67–68, 92

Thomas, William, 129

Thomas Aquinas. *See* Aquinas, Thomas

Tom a Lincoln (Johnson), 16

"To Mistress Wilkinson and Mistress Warcup" (Bradford), 10

tragedy, 113–14, 123–26, 140–41

tragicomedy: interplay of race, gender, and infidel-conversion motif in, 142–44, 155–56, 171–72; linked to martyrdom and the threat of death, 160–62

transformative romance, 126–33

translation. *See* reading and translation

Traub, Valerie, 120

Trubowitz, Rachel, 155

Turks: Christian arguments over baptism and conversion of, 115–16; early modern racial characterizations, 72; as figures of alterity in English baptismal theology, 53–58; race, religion, and geography in *The baptizing of a Turke*, 116–18, 121–23

turning-Turk motif, 23–24, 155–56, 158–59

Tyndale, William: on allegory and correct reading of Scripture, 91; circumcision/baptism analogy, 39, 49–51; reformed sacramental theology of, 37; on Turks and Turk/infidel salvation without baptism, 53–54, 55–56, 57, 91, 114–15

vernacular Bibles, 94–95

Vicary, Thomas, 153

Vitkus, Daniel, 125

Watkins, John, 86

Weinberg, Bernard, 124

Werth, Tiffany Jo, 21, 98, 100

Whitgift, John, 115–16, 194–95n33

Whitney, Geffrey, 1–3, 4

Wofford, Susanne, 77, 80

Zwingli, Ulrich, 35